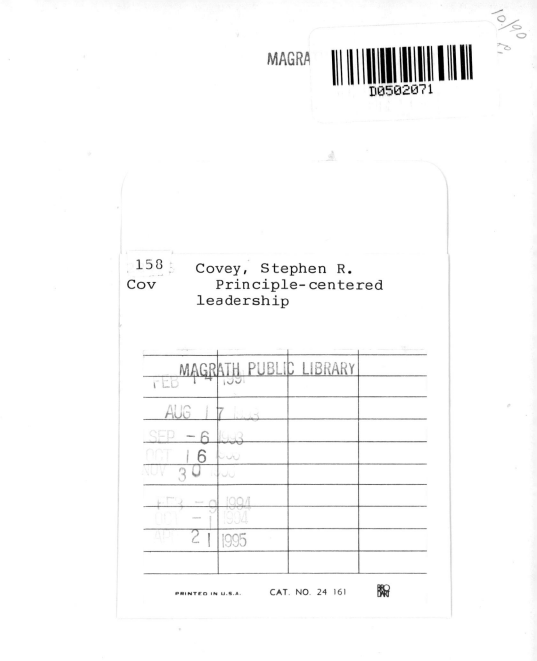

PRINCIPLE-CENTERED LEADERSHIP

Teaching People How to Fish

PRINCIPLE-CENTERED LEADERSHIP

Teaching People How to Fish

Stephen R. Covey

*"Give a man a fish
and you feed him for a day;
teach him how to fish
and you feed him for a lifetime."*

THE INSTITUTE
FOR PRINCIPLE-CENTERED
LEADERSHIP

THE INSTITUTE FOR PRINCIPLE-CENTERED LEADERSHIP
The Covey Leadership Center Building at Jamestown Square
3500 North University Avenue, Provo, Utah 84604 · 1-800-331-7716 and 1-801-377-1888

First Edition

Published by
THE INSTITUTE FOR PRINCIPLE-CENTERED LEADERSHIP
in cooperation with
EXECUTIVE EXCELLENCE   2622

10   9   8   7   6   5   4   3   2   1
ISBN 0-916095-31-2

ALSO BY
STEPHEN R. COVEY

Spiritual Roots of Human Relations
How to Succeed with People
The Divine Center
Marriage & Family Insights
The Seven Habits of Highly Effective People

CONTENTS

Part Three: Managerial Effectiveness 155

Part Four: Organizational Leadership 215

FOREWORD

On Bottoms, Tops and Pops

by Ken Shelton
Editor of Executive Excellence ®

Once on a visit to Manhattan, I attended a New York Pops concert at Carnegie Hall, the venerable edifice saved from certain destruction by performing artists and philanthropists. Conductor Skitch Henderson and guest Steve Allen both paid tribute to those who donated money, time and effort to restore the hall: so much would have been lost had it been bulldozed.

After the concert, I chatted with a cellist whose instrument was crafted in 1670.

"Why play an antique?" I asked him.

"Simply because you can't get the same quality sound from a modern instrument," he replied.

Although in this book of articles, originally published in *Executive Excellence,* Stephen R. Covey begins by discussing "A Break with the Past" and "How to Overcome the Pull of the Past," he is no modernist but very much the classicist whose ambition is "to restore the American character."

Playing with Principles

Covey's instruments — natural laws, governing social values and principle-centered leadership — have also stood the test of time. He, in fact, seeks and teaches the timely application of timeless truths, preserved from the rush of traffic and the trade of business, serving collectively, in a sense, as Central Park: a spacious island of sanity and serenity amid a crowded, jaded and congested city.

On that same trip to New York, I spoke with a young woman, an 18-year-old Japanese-American, who was studying music at Julliard. She, too, played the cello. She reported that the training at Julliard is very individualized, based on an objective assessment of one's current level of achievement and of one's ultimate potential. The methodology is continuous improvement, step by step, day by day, working on different things until the total performance comes together.

So, too, is the Covey leadership training technology. Whether on a personal or an organizational level, his counsel is to lay a solid foundation of character and then to build wisely upon it. As a metaphor, he writes about the "Six Days of Creation," suggesting that much of substance and worth can come from vision and a strong work ethic.

What separates Covey from many of his colleagues in the academic and professional fields of business management and organizational behavior is his center. He looks first to scripture and then to other texts. He invites top business executives and university students alike to center their lives on the classic principles of effective human behavior — on basic, bottom-line things that do not change — and then to monitor their progress by checking sure signs of internal (private) and external (public) growth.

Covey's path to quality is continuous improvement, daily progress, working from the inside out, from the circle of influence, from the foundation of character. Once the basic habits are well established, he talks about style, personality and individual interpretation or arrangement. In effect, he seeks modern applications of classic principles, the greatest hits in history, from Aesop to Tom Peters, with a dose of Drucker and a dash of Deming.

When Covey integrates new material into his presentations, he gives proper attribution. Perhaps a result of his Harvard training, he is respectful of original sources; in fact, in any given speech, he may reference six or more books written by other people and ask his audience to go buy and read them.

But as Covey draws ideas from disparate sources — digesting an amazing breadth of thought — he adds depth by presenting them within the context of his own personal experience with people and organizations. Together these ideas and life experience create a unique Covey paradigm of leadership, quality and excellence based on the principle of continuous improvement. Covey suggests as a theme in this book that no person or company should be content to stay where they are, no matter how successful they now appear to be. He sees the goals of excellence and total quality as expressions of an innate human need for progress and improvement in personal, interpersonal, managerial and organizational areas.

Personal. The personal side of leadership means total integrity around your value system, even when it's not pleasant or popular. It also means being open to critical feedback. Feedback is not just "the breakfast of champions," says Covey; "it is the breakfast, lunch and dinner of champions." Leaders are continuously wanting and getting feedback, he says. They have sufficient internal security to be open to it and not be threatened by it.

Interpersonal. Leaders make constant deposits into the emotional bank accounts of others, particularly key stake-holders. They negotiate in good faith, not in fear. They live more from imagination than memory. They operate around a mission, organize around roles and schedule around goals and priorities. They practice the skills of empathy and synergy.

Managerial. The Covey rule here is to manage others with an abundance mentality through win-win performance agreements, maintaining balance between production and production capability. It's a release style that focuses on results not methods and requires boss and subordinate to work toward mutual trust and respect. The boss involves people meaningfully in the mission and work of the organization; and the subordinate performs completed staff work.

Organizational. Leaders of organizations, notes Covey, are to work on six conditions to prevent seven chronic problems. He does allow for fishing and golfing; but, unfortunately, these are meant as metaphors for monitoring the stream of stake-holder information and solving problems around the "executive nine," the people, style, structure, systems, etc.

Life-Long Learning

The Covey leadership paradigm is not in the mind of most modern managers, which is why so many hit and miss, start and stop and madly dash about without making any real progress. With limited vision, top-down mission and no disciplined systems, you get violated expectations, disillusionment and cynicism.

The solution, suggests Covey, is not a human relations or even a human resource approach to learning, problem solving, producing and serving customers — it is a principle-centered solution. Quality is not some program of the company — it is the philosophy of the company, and it beats within the heart of every person identified or associated with the company.

In writing these articles, Covey puts down the short-term view and the short-cut approach. He advocates life-long learning and teaches others how to fish for their own satisfying results.

In reading these articles, please pick up the challenge to change some bad habits and start some new patterns, to have your own Julliard finishing school, your own timeless instruments and your own concerts in Carnegie Hall.

PREFACE

Cosmetics vs. Character

In 1976, I conducted a fascinating, bicentennial research project: a review of the popular success literature of the United States published since 1776. My study brought me into contact with thousands of books, magazines, and digests devoted to success principles and practices.

This is what I found: For the first 150 years, the primary focus was the *character ethic.* The character ethic deals with the development of fundamental traits such as service, honesty, industry, charity, chastity, patriotism, integrity, benevolence, thrift, self-discipline, self-sacrifice, and so on.

About 50 years ago, a highly significant new trend began to eclipse or subordinate this character ethic, and the trend has continued to form the *personality ethic.* It focuses primarily on human relations techniques, on influence strategies, on image building, on getting what you want, on self-actualization, on assertiveness skills, on positive mental attitude, on success programming and people manipulation tactics.

With this trend, many self-centered cults and fads have moved into the literature and into corporate life, promising their adherents self-realization, enlightenment, peace of mind or vital health. These concepts and systems may have some genuine merit to commend them, but when they become ends in themselves they create an absolute distortion of life, an aberrant behavior and addiction.

During the early decades of America's history, before scientific empiricism became so pervasive in academic circles, much of the success literature was taught in our schools, beginning in the early grades and continuing through college. Most church-related universities focused explicitly on character development, and many other institutions of higher learning were either founded on or dedicated to the idea of training the whole person, including the moral or spiritual dimension.

The success literature of our nation's formative years reflects this emphasis. Books dealing with self-improvement and achievement focused primarily on such character traits as sincerity, humility, courage, integrity, fidelity, honesty, simplicity, thrift, and discipline. Personality attributes and human relations skills were seen as the natural fruits of these character roots. Typical of this literature is Benjamin Franklin's *Autobiography*, wherein he tells how he systematically inculcated some of the virtues and character traits essential for success.

More recently, the primary thrust of higher education, including that of most church-related universities, has shifted from moral to mental — and most management literature reflects this movement. We see the emergence of human relations technologies that secure cooperation, support, acceptance, and favorable opinion; and we see the growing popularity of "positive mental attitude" and "power of constructive imagination" approaches to personal development and achievement, wherein mental images of success are planted in the subconscious mind to organize thoughts and accomplish goals.

By taking a casual survey of book titles in the areas of popular psychology, self-improvement or human interaction, I find that many of these books deal with such topics as successful living, self-esteem, communication, and marriage relations. Such books as *How to Win Friends and Influence People* and *Psycho-cybernetics* helped establish the personality ethic; they only give lip service to the principles of character development.

The shift in focus is symptomatic of the gradual secularization of the American culture: we have gone from a moral to a mental to a social orientation. I suggest that the depth and pervasiveness of the social problems in our society are other symptoms of the same problem which stems from the same underlying cause.

Henry David Thoreau said it well: "For every thousand hacking at the leaves of evil, there is one striking at the root."

The popular success literature only mirrors the symptoms (the leaves) without dealing with the causes (the roots). It features a futile Band-aid approach to curing deep-seated problems with individuals and institutions. For when the personality ethic is separated, severed, or truncated from its character roots, it yields a

xii

kind of manipulative personality, one that knows how to trigger desired responses by employing various influence strategies and mental calculations.

Fortunately, I detect a better balance between character and personality in some recent management literature. I attribute this trend to more intense competition in the international marketplace. Global competition rewards quality, service, productivity and stability. To be competitive, management must focus on principles, and not so much on practices. Practices are culturally indigenous, but principles are transferable, universal, general laws which govern all of life.

In their landmark, best-selling book, *In Search of Excellence*, Tom Peters and Bob Waterman reported that most well-managed companies are value-driven or value-governed and that their leadership is committed to certain basic principles, beliefs, or values which they attempt to translate into purposes, policies, programs, and practices. They write:

> *Some colleagues who have heard us expound on the importance of values have said, in effect, "That's swell, but isn't it a luxury? Doesn't the business have to make money first?" The answer is that, of course, a business has to be fiscally sound and the excellent companies are among the most fiscally sound of all. But their value set integrates the notions of economic health, serving customers, and making money down the line. As one executive said to us, "Profit is like health. You need it and the more the better, but it's not why you exist." Moreover, in a piece of research that preceded this work, we found that companies whose only articulated goals were financial did not do nearly as well financially as companies that had broader sets of values.*

Indeed, the best managed companies are still value-driven. Their leaders are committed to certain basic principles or values which they translate into organizational policies and programs.

In my mind, these findings signal the return to a character ethic in the excellent companies of today, and, for institutional purposes, also a need to interact with others in ways that motivate and lift them to higher levels of moral performance.

My experience tells me that already people have a kind of inner extra-sensory perception whereby they instinctively trust those whose personality is founded upon correct principles and distrust others. We have evidence of this in our long-term relationships. We learn that communication technique is relatively unimportant compared to the trust level, which is the result of our interactive trustworthiness over time. When trust is high, we communicate easily, effortlessly, instantaneously. We even make mistakes and others will still capture our meaning. But when trust is low, communication is exhausting, time-consuming, ineffective, and inordinately difficult.

It's relatively easy to work on personalities: all we have to do is learn some new skill, rearrange language patterns, adopt human relations technologies, employ visualization affirmations, or strengthen our self-esteem.

It's a different matter to change habits, develop virtues, learn basic disciplines, keep promises, be faithful to vows, exercise courage, or be genuinely considerate of the feelings and convictions of others. Nonetheless, it's the true test and manifestation of our maturity.

To value oneself and, at the same time, subordinate oneself to higher purposes and to other people's interests is the paradoxical essence of highest humanity and the foundation of effective leadership.

Part 1:

PERSONAL DEVELOPMENT

I have long advocated a natural, gradual, day-by-day, step-by-step, sequential approach to personal development. My feeling is that any product or program — whether it deals with losing weight or mastering skills — that promises "quick, free, instant and easy" results is probably not based on correct principles. And yet virtually all advertising uses one or more of these words to entice us to buy. Small wonder many of us are addicted to "quick fix" approaches to personal development.

In this section, I suggest that real character and skill development is irrevocably related to natural laws and governing principles; when we observe these, we gain the strength to break with the past, to overcome old habits, to change our paradigms and to achieve primary greatness.

Chapter 1

A Break with the Past

Almost every significant breakthrough is the result of a courageous break with traditional ways of thinking.

In scientific circles, dramatic transformations, revolutions of thought, great leaps of understanding, and sudden liberations from old limits are called paradigm shifts. These offer distinctively new ways of thinking about old problems.

The word *paradigm* is from the Greek word, *paradigma*: a pattern or map for understanding and explaining certain aspects of reality. While a person may make small improvements by developing new skills, quantum leaps in performance and revolutionary advances in technology require new maps, new paradigms, new ways of thinking about and seeing the world.

For example, some 500 years ago, people had a certain map, which reflected their understanding of the world at that time. It wasn't changed until an expert navigator and courageous seaman, Christopher Columbus (1451-1506), challenged the conventional wisdom by sailing due west in hopes of discovering a new route to the Indies. While he failed to discover the Indies, he certainly changed the map, the paradigm, of the world. And his break-with resulted in a most significant break-through in world history.

Once Columbus was invited to a banquet where he was assigned the most honorable place at the table. A shallow courtier who was meanly jealous of him abruptly asked: "Had you not discovered the Indies, are there not other men in Spain who would have been capable of the enterprise?"

Columbus made no reply, but took an egg and invited the company to make it stand on end. They all attempted, but in vain; whereupon, he tapped it on the table, denting one end, and left it standing.

3

"We all could have done it that way!" the courtier accused.

"Yes, if you had only known how," retorted Columbus. "And once I showed you the way to the new world, nothing was easier than to follow it."

With the upcoming 500-year anniversary of the voyage of Columbus, I celebrate with all Americans the spirit of exploration and renaissance — a spirit that distinguishes the best organizations in the world.

A Set of Principles at the Center

Another renaissance man, Nicolas Copernicus (1473-1543) developed a new map for the stars, as Columbus had developed a new map of the seas.

At the time, astronomers generally accepted the theory of Egyptian astronomer Ptolemy, that the earth was the center of the universe and had no motion. Copernicus proved that the earth moved rapidly through space and that the sun was at the center. Although his sun-at-the-center paradigm was considered scientific heresy by some and spiritual blasphemy by others, Copernicus bravely broke with tradition and started a revolution that marks the beginning of modern science.

In his writings, *De Revolutionibus Orbium Caelestium*, Copernicus noted, "To ascribe movement to the earth must seem absurd to those who for centuries have consented that the earth is placed immovably as the central point of the universe. But I shrink not from any man's criticism. By long and frequent observations and by following a set of fixed principles, I have discovered not only that the earth moves but also that the orders and magnitudes of all stars and spheres, nay the heavens themselves, are so bound together that nothing in any part thereof could be moved from its place without producing confusion in all the parts of the Universe as a whole."

Throughout history, leaders have used various models and "maps" to manage people. These range from the primitive "carrot-and-stick" paradigm, where rewards and punishments are used to generate productivity, to more sophisticated human relations and human resource models based on influence strategies and involvement techniques.

My hope is to help bring about a paradigm shift in management training by focusing on a new map, "Principle-Centered Leadership." Using this paradigm, leaders can expect to transform their organizations and their people by communicating vision, clarifying purposes, making behavior congruent with belief, and aligning procedures with principles, roles and goals. People may then achieve a heightened sense of personal contribution through their commitment to the organization's mission.

Often we can't embrace a new paradigm until we let go of the old one. Likewise, until we drop unwarranted assumptions about people, we can't expect to bring about lasting improvements in our organizations: we can't magnify our human resources using manipulative management techniques any more than we can repair Humpty Dumpty with more horses and more men. Nevertheless, in this topsy-turvy world, matters often get turned around. We confuse efficiency for effectiveness, expediency for priority, imitation for innovation, cosmetics for character, or pretense for competence.

Ultimately, the leadership style one adopts springs from one's core ideas and feelings about the nature of man. Whatever a person has at the center of his life — work or pleasure, friend or enemy, family or possessions, spouse or self, principles or passions — will affect his perception. And it is perception that governs beliefs, attitudes, and behaviors.

I endorse the idea — I teach them correct principles, and they govern themselves — as an enlightened approach to management and leadership. Individuals and organizations ought to be guided and governed by a set of proven principles. These are the natural laws and governing social values that have gradually come through every great society, every responsible civilization over the centuries. They surface in the form of values, ideas, norms, and teachings that uplift, ennoble, fulfill, empower and inspire people.

Like the paradigm shift in science, this shift in management pattern can completely change one's outlook on the world and eventually transform one's organization. While managers must focus on the bottom line, leaders must look to the top line for clear vision and direction.

Where there is no vision, says the Proverb, people perish. That's because they select goals and begin pursuing them — climbing the proverbial ladder of success — before they define missions and clarify values. Consequently, upon reaching the top rung, they often discover to their dismay that the ladder is leaning against the wrong wall.

Processes for Releasing Potential

In physics, Newton neatly packaged the laws of force and gravity into an all-inclusive theory, adequate for his day. But the enormous energy locked within the atom remained untapped until Albert Einstein (1879-1955) found the key. His principle of relativity treated matter and energy as exchangeable, not distinct, and revolutionized scientific thought with new conceptions of time, space, mass, motion, and gravitation.

In his *Autobiographical Notes*, Einstein wrote: "Newton, forgive me. You found the only way that, in your day, was at all possible for a man of the highest powers of intellect and creativity. The concepts that you created still dominate the way we think in physics, although we now know that they must be replaced by others farther removed from the sphere of immediate experience if we want to try for a more profound understanding of the way things are interrelated."

Of course, when the tiny atom was split, enormous energy and power were unleashed. Likewise, the aim of any human resource development program ought to be to release the tremendous creative power and potential of people by involving them in a meaningful change and development process.

Principle-centered leadership suggests that the highest level of human motivation is a sense of personal contribution. It views people as the most valuable organizational assets — as stewards of certain resources — and stewardship as the key to discovering, developing and managing all other assets. Each person is recognized as a free agent, capable of immense achievement, not as a victim or pawn limited by conditions or conditioning.

The training design that matches this paradigm is process, not product, oriented. The organizational development process is first to gather and diagnose the data; second, to select priorities, values and objectives; third, to identify and evaluate alternatives; fourth, to plan and decide action steps; and fifth, to compare results with original goals and objectives.

The following five-step individual development process should be an integral part of any on-going training program: first, capture the content of the material, the essence of what is presented — seeking first to understand the basic principles; second, expand on what you have learned — adding your own ideas and thoughts; third, teach the material — sharing what you have learned with others to increase understanding, to create a common vocabulary for change, and to unlock the perceptions that others have of you; fourth, apply the principles — putting them to the test in your immediate circumstances; and fifth, monitor the results.

All real growth is characterized by this step-by-step developmental process. When individuals are trained in management principles through this process, they are liberated from old limits, old habit patterns, and are increasingly motivated and directed from within. And when people in organizations are thus trained, they find ways to make their structure, systems and style increasingly congruent with their mission, values, roles and goals.

Programs for Breaking Barriers

Pilot Chuck Yeager (1923-) launched an era of supersonic flight on October 14, 1947, when he cracked the sound barrier and its "invisible brick wall." Some prominent scientists had "hard data" that the barrier was impenetrable. Others direly predicted that both pilot and plane would disintegrate at Mach 1 or that the pilot would lose his voice, revert in age, or be severely buffeted. Notwithstanding, on that historic day, Yeager attained an air speed of 700 miles per hour (Mach 1.06) in his Bell Aviation X-1 plane.

Three weeks later, he streaked to Mach 1.35; six years later, he flew at an incredible 1,612 miles per hour (Mach 2.44), putting to rest the myth of an impenetrable barrier.

In his autobiography, he writes: "The faster I got, the smoother the ride. Suddenly the Mach needle began to fluctuate. It went up to .965 Mach — then tipped right off the scale. I thought I was seeing things! We were flying supersonic, and it was as smooth as a baby's bottom: Grandma could be sitting up there sipping lemonade. I was thunderstruck. After all the anxiety, after all the anticipation, breaking the sound barrier was really a let-down. The sonic barrier, the unknown, was just a poke through Jello, a perfectly paved speedway. Later I realized that this mission had to end in a let-down because the real barrier wasn't in the sky but in our knowledge and experience of supersonic flight."

Having broken the "sound barrier," we yet face what many consider an even more imposing obstacle to progress — the "human barrier." For many managers today, breaking the "human barrier" or status quo performance is as difficult as breaking the "sound barrier" was for aeronautical engineers four decades ago.

Why? Because people are often seen as limitations, if not liabilities, rather than advantages and assets. Thus, low performance is often institutionalized in the structure and systems, procedures and processes of the organization. Some executives pilot their single-engine, propeller-driven firms at slow speeds and low altitudes, cocksure that anything smacking of high performance would cause them to lose control and crash.

Meanwhile, a few well-trained and courageous managers are breaking the mythical human barrier and proving that gains in human performance of 500 percent — not just five percent — are possible, without anyone losing his voice, reverting to adolescence or experiencing violent buffeting. In fact, people in high performing organizations tend to be much healthier and happier. Because they are treated as the most valuable resource of the organization, they assist each other in making quantum leaps in quality and productivity. They also seek training in the principles and practices of supersonic management and have simple faith in the soaring potential of their people.

Training and development programs should evolve naturally from the company's mission, principles and values. Programs should attempt to empower people to soar, to sail, to step bravely forward into the unknown, being guided more by imagination than memory, and ultimately to reach beyond their fears and past failures.

I believe it's high time for many individuals and companies to make a quantum leap in performance, a healthy change of habits, a major shift in patterns; otherwise, it's business as usual — and that's simply not cutting it anymore.

Chapter 2

How to Overcome the Pull of the Past

To succeed at breaking old habits and making new ones, learn how to handle the restraining forces and harness the driving forces to achieve the daily private victory.

Overcoming the pull of the past is in large part a matter of having clear identity and strong purpose — of knowing who you are and what you want to accomplish. Poor performance can often be attributed to poor prioritization and organization. Weak resolve is easily uprooted by emotion, mood and circumstance.

Highly effective people carry their agenda with them. Their schedule is their servant, not their master. They organize weekly, adapt daily. However, they are not capricious in changing their plan. They exercise discipline and concentration and do not submit to moods and circumstances. They schedule blocks of prime time for important planning, projects and creative work. They work on less important and less demanding activities when their fatigue level is higher. They avoid handling paper more than once and avoid touching paperwork unless they plan on taking action on it.

I define discipline as the ability to make and keep promises and to honor commitments. It's the key to overcoming the pull of the past. If we begin small, we can gradually strengthen our sense of personal honor and build our capacity to make and keep large promises. Eventually, our sense of personal honor becomes stronger than our moods. We will then make promises sparingly because we keep the ones we make.

It often helps to write commitments down and keep them in front of us. We recently developed our own tool for doing that —

the Seven Habits Organizer. Recording our roles and goals strengthens our resolve and reminds us to budget time and other resource to fulfill promises.

You might start this process by promising to get up at a certain time in the morning, regardless of how you feel. Next promise that you will use that first waking hour in a very profitable way — planning and preparing for the day. And then do it. You will find that there is enormous power in the principle of keeping promises and honoring commitments. It leads to strong self-esteem and personal integrity, the foundation of all true success.

Three Great Forces

In astronautics, we learn that more power and energy is expended during liftoff and in clearing the earth's gravity than in navigating a million miles and returning again to earth.

Similarly, we expend more effort and energy in starting a new behavior. Old habits exert a powerful pull. We may one day resolve to break the habit of overeating, for example, only to renew the resolve the very next day. We may promise to stop procrastinating by writing those overdue letters and getting at those important but not urgent projects, only to break the resolve and start the circular, self-defeating habit of making resolutions only to break them again. We may then begin to wonder if it's worth making any commitments.

How can we break bad habits and form healthy new ones? We must first sit down and count the costs, lest we make a public statement and lay the foundation but are not able to finish. If we do not finish what we start, we are mocked, either by others or by ourselves. We simply must sit down first and count the costs and calculate the restraining forces to ensure that we have sufficient thrust.

Force field analysis teaches us that in every environment there are powerful restraining forces at work to pull down any new thrust. Any serious effort to change a habit should take these forces into account. For example, if we resolve to change our diet, we should consider the times and places and situations where we slip. We can then avoid those things that trip us and add things that help us to progress and carry out resolutions.

Old habits have a tremendous pull. Breaking deeply imbedded habits of procrastination, criticism, overeating or oversleeping involves more than a little will power. We may be dealing with basic character issues and need to achieve some basic reorientation or transformation.

Often our own resolve and will power are not enough. We may need the transforming power of an alliance with other people who are similarly committed — relationships where we contract to do something. The success of groups like Alcoholics Anonymous attest to the power of reinforcing associations.

Still, change will be difficult at first. Once we decide to change, to lift off, we may have to sacrifice our "freedom" to do as we please or to do what comes naturally until new habits are firmly formed and our desires for the old ways abated. We'll go through withdrawal — dealing with cravings and routines and tendencies. And just as astronauts are buffeted by the forces of nature as they clear the pull of "g-forces" of gravity, so must we experience some rigors as we attempt to overcome the pull of the past.

Grounding us to our bad habits are three great forces: appetite, pride and ambition.

First, appetites and passions. We all succumb at times to the pull of appetites — our physiological cravings and longings for food and drink, for example. Many people are slaves to their stomach and to their addictions. Their stomach controls their mind and body, not without consequence. When we overindulge, we are less sensitive to the needs of others. We become angry with ourselves and take that anger out on others, sometimes at the slightest provocation. Hence, when we are controlled by our appetites and passions, we inevitably have relationship problems.

Sir Walter Scott noted, "He who indulges his sense in any excess renders himself obnoxious to his own reason; and to gratify the brute in him, displeases the man and sets his two natures at variance."

Sleep is another strong appetite. Often we want to get the day organized and have an orderly breakfast and a peaceful moment of meditation. But when the mental or mechanical alarm goes off, good resolves dissipate and often dissolve. We get up late and frantically get dressed and fed and off to work, impatient and frayed, short-tempered and ill-suited to meet the challenges of the day. For this reason, "extra" sleep is hardly ever worth it. What a difference when we organize and arrange our affairs to get to bed early and arise early and get organized.

Second, pride and pretension. If we are not secure in our self-definition, we look to the social mirror for our identity and approval. Our concept of ourselves comes from what others think of us. We find ourselves gearing our lives to meet their expectations. The more we live what others expect of us, the more insecure and pretentious we become. Expectations change. Opinion is fickle. And as we go on playing games and roles, giving in to vanity and pride, we deceive ourselves and, feeling threatened, fight to maintain the false front.

Third, aspiration and ambition. When we are blinded by ambition, we seek first to be understood and to get glory, position, power, and promotion rather than looking at time, talents and possessions as a stewardship for which we must account. The aspiring individual is deeply possessive. He interprets everything in terms of what it will do for him. Everyone becomes a competitor. His relationships — even close, intimate ones — tend to be competitive. He uses various methods of manipulation to achieve his ends.

The Daily Private Victory

If we can overcome the pull of the flesh to arise early in the morning — putting mind over mattress — we will experience our first victory of the day. We can then move on to other things. For by small means are great things accomplished.

Such an early morning victory gives a sense of conquering, of overcoming, of mastering — and this sense propels one to further conquer difficulties and clear hurdles throughout the day. Starting the day with a private victory over self is one good way to break old habits and make new ones.

Our ability to do more and perform better will increase as we exercise the discipline of doing important and difficult work first, when we are fresh, and deferring routine jobs to other times. In this way, we are products of our decisions, goals and plans, not of our moods and circumstances.

All of us have our private battles. And we all have the chance to live out our public battles in our minds before we ever come to them in fact. In this way, we can actually live out the challenges of our day before they come. We can deal with aspirations, selfishness, negative inclinations, impatience, anger, procrastination, and irresponsibility — fight these things out and win the battle vicariously before we do in fact.

Then when the public battles come — the pressures and stresses that descend upon our lives — we will have the internal strength to deal with them from a set of correct principles. Winning the private battle before going into the public arena is another key to breaking old habits and making new ones. I have learned that we do not have lasting public victories until we have successful private victories.

Conditioning is All Important

We increase our capacity to make and break habits much as we increase our lung capacity — we begin with a program of aerobics.

Certainly, we can't run faster than we have strength. We must build up gradually. Aerobics means an active exercise program based on the idea of an incremental build-up of reserve power in the body to supply necessary oxygen to the systems. Anyone who leads a sedentary lifestyle and is then physically put to the test finds that his body cries for oxygen. But his circulatory system is underdeveloped, and a serious deficiency may bring stroke, heart attack, or death.

So the principle is to build up regularly, gradually, through daily exercise of emotional fiber. Build reserves of emotional stamina to be called on in times of stress.

With regard to making new habits, the aerobic exercise I recommend is to daily do two things: 1) gain perspective and 2) make some decisions and commitments in light of that perspective. People have the capability to transcend themselves, to rise above the moment and see what's happening and what should be happening. We need to take time to plan and make some decisions in light of this understanding. For as Goethe put it, "Things which matter most must never be at the mercy of things which matter least." Careful planning helps us maintain a sense of perspective, purpose and ordered priorities.

Five Suggestions

If we will do the following five things, we will have the strength to be strong in hard moments, in testing times.

- Never make a promise we will not keep.

- Make meaningful promises, resolutions and commitments to do better and to be better — and share these with a loved one.

- Use self-knowledge and be very selective about the promises we make.

- Consider promises as a measure of our integrity and faith in ourselves.

- Remember that our personal integrity or self-mastery is the basis for our success with others.

One simple practice can propel you forward in your long-term quest for excellence and in your struggle for true maturity (courage balanced with consideration) and for integrity. It is this: before every test of your new habit or desired behavior, stop and get control. Plumb and rally your resources. Set your mind and heart. Choose your mood. Proactively choose your response. Ask, "How can I best respond to this situation?" Choose to be your best self, and that choice will arrest your ambivalence and renew your determination.

When everything is ready for take-off, the astronauts say, "All systems go." That means that everything is in proper balance and working order. They can have a launch from the pad or they can make some significant maneuvers in space because everything is coordinated, harmonized and prepared to move ahead.

"All systems go" might be a good expression for us to indicate that all systems are ready to take us to the height planned. When our habit system and value system are not synchronized, we are subject to internal doubts and resistance, and often the mission is aborted. Active, positive behavior reinforces our good intentions and resolutions. Actions — actual doing — can change the very fiber of our nature. Doing changes our view of ourselves. Our personal behavior is largely a product of such self-made fuel.

Consequently, if a person makes a promise but does not fulfill that promise, there is a danger of a basic breakdown in his character. His honor and integrity are threatened. His self-esteem tends to diminish. He eventually creates a different picture of himself and conforms his behavior to that picture. But if we deal well with each new challenge and overcome it, we unleash within ourselves a new kind of freedom, power and capacity to soar to heights previously undreamed of.

Chapter 3

Six Days of Creation

All real growth and progress is made step by step, following a natural sequence of development.

As recorded in *Genesis*, the earth was created in six days. Each day or time period was important, each in its own time: the light, the land, the plants and animals, and finally man.

This sequential development process is common to all of life.

• As children, we learn to turn over, to sit up, to crawl, then to walk and run. Each step is important. No step can be skipped.

• In school, we study mathematics before algebra, algebra before calculus. We simply can't do calculus until we understand algebra.

• In construction, we build a strong foundation before doing any framing and finishing work.

We know and accept this step-by-step process in physical and intellectual areas because things are seen and constant evidence supplied. But in other areas of human development and in social interaction, we often attempt to shortcut natural processes —

substituting expediency for priority, imitation for innovation, cosmetics for character, style for substance and pretense for competence. We often skip some vital steps to save time and effort and still hope to reap the desired rewards.

But such hope is vain. We find there are no shortcuts in the development of professional skills, of talents such as piano playing and public speaking, or of our minds and characters. In all of life, there are stages or processes of growth and development; and at every step, the concept of *the six days of creation* applies.

For example, what happens when a person attempts to shortcut this day-by-day process in developing his or her tennis game? If a person is an average tennis player — at *day three* — but decides one day to play at *day six* to make a better impression, what will result?

What would happen if you were to lead your friends to believe you could play the piano at *day six*, while your actual present skill was at *day two*?

If you are at *day three* in golf and competing against someone at *day five*, would positive thinking alone beat him?

The answers are obvious. It is simply impossible to violate, ignore, or shortcut this development process. It is contrary to nature, and any attempt to seek such a shortcut will result in confusion and frustration. If I am at *day two*, in any field, and desire to move to *day five*, I must first take the step toward *day three*. No bypassing, no shortcutting, no pretending or appearing, no making impressions, no amount of "dressing for success" will compensate for lack of skill and judgment.

Progress involves accepting the fact that I am currently at *day two* and refusing to pretend to be anywhere else.

If students won't let a teacher know what level they are on — by asking a question, or revealing their ignorance — they will not learn or grow. People cannot pretend for long; they will eventually be found out. Often an admission of our ignorance is the first step in our education.

Internal Growth

Now, instead of considering skill or knowledge growth, let us consider the internal growth of an individual. For example, suppose that a particular person is at *day five* intellectually but at *day two* emotionally. Everything is okay when the sun is shining or when things go well. But what happens when fatigue, marital problems, financial pressure, uncooperative teenagers, screaming kids, and ringing telephones join together?

The emotionally immature person may find himself or herself absolutely enslaved by the emotions of anger, impatience, and criticalness. And yet in public, when things are going well, one may never detect this internal deficiency, this immaturity.

Shortcircuiting the natural development process is not always obvious in emotional, social and spiritual areas. We can "pose," and we can pretend. And for a while, we can get by on "one-night stands." We might even deceive ourselves. Yet most of us know what we really are inside, as do some of those we live with and work around.

To relate effectively with our colleagues, spouse or children requires emotional strength, because we must learn to listen. Listening involves patience, openness, and the desire to understand. When we are open, we run the risk that we may be changed — we may be influenced. And if we are sure that we are right, we don't want to change. We find it easier to be closed and to tell and dictate. It is easier to operate from our *day two* emotional level and to give *day six* advice.

Possessing Precedes Giving

I once tried to teach the value of sharing to my daughter at a time when she was not ready to receive it. In effect, I was attempting to move her from *day two* to *day five* on command.

One day I returned home to my daughter's third-year birthday party only to find her in the corner of the front room defiantly grasping all of her presents, unwilling to let the other children play with them. I sensed the presence of several parents witnessing this selfish display. I was embarrassed because I was a professor in the field of human relations, and I felt that these people expected more of me and my children.

The atmosphere in the room was charged, as the other children crowded around my daughter with their hands out, asking to play with the presents they had just given her; and, of course, my daughter adamantly refused to share anything. I said to myself, "Certainly I should teach my daughter to share. The value of sharing is one of the most basic things we believe in." So I proceeded through the following process.

My first method was simply *to request*: "Honey, would you please share with your friends the toys they've given you?"

A flat "No."

My second method was *to reason*: "Honey, if you learn to share your toys with them when they are at your home, then when you go to their homes they will share their toys with you."

Again, "No!"

I was becoming a little more embarrassed, as it was evident I was having no influence. The third method was *to bribe*: "Honey, if you will share, I've got a special surprise for you. I'll give you a piece of gum."

"I don't want a piece of gum!" she exploded.

Now I was becoming exasperated. My fourth method was *to threaten*: "Unless you share, you will be in real trouble!"

"I don't care. These are my things. I don't have to share!"

Last method was *to force*. I merely took some of the toys and gave them to the other kids. "Here, kids, play with them."

Perhaps my daughter needed the experience of possessing the things before she could give them — unless we possess something, we can never really give it. But at that moment, I valued the opinion of those parents more than the growth and development of my child and our relationship. I made an initial judgment that I was right — she should share — and that she was wrong in not doing so. Based on that judgment, I proceeded to manipulate her until I ultimately forced her.

She was at *day two*, and I imposed a *day five* expectation, simply because on my own scale I was at *day two* emotionally. I was unable or unwilling to give patience or understanding, but I expected her to give! If I had been more mature, I may have allowed her to choose to share or not to share. Perhaps after reasoning with her, I could have attempted to turn the attention of the children to an interesting game, thus taking all of the emotional pressure off my child. I've since learned that once my children gain a sense of real possession, they share naturally, freely, and spontaneously.

There are times to teach and train and times not to teach. When relationships are strained and charged with emotion, attempts to teach or train are often perceived as a form of judgment and rejection. A better approach is to be alone with the person and to discuss the principle privately. But again, this requires patience and internal control — in short, emotional maturity.

Borrowing Strength Builds Weakness

In addition to parents, many employers, leaders, and others in positions of authority may be competent, knowledgeable, and skillful (at *day six*) but are emotionally and spiritually immature (at *day two*). They, too, may attempt to compensate for this deficiency, or gap, by borrowing strength from their position or their authority.

How do immature people react to pressure? How does the boss react when subordinates don't do things his way? The teacher when the students challenge her viewpoint?

How would an immature parent treat a teenage daughter when she interrupts with her problems? How does this parent discipline a bothersome younger child? How does this person handle a difference with a spouse on an emotionally explosive matter? How does the person handle challenges at work?

An emotionally immature person will tend to *borrow strength* from position, size, strength, experience, intellect or emotions to make up for a character imbalance. And what are the consequences? Eventually, this person will build weakness in three places:

First, he builds weakness in himself. Borrowing strength from position or authority reinforces his own dependence upon external factors to get things done in the future.

Second, he builds weakness in the other people. Others learn to act or react in terms of fear or conformity, thus stunting their own reasoning, freedom, growth and internal discipline.

Third, he builds weakness in the relationship. It becomes strained. Fear replaces cooperation. Each person involved becomes a little more arbitrary, a little more agitated, a little more defensive.

To win an argument or a contest, he may use his strengths and abilities to back people into a corner. Even though he wins the argument, he loses. Everyone loses. His very strength becomes his weakness.

In fact, whenever we borrow strength from our possessions, positions, credentials, appearance, memberships, status symbols or achievements, what happens to us when these things change or are no longer there?

Obviously, we remain stuck with the weaknesses we have developed in ourselves, in our relationships and in others. In fact, people who have the habit of borrowing strength will eventually lose influence with those they most what to impress. Their children may feel belittled and crushed, with little sense of worth, identity or individuality. Their coworkers may become rebellious and strike back in their own way, often at the very things that are treasured the most.

From what sources, then, can we borrow strength without building weakness? Only from sources that build the internal capacity to deal with whatever the situation calls for. For instance, a surgeon borrows strength from his developed skill and knowledge; a runner from his disciplined body, strong legs and powerful lungs.

In other words, we ask the question: What is it that the situation demands? What strength, what skill, what knowledge, what attitude? Obviously the possessions, the appearances, or the credentials of the surgeon or the athlete are only symbols of what is needed and are therefore worthless and deceiving without the substance.

Implications for Personal Growth

I see six significant implications of the "six-day" development process:

• *Growth is a natural process* — you reap as you sow; algebra before calculus; crawling before walking.

• *We all are at different "days"* (levels of growth) in the physical, social, emotional, intellectual, and spiritual areas. If I am at a different level than you, perhaps the things I need to work on and overcome you have already conquered, and vice versa. Your *day four* may be my *day two*.

• *Comparisons are dangerous.* Comparisons breed insecurity, and yet we commonly make them between our children, coworkers, and other acquaintances. If our sense of worth and personal security comes from such comparisons, how insecure and anxious we will be — feeling superior one minute and inferior the next. Opinions, customs, fashions are fickle, always changing. There is no security in changing things. Internal security simply does not come externally. Borrowing strength from any source that does not build and internally strengthen the borrower will internally weaken him.

Moreover, comparing and borrowing breeds complacency and vanity on the one hand, and discouragement and self-dislike on the other. It encourages people to seek short-cuts, to be ruled by opinion, to live by appearances, and to borrow more strength from external sources.

It's best to compare ourselves only with ourselves. We can't focus or base our happiness on another's progress; we can focus only on our own. We should compare people against their own potential and then constantly affirm that potential and their efforts toward reaching it. We should ask, "How is he doing with what he's got?" instead of comparing one person against another and meting out love or punishment on the basis of that comparison.

• *There is no shortcut.* If I am at *day two* (to continue the metaphor) and desire to move to *day six,* I must go through *days three, four,* and *five.* If I pretend to be at *day six* in order to impress others, eventually I will be found out. Trying to be all things to all people results in the loss of everybody's respect, including one's own. If some people are at *day three,* it is futile and hurtful to compare and criticize them because they aren't at *day five* or *six.* There simply is no shortcut.

• *To improve, we must start from where we are,* not from where we should be, or where someone else is, or even from where others may think we are. By doing one more pushup each day, I could do 30 in a month. Likewise, in any area of improvement, I could also exercise a little more of what it takes, such as a little more patience, understanding, courage, slowly increasing my capacity through daily effort and discipline.

I believe that *day one* and *day two* for most of us involve getting more control over the body — getting to bed early, arising early, exercising regularly, eating in moderation, staying at our work when necessary even though tired, etc. Too many are trying to conquer *day four, five,* and *six* problems, such as procrastination, impatience, or pride, while still a slave to their appetites. If we can't control the body and its appetites, how can we ever control our tongue or overcome our passions and the emotions of anger, envy, jealousy, or hatred. Algebra precedes calculus.

Many aspire to the fruits of *days five* and *six* (love, spirituality, wisdom in decision-making) and yet are unwilling to obey the laws of *day one* (mastering of appetites and passions).

• *Introspection gives us an accurate understanding of our weaknesses and the power to overcome them.* Many of us simply don't know where to start. We don't always know what things come before other things. Someone else's pattern and process may differ from ours. What is someone else's *day five* may be our *day two.* We may be at *day four* one time and at *day one* another time —

even on the same matter! At times we will need to do some work at each level simultaneously.

But the key to our growth and development is always to begin where we are, at our *day one*.

Chapter 4

The Centered Life

Whatever lies at the center of a person's life becomes the primary source of his life-support system. In large measure, I believe, that system is represented by four fundamental dimensions: security, guidance, wisdom, and power.

Four Dimensions

Security represents a person's sense of worth, his identity, his emotional anchorage, his self-esteem, his basic personal strength or lack of it. Security is not an all-or-nothing matter: it lies somewhere on a continuum between a deep sense of high intrinsic worth on one end and on the other end, extreme insecurity wherein a person's life is buffeted by all the fickle forces that play upon it.

Guidance means direction one receives in life. Encompassed by our map, our internal frame of reference that interprets for each of us what is happening out there, are standards or principles or criteria that govern decision-making and doing. Over time, this internal monitor becomes our source of guidance. It serves as a conscience.

If we represent guidance on a continuum, the lower end will show strong addictions and dependencies, conditioned by the person's centering on selfish, sensual or subsistence living. A position toward the middle of the continuum would represent development of the social conscience, the conscience which has been educated and cultivated by centering on human institutions, traditions, and relationships. On the other end of the continuum is the spiritual conscience, wherein a person's guidance comes from inspired or inspiring sources.

Wisdom indicates perspective on life, a sense of balance, an understanding of how the various parts and principles apply and relate to each other. It embraces judgment, discernment, comprehension. It is a gestalt or oneness, an integrated wholeness. The low end of the wisdom continuum is represented by a completely inaccurate map, such that the person's actions and thinking are based on distorted, discordant principles.

The upper end of the wisdom continuum would represent a perfectly accurate, and complete map of life wherein all the parts and principles are properly related to each other. In moving toward that end, there is a clear sense of increasing idealism and purpose (things as they should be) as well as a sensitive, practical approach to realities (things as they are).

Power is the faculty or the capacity to act, the strength and potency to accomplish something. It is the vital energy to make choices and decisions. It also represents the capacity to overcome deeply embedded habits and to cultivate higher, more effective habits. Such power includes the wisdom to discern pure joy and happiness as distinct from temporary pleasure.

At the lower end of the power continuum would be the person who is essentially powerless. He is insecure and completely a product of what happens or has happened to him. He is dependent on circumstances and on others. He may be a total reflection of other people's opinions and directions. He finds himself repeating the same mistakes. He has no real comprehension of what true joy and happiness are.

At the upper end of the continuum is the person who possesses greatly developed powers — one with a high level of self-discipline whose life is a functional product of his decisions rather than of external conditions. Such a person causes things to happen. He is proactive rather than reactive; he chooses his response to any given situation based upon principles, standards, or criteria which he has made an integral part of himself. He takes responsibility not only for his response to what happens to him but in a large measure for what happens to him. He takes responsibility for his feelings and moods and attitudes as well as his thoughts and actions. The four factors defined above — security, guidance, wisdom, and power — are interdependent. Security and well-founded guidance bring true wisdom, and wisdom becomes the spark or catalyst to release and direct power in the person. When these four factors are present together, harmonized and enlivened by each other, they create the great force of a noble personality, a balanced character, a beautifully integrated individual.

Alternate Life Centers

Now let's look at several possible life centers and see how they measure up as promoters of these four fundamental dimensions of personality.

Spouse. It might seem natural and proper to become centered on one's husband or wife. However, I have observed a certain weakness in most spouse-centered relationships — a strong emotional dependence. When a person's sense of emotional worth comes primarily from the marriage relationship, then he or she becomes highly dependent upon that relationship. And that makes him or her extremely vulnerable to the moods and feelings, the behavior and treatment, of the partner, or to any external event which may impinge on the relationship — a new child, in-laws, economic setbacks, social successes, and so forth.

Work or Money.   Another common center to people's lives is work or money.   Our culture encourages us to become centered on work or money-making, and many people adopt this center, often out of a deep desire to provide better for one's family.   But as with other alternative centers, this too will bring about its own undoing. Many people derive much of their security from their employment or from their income or net worth.   And since many factors affect these economic foundations, people become anxious and uneasy, protective and defensive, about anything which may affect those foundations.

When a person's sense of personal worth comes from his net worth, when it is the ground of his being, then he is totally vulnerable to anything that will affect that net worth.   But work and money per se provide no wisdom, no guidance, and only a limited degree of power and security.   All it takes to bring to surface the limitations of a material world is a crisis in a person's life or in the life of a loved one.

Possessions.   Closely allied to the money center, and one of the most common centers and driving forces of materialistic people, is that of possessions.   I speak not only of material possessions but also of the intangible possession of fame or glory or social prominence;   each carries similar seeds of instability and disillusionment.   Through sad experiences, many people learn how flawed this center is; it can vanish rapidly and is influenced by a multitude of forces that can play upon it.

When a person's sense of security lies in his reputation or possessions, his life will be in a constant state of threat and jeopardy, since these possessions may be lost or stolen or devalued.   When his wealth is equated with his net worth, he may feel inferior in the presence of someone of greater wealth and superior in the presence of a person of lesser wealth.   Similarly with the intangibles of position, fame, status, his sense of self-worth depends on whom he is with.   This situation does not permit any feeling of constancy or anchorage or persistent selfhood. It becomes a life of constant threat and worry and of developing various ways of trying to protect and insure these assets, properties, or securities, this position or reputation.

We hear stories of people committing suicide after losing their fortunes in a significant stock decline or their fame in a political reversal. But perhaps the more subtle material vanities have to do with the fashionableness of our clothing, our good looks, the status symbols we surround ourselves with — elegant homes, cars, boats, jewelry, and so on. We simply cannot safely build our security upon such transitory things.

Pleasures. Another very common center, closely allied with material possessions, is that of fun and pleasure. We live in a world where instant gratification is always available, and many become impatient with the natural "law of the harvest," the law of justice. They don't plan to wait for any harvest, or indeed to reap only what they sow. They want what they want, and they want it now. If they don't get it they scream and pout, or they intimidate and condemn and manipulate.

Too much idleness, sports spectating, movie viewing, game playing — too much undisciplined leisure time in which a person continually takes the course of least resistance — gradually wastes a life, a career, a family. It ensures that one's capacities stay dormant, talents remain undeveloped, the mind and spirit become lethargic, and the heart is unfulfilled. Such a life gives no service, makes no contribution, enjoys no larger vision; and short of change, it slips away to decay and death. And the tragic loss or rejection of all the promise and potential will some day bring the recognition indicated by Whittier:

> *Of all sad words of tongue and pen,*
> *The saddest are these — It might have been.*

Leaders. Another popular center is leaders or heroes. Many people are very susceptible to the teachings and examples of people who embody the values they admire. They identify with these people. They then build their security on such expectations and hopes and thereby become dependent and vulnerable. They can be terribly hurt and disillusioned when a particular leader, teacher, mentor, or hero of some kind "doesn't come through." They forget or do not understand that almost everyone has his Achilles' heel and therefore may not be able to measure up to the standard of perfection in every observed situation.

Friends. Young people are particularly susceptible to becoming friend-centered. Acceptance and belonging to a peer group can become supremely important to a young person. Anything that would cause embarrassment to self or to the group becomes the ultimate sin. In that situation, the person's frame of reference becomes more like a straightjacket, through which he deals with life. Often this results in losing the very thing desired, as he strives to become all things to all people. He ends up becoming nothing to everyone, including himself.

Enemies. No one would consciously want to put an enemy at the center of his life, and yet enemy-centering is a very common thing, particularly when there is frequent interaction between people who are in real conflict with each other. When someone feels he has been unjustly dealt with by an emotionally or socially significant person, it is very easy for him to become preoccupied with the injustice and make the other person the center of his life.

For example, in organization life, some become obsessed with the particular weaknesses of their bosses or their working associates — almost paranoid in some instances. They think and talk of almost nothing else, constantly looking for evidence, reading in motives, seeking validation and sympathy from others, planning defensive maneuvers, and so forth.

Self. Another option is self-centeredness. It lies at the heart of most of the centers already described. We tend to equate self-centeredness with selfishness, which we think of as bad. And yet, if we closely examine many of the popular approaches to growth, enlightenment, and self-fulfillment, we often find self-centering at their core. Nevertheless, the approaches continue to find public acceptance. It's as if self-centeredness in the raw — as in a husband indulging his expensive tastes while denying his wife necessities — is clearly objectionable, while giving it another name, such as "personal development," endows it with respectability. "How could it be wrong when it feels so good?"

On the low end of the self-centered continuum is a kind of egocentrism wherein the person is concerned only with his own activities and wants. Also on the lower end would be a kind of philanthropic hedonism or pleasure seeking, an attempt to satisfy one's own wants in the guise of helping others. The higher forms of humanism would be at the upper end of the continuum. Even though the altruistic or humanistic approach appears to be other-centered, in that it focuses on doing good to others, its basic method is still self-centered.

Combination. In this condition, people are so much a function of the influences that play upon their lives that their center often becomes a blending or mixing of many of the centers discussed above. Depending upon what condition (external and/or internal) the person may be in, different centers are activated until each is played out as the person's underlying needs are satisfied, then another center becomes the compelling force. Such fluctuations may take place even on the same day.

One of the main problems with an eclectic-approach or combination center is the continual shifting of the perspective of the map, resulting in relativism and a lack of consistency in basic values, standards and direction. It is like roller-coasting through life: high one moment, low the next, making efforts to compensate for one weakness by borrowing strength from another weakness. It offers no consistent sense of direction, no persistent wisdom, no steady power supply or sense of personal, intrinsic worth and identity.

Church. Suppose, then, that we consider putting a church at the center of our lives. This has the appearance of logic for church members who believe that the church is God's kingdom on earth.

Nevertheless, it should be apparent that the church is a means to an end, not an end in itself. The church is the instrument. And, as members of every church know, there is a difference between being active in the church and being active in the gospel. In the narrow sense, activity in the church means attending meetings and observing well-defined and minimal laws and rituals. Activity in the gospel means much more, having more to do with the heart and mind.

Family. How about family-centeredness? Surely this is safe. After all, we hear that "the family is the most important organization in society" and that "no other success can compensate for failure in the home" and that "the most important work we will ever do will be within the walls of our own homes."

These statements have great merit, but there's a paradox at play here: the ultimate result of family-centeredness can be the loss of the family. For example, a family-centered person may come to resent job demands and to reject opportunities to serve in volunteer organizations and become a law unto himself.

I personally know of several individuals who put their families first, who made continuous efforts to keep the family happy and together, but who in the process neglected other important responsibilities and duties. They stopped being models of service and sacrifice outside the family. In each case, these individuals have weakened, not strengthened their family ties because they were building too much on family conveniences and pleasures instead of on correct principles. "Me and mine" can be as selfish as "me."

Principle-Centered Life

My experience leads me to believe that when a person centers his life on correct principles and their source, he becomes more balanced, unified, organized, anchored, rooted. He finds a foundation and cornerstone of all his activities, relationships, and decisions. Such a person will have a sense of stewardship about everything in his life, including time, talents, money, possessions, relationships, his family, his body, and so forth. He recognizes the need to use them for good purposes and, as a steward, to be accountable for their use.

When we are anchored to social mirrors and models, however, we empower circumstances to guide and control us. We become reactive rather than proactive; we reflect what happens to us; we respond to external conditions and stimuli rather than choose our own responses or to cause things to happen.

Because of a lack of wisdom (of accurate maps), our reactions will often tend to be either overreactive or underreactive instead of appropriately proactive. A proactive stance means that we act on the basis of our own decisions and values, not on the basis of our external conditions or internal moods. To put it another way, we subordinate moods and feelings to higher values and commitments.

One common reactive pattern is to live in compartments, such that one's behavior is based largely on the role expectations in each compartment — husband, father, son, business executive, community leader, and so on. But each of these compartments carries its own value system, in which case the person may find himself meeting different expectations and living by differing values based on the role or the environment he is in at any particular time. A life centered on unchanging principles, on the other hand, brings permanency into one's life.

As I review my life, I conclude that at one time or another I have experienced just about every center described in this chapter — and every consequence of that centering. And I conclude that the principle-centered life is the only abundant one.

Chapter 5

Signs of Progress

From study and observation and from my own strivings, I have isolated eight discernible characteristics of people who are principle-centered leaders.

These traits not only characterize effective leaders, they also serve as signs of progress for all of us. I will briefly discuss each in turn.

They Are Continually Learning

Principle-centered people are constantly educated by their experiences. They read, they seek training, they take classes, they listen to others, they learn through both their ears and their eyes. They are curious, always asking questions. They continually expand their competence, their ability to do things. They develop new skills, new interests. They discover that the more they know, the more they realize they don't know; that as their circle of knowledge grows, so does its outside edge of ignorance. Most of this learning and growth energy is self-initiated and feeds upon itself.

You will develop your abilities faster by learning to make and keep promises or commitments. Start by making a small promise to yourself; continue fulfilling that promise until you have a sense that you have a little more control over yourself. Now take the next level of challenge. Make yourself a promise and keep it until you have established control at that level. Now move to the next level; make the promise, keep it. As you do this, your sense of personal worth will increase; your sense of self-mastery will grow, as will your confidence that you can master the next level.

Be serious and intent in the whole process, however, because if you make this commitment to yourself and then break it, your self-esteem will be weakened and your capacity to make and keep another promise will be decreased.

They are Service Oriented

Those striving to be principle-centered see life as a mission, not as a career. Their nurturing sources have armed and prepared them for service. In effect, every morning, they "yoke up" and put on the harness of service, thinking of others.

See yourself each morning, yoking up, putting on the harness of service in your various stewardships. See yourself taking the straps and connecting them around your shoulders as you prepare to do the work assigned to you that day. See yourself allowing someone else to adjust the yoke or harness. See yourself yoked up to another person at your side — a coworker or spouse — and learning to pull together with that person.

I emphasize this principle of service or yoking up because I have come to believe that effort to become principle-centered without a load to carry will simply not succeed. We may attempt to do it as a kind of intellectual or moral exercise, but if we don't have a sense of responsibility, of service, of contribution, something we need to pull or push, it becomes a futile endeavor.

They Radiate Positive Energy

The countenances of principle-centered people are cheerful, pleasant, happy. Their attitude is optimistic, positive, upbeat. Their spirit is enthusiastic, hopeful, and believing.

This positive energy is like an energy field or an aura that surrounds them and that similarly charges or changes weaker, negative energy fields around them. They also attract and magnify smaller positive energy fields. When they come into contact with strong, negative energy sources they tend to either neutralize or sidestep this negative energy. Sometimes they will simply leave it, walking away from its poisonous orbit. Wisdom gives them a sense of how strong it is and a sense of humor and of timing in dealing with it.

Be aware of the effect of your own energy and understand how you radiate and direct it. And in the middle of confusion or contention or negative energy, strive to be a peacemaker, a harmonizer, to undo or reverse destructive energy. You will discover what a self-fulfilling prophecy positive energy is when combined with the next characteristic.

They Believe in Other People

Principle-centered people don't over-react to negative behaviors, criticism, or human weaknesses. They don't feel built up when they discover the weaknesses of others. They are not naive; they are aware of weakness. But they realize that behavior and potential are two different things. They believe in the unseen potential of all people. They feel grateful for their blessings and feel naturally to compassionately forgive and forget the offenses of others. They don't carry grudges. They refuse to label other people, to stereotype, categorize, and prejudge. Rather, they see the oak tree in the acorn and understand the process of which they can be a part in helping this acorn become a great oak.

Once my wife and I felt uneasy about the labels we and others had attached to one of our sons, even though these labels were justified by his behavior. By visualizing his potential, we gradually came to see him differently. When we believed in the unseen potential, the old labels naturally vanished, and we stopped trying to change him overnight. We simply knew that his talent and potential would come in its own time. And it did, to the astonishment, frankly, of others, including other family members. We were not surprised because we knew who he was.

Truly, believing is seeing. We must, therefore, seek to believe in the unseen potential. This creates a *climate for growth and opportunity.* Self-centered people believe that the key lies in them, in their techniques, in doing "their thing" to others. This works only temporarily. If you believe it's "in" them, not "in" you, you relax, accept, affirm, and let it happen. Either way, it is a self-fulfilling prophecy.

They Lead Balanced Lives

They read the best literature and magazines and keep up with current affairs and events. They are active socially, having many friends and a few confidants. They are active intellectually, having many interests. They read, watch, observe, and learn. Within the limits of age and health, they are active physically. They have a lot of fun. They enjoy themselves. They have a healthy sense of humor, particularly laughing at themselves and not at others' expense. You can sense they have a healthy regard for and honesty about themselves.

They can feel their own worth, which is manifest by their courage and integrity and by the absence of a need to brag, to drop names, to borrow strength from possessions or credentials or titles or past achievements. They are open in their communication, simple, direct, nonmanipulative. They also have a sense of what is appropriate, and they would sooner err on the side of understatement than on the side of exaggeration.

They are not extremists — they do not make everything all or nothing. They do not divide everything into two parts, seeing everything as good or bad, as either/or. They think in terms of continuums, priorities, hierarchies. They have the power to discriminate, to sense the uniquenesses, similarities, and differences in each situation. This does not mean they are relativists, seeing everything in terms of situational ethics. They fully recognize absolutes and courageously condemn the bad and champion the good.

Their actions and attitudes are proportionate to the situation—balanced, temperate, moderate, wise. For instance, they're not workaholics, religious zealots, political fanatics, diet crashers, food bingers, pleasure addicts, fasting martyrs. They're not slavishly chained to their plans and schedules. They don't condemn themselves for every foolish mistake or social blunder. They don't brood about yesterday or daydream about tomorrow. They live sensibly in the present, carefully plan the future, and flexibly adapt to changing circumstances. Their self-honesty is revealed by their sense of humor, their willingness to admit then forget mistakes, and to cheerfully do the things ahead which lie within their power.

They have no need to manipulate through either intimidating anger or self-pitying martyrdom. They are genuinely happy for others' successes and do not feel in any sense that these take anything from them. They take both praise and blame proportionately without head trips or overreactions. They see success on the far side of failure. The only real failure for them is the experience not learned from.

They See Life as an Adventure

Principle-centered people savor life. Because their security comes from within instead of from without, they have no need to categorize and stereotype everything and everybody in life to give them a sense of certainty and predictability. They see old faces freshly, old scenes as if for the first time. They are like courageous explorers going on an expedition into uncharted territories; they are really not sure what is going to happen, but they are confident it will be exciting and growth-producing and that they will discover new territory and make new contributions. Their security lies in their initiative, resourcefulness, willpower, courage, stamina, and native intelligence rather than in the safety, protection, and abundance of their home camps, of their comfort zones.

They rediscover people each time they meet them. They are interested in them. They ask questions and get involved. They are completely present when they listen. They learn from them. They don't label them from past successes or failures. They see no one bigger than life. They are not overawed by top government figures or celebrities. They resist becoming any person's disciple. They are basically unflappable and capable of adapting to virtually anything that comes along. One of their fixed principles is flexibility. They truly lead the abundant life.

They are Synergistic

Synergy is the state in which the whole is more than the sum of the parts. Principle-centered people are synergistic. They are change catalysts. They improve almost any situation they get into. They work as smart as they work hard. They are amazingly productive, but in new and creative ways.

In team endeavors, they build on their strengths and strive to complement their weaknesses with the strengths of others. Delegation for results is easy and natural to them, since they believe in others' strengths and capacities. And, since they are not threatened by the fact that others are better in some ways, they feel no need to supervise them closely.

When principle-centered people negotiate and communicate with others in seemingly adversarial situations, they learn to separate the people from the problem. They focus on the other person's interests and concerns rather than fight over positions. Gradually, others discover their sincerity and become part of a creative problem-solving process. Together, they arrive at synergistic solutions, which are usually much better than any of the original proposals, as opposed to compromise solutions wherein both parties give and take a little.

They Exercise for Self-Renewal

Finally, they regularly exercise the four dimensions of the human personality: physical, mental, emotional, and spiritual.

They participate in some kind of balanced, moderate, regular program of aerobic exercise, meaning cardiovascular exercise — using the large leg muscles and working the heart and lungs. This provides endurance — improving the capacity of the body and brain to use oxygen — along with many other physical and mental benefits. Also valuable are stretching exercises for flexibility and resistance exercises for strength and muscle tone.

They exercise their minds through reading, creative problem-solving, writing, and visualizing. Emotionally, they make an effort to be patient, to listen to others with genuine empathy, to show unconditional love, and to accept responsibility for their own lives and decisions and reactions. Spiritually, they focus on prayer, scripture study, meditation, and fasting.

I'm convinced that if a person will spend one hour a day on these basic exercises, he or she will improve the quality, productivity, and satisfaction of every other hour of the day, including the depth and restfulness of sleep.

No other single hour of your day will return as much as the hour you invest in sharpening the saw, that is, exercising these four dimensions of the human personality. If you will do this daily, you will soon experience the impact for good on your life.

Some of these activities may be done in the normal course of the day; others will need to be scheduled into the day. They take some time, but in the long run they save us a great deal of time. We must never get too busy sawing to take time to sharpen the saw; never too busy driving to take time to get gas.

I find that if I do this hour of exercise early in the morning, it is like a private victory and that it just about guarantees public victories throughout the day. But if I take the course of least resistance and neglect all or part of this program, I forfeit that private victory and find myself uprooted by public pressures and stresses through the day.

These principles of self-renewal will gradually produce a strong and healthy character with a powerfully disciplined, service-focused will.

Chapter 6

Primary Greatness

In his work and writings, Erich Fromme has observed that self-alienation is largely a fruit of how oriented we are to the human personality market, to selling ourselves to others.

He notes: "Today we come across an individual who behaves like an automaton, who does not know or understand himself, and the only person that he knows is the person that he is supposed to be, whose meaningless chatter has replaced communicative speech, whose synthetic smile has replaced genuine laughter, and whose sense of dull despair has taken the place of genuine pain."

Positive personality traits, while often essential for success, constitute secondary greatness. To focus on personality before character is to try to grow the leaves without the roots.

If we consistently use personality techniques and skills to enhance our social interactions, we may truncate the vital character base. We simply can't have the fruits without the roots. Private victory precedes public victory. Self-mastery and self-discipline are the character roots of good relationships with others.

If we use human influence strategies and tactics to get other people to do what we want, we may succeed in the short-term; but over time, our duplicity and insincerity will breed distrust. Everything we do will be perceived as manipulative. We may have the "right" rhetoric, style and even intention, but without trust, we won't achieve primary greatness or lasting success. To focus on technique is like cramming your way through school. You sometimes get by, perhaps even get good grades, but if you don't pay the price, day in and day out, you never achieve true mastery of the subjects. Could you ever "cram" on the farm — forget to plant in the spring, play all summer and then race in the fall to bring in the harvest? No, because the farm is a natural system. You must pay the price

47

and follow the process. You reap what you sow; there is no shortcut.

The law of the harvest also operates in long-term human relationships. In a social or academic system, you may get by if you learn how to "play the game." You may make favorable first impressions through charm; you may win through intimidation. But secondary personality traits alone have no permanent worth in long-term relationships. If there isn't deep integrity and fundamental character strength, true motives will eventually surface and human relationships will fail.

Many people with secondary greatness — that is, social status, position, fame, wealth or talent — lack primary greatness or goodness of character. And this void is evident in every long-term relationship they have, whether it is with a business associate, a spouse, a friend or a teenage child. It is character that communicates most eloquently. As Emerson once put it, "What you are shouts so loud in my ears I cannot hear what you say."

Of course, people may have character strength but lack key communication skills — and that undoubtedly affects the quality of their relationships as well. But in the last analysis, what we are communicates far more eloquently than anything we say or do.

How We See Ourselves

The view we have of ourselves affects not only our attitudes and behaviors but also our views of other people. In fact, until we take how we see ourselves — and how we see others — into account, we will be unable to understand how others see and feel about themselves and their world. Unaware, we will project our intentions on their behavior and think ourselves objective.

If the vision we have of ourselves comes from the social mirror — from the opinions, perceptions and paradigms of the people around us — our view of ourselves is like a reflection in the crazy mirror at the carnival. Specific data is disjointed and out of proportion:

"You're never on time."

"Why can't you ever keep things in order?"

"This is so simple. Why can't you understand it?"

Such data is often more projection than reflection. It projects the concerns and character weaknesses of people giving the input, rather than accurately reflecting what we are.

When the basic source of a person's definition of himself is the social mirror, he may confuse the mirror reflection with his real self; in fact, he may begin to believe and accept the image in the mirror, even rejecting other, more positive views of himself unless they show the distortions he has come to accept.

From time to time, I conduct a little experiment. I ask people to list others' perceptions of them, and then compare these with their own self-concept. Typically, more than half are shocked to realize that to a large degree, their self-image has come from the social mirror. It has come slowly, gradually, imperceptibly. And unless it changes, it will severely handicap them for life.

One antidote for a poisoned self-image is the affirmation of your worth and potential by another person. In the play *Man of La Mancha*, Don Quixote slowly changes the self-concept of the prostitute by constantly, unconditionally affirming her. When she starts to see herself differently, she starts to act differently. He even gives her a new name, Dulcinea, so that she will ever be reminded of her new identity and potential.

To affirm a person's worth or potential, you may have to look at him with the eye of faith and treat him in terms of his potential, not his behavior. Goethe put it this way, "Treat a man as he is, and he will remain as he is; treat a man as he can and should be, and he will become as he can and should be." This isn't to say that we trust him unconditionally, but it does mean that we treat him respectfully and trust him conditionally.

Some people say that you have to like yourself before you can like others. That idea has merit, but if you don't know yourself, if you don't control yourself, if you don't have mastery over yourself, it's very hard to like yourself, except in some superficial way.

Real self-respect comes from dominion over self, from true independence and win-win interdependence. If our motives, words and actions come from human relations techniques (the personality ethic) rather than from our own inner core (the character ethic), others will sense that insecurity or duplicity. We simply won't be able to create and sustain effective, win-win relationships.

The place to begin building any relationship is inside ourselves, inside our circle of influence, our own character. As we become independent — proactive, centered in correct principles, value-driven and able to organize and execute around the priorities in our life with integrity — we then can choose to become interdependent: capable of building rich, enduring, productive relationships with other people.

Acute and Chronic Pain

While our relationships with other people open up tremendous possibilities for increased productivity, service, contribution, growth and learning, they may also cause us the greatest pain and frustration — and we're very aware of that pain because it's acute.

We may live for years with chronic pain caused by a lack of vision, leadership or management in our personal lives. We may feel vaguely uneasy and uncomfortable and occasionally take steps to ease the pain, and yet, because the pain is chronic, we get used to it, gradually learning to live with it.

But when we have problems in our relationships with other people, we're very aware of the pain — it's often intense, acute, and we want it to go away. That's when we try to treat the symptoms with quick-fix techniques — the Band-aids of the personality ethic. We don't understand that the acute pain is an outgrowth of the deeper, chronic problem. And until we stop treating the symptoms and start treating the problem, our efforts will be counter-productive. We will only obscure the chronic pain even more.

Personal effectiveness is the foundation of interpersonal effectiveness. Private victory precedes public victory. Strength of character and independence form the foundation for authentic, effective interaction with others.

Dag Hammarskjold, past Secretary-General of the United Nations, once made a profound, far-reaching statement: "It is more noble to give yourself completely to one individual than to labor diligently for the salvation of the masses."

In other words, I could devote eight, ten or twelve hours a day, five, six or seven days a week to the thousands of people and projects "out there" and still not have a deep, meaningful relationship with my own spouse, teenage son or close working associate. And it would take more nobility of character — more humility, courage and strength — to rebuild that one relationship than it would to continue putting in all those hours for all those people and causes.

Many problems in organizations stem from poor relationships at the very top — between two partners in a firm, between the owner and president of a company, between the president and an executive vice-president. And it takes more nobility of character to confront and resolve those issues than it does to work diligently for the many people and projects "out there."

Three Character Traits

The following three character traits are essential to primary greatness.

Integrity. I define integrity as the value we place on ourselves. As we clearly identify our values and proactively organize and execute around our priorities on a daily basis, we develop self-awareness and self-value by making and keeping meaningful promises and commitments. If we can't make and keep commitments to ourselves as well as to others, our commitments become meaningless We know it, and others know it. They sense our duplicity and become guarded.

Maturity. I define maturity as the balance between courage and consideration. If a person can express his feelings and convictions with courage balanced with consideration for the feelings and convictions of another person, he is mature. If he lacks internal maturity and emotional strength, he might try to borrow strength from his position, power, credentials, seniority, or affiliations.

While courage may focus on getting bottom-line results, consideration deals more with the long-term welfare of other stakeholders. In fact, the basic mission of mature management is to increase the standard of living and the quality of life for *all* stakeholders.

Abundance Mentality. Our thinking is that there is plenty out there for everybody. This abundance mentality flows out of a deep sense of personal worth and security. It results in sharing recognition, profits and responsibility. It opens up creative new options and alternatives. It turns personal joy and fulfillment outward. It recognizes unlimited possibilities for positive interaction, growth and development.

Most people are deeply scripted in the scarcity mentality. They see life as a finite pie: if someone gets a big piece of the pie, it means less for everybody else. It's the zero sum paradigm of life. People with a scarcity mentality have a hard time sharing recognition, credit, power or profit. They also have a tough time being genuinely happy for the success of other people — even, and sometimes especially, members of their own family or close friends and associates. It's almost as if something is being taken from them when someone else receives special recognition or success.

A character rich in integrity, maturity and the abundance mentality has a genuineness that goes far beyond technique. Your character is constantly radiating, communicating. From it, people come to trust or distrust you. If your life runs hot and cold, if you're both caustic and kind, if your private performance doesn't square with your public performance, people won't open up to you, even if they want and need your love or help. They won't feel safe enough to expose their opinions and tender feelings.

Inside-out Vs. Outside-in

Lasting solutions to problems, lasting happiness and success come from the inside-out. What results from the outside-in is unhappy people who feel victimized and immobilized, focused on all the weaknesses of other people and the circumstances they feel are responsible for their own stagnant condition. It results in unhappy marriages where each spouse wants the other to change, where each is confessing the other's weaknesses, where each is trying to shape up the other. It results in labor-management disputes where people spend much time and energy lobbying or fighting to get their way.

Members of our family have lived in three of the world's trouble spots — South Africa, Israel and Ireland — and I believe that the source of the continuing problems in each of these places is the dominant social paradigm of outside-in.

Inside-out suggests that if you want to have a happy marriage, be the kind of person who generates positive energy and sidesteps negative energy. If you want to have a more cooperative teenager, be a more understanding parent. If you want to have more freedom or more latitude in your job, be more responsible and make a greater contribution.

Inside-out suggests that if we want to develop the trust that results in win-win agreements and synergistic solutions, we must control our own lives and subordinate short-term desires to higher purposes and principles. Private victories precede public victories. Making and keeping promises to ourselves precedes making and keeping promises to others. And it's a continuing process, an upward spiral of growth that leads to progressively higher forms of independence and interdependence.

Educating and Obeying the Conscience

The key to working from the inside-out, the paradigm of primary greatness, is to educate and obey the conscience — that unique human endowment that senses congruence or disparity with correct principles and lifts us toward them.

Just as the education of nerve and sinew is vital to the athlete and education of the mind is vital to the scholar, education of the conscience is vital to primary greatness. Training the conscience, however, requires even more discipline. It requires honest living, reading inspiring literature and thinking noble thoughts. Just as junk food and lack of exercise can ruin an athlete's condition, things that are obscene, crude or pornographic can breed an inner darkness that numbs our highest sensibilities and substitutes the social conscience of "Will I be found out?" for the natural conscience of "What is right and wrong?"

The education of conscience begins in the family in one's earliest months and continues there indefinitely through parental example and precept. But when a person becomes converted to the need, he seeks to advance that education himself. He finds that moving along the upward spiral involves learning, committing and doing — and learning, committing and doing again at increasingly higher levels.

People with primary greatness have a sense of stewardship about everything in life, including their time, talents, money, possessions, relationships, family and even their bodies. They recognize the need to use all their resources for positive purposes; and they expect to be held accountable.

People with primary greatness return kindness for offense, patience for impatience. They bring out the best in those around them by seeking to bless when being cursed, to turn the other cheek, to go the second mile, to forgive and forget, to move on in life with cheerfulness, believing in the potential goodness of people and the eventual triumph of truth.

The moment a person attempts to become his own advocate, seeking to defend or justify himself or to return in kind the treatment he receives, he becomes caught up in the exchange of negative energy. He and his enemy are then on the same turf, and they will either fight or flee in such destructive ways as manipulation, violence, withdrawal, indifference, litigation or political battles (witness the political campaigns of 1988).

As we give grace to others, we receive more grace ourselves. As we affirm people and show a fundamental belief in their capacity to grow and improve, as we bless them even when they are cursing or judging us — we build primary greatness into our personality and character.

Chapter 7

Making Champions of Your Children

Sandra and I have nine children, and we consider all of them champions. Of course, neither they nor we have arrived; daily, we pray for wisdom, strength, forgiveness and the power to do better.

In this chapter, I'll write about what we have tried to do in various ways with each of our children to make them champions.

The following 10 keys, incidentally, also apply to making champions of the people you employ, manage or lead.

First, we work to build our children's self-esteem, from the day they are born, by affirming them a great deal, believing in them, and giving them a lot of positive feedback. We express confidence in them and in their potential. We try not to compare them with each other or with other people.

I have always believed that how people feel about themselves inside is the real key to using their talent and releasing their potential. And how they feel about themselves is largely a function of how they are seen and treated by others, particularly their parents.

When our children were young — preschool ages — we tried to build their self-esteem by spending a lot of time with them, listening to them, playing with them, and affirming them. For example, I still spend a tremendous amount of time with our youngest child, eight-year-old Joshua, and I thoroughly enjoy it. When I return from a trip — even if I'm only gone one day — we celebrate by going to a neighborhood store for a treat. As soon as we're in the car together, he'll nuzzle up to me and say, "Oh, we're here together again, just you and me." And then I start going, "ah, oh." By the time we get to the store, we're just filled with each other. And then at night, he says, "Will you tell me a story again tonight, dad?" I say, "Oh, of course, son." So he gets right next to me, and I tell him stories.

Second, we encourage primary greatness. We teach them that there are two kinds of greatness: primary greatness — which is the principle-centered character — and secondary greatness, which is the greatness that the world acknowledges. That's been a constant theme. We try to inspire them to go for primary greatness first and not to compensate for character weakness by substituting or borrowing strength from secondary sources (popularity, reputation, possessions, natural talents, etc.)

Our son Sean showed primary greatness scores of times while on his mission to South Africa — constantly denying himself, disciplining himself, loving others, affirming every one he worked with, and finally extending his mission to influence more people. He learned, often the hard way, that the critical issues of life revolve around God's opinion and glory, not man's opinion and glory.

Sean has also shown primary greatness in his courage to make tough decisions in the face of tremendous pressure. As a quarterback on the BYU football team, he learned to read the defense and audibilize when he felt that the play sent in was not going to work. He developed poise, patience, and skill to read coverage and throw to the open receiver. When he sensed the team getting low, he returned to the huddle high and exuded an attitude of, "We're going to score — we're going to make something happen." When he was sacked, he'd hop back up, pat the tackler on the back, and say, "Good hit." He tried to get close to a player who was discouraged and had lost faith in himself.

While he wants to play well and win games, his primary goal in college is to prepare for life and for graduate school. Right now he's not thinking in terms of a long-term football career, knowing that a serious injury can change everything anyway.

Third, we encourage them to develop their own interests. For instance, when Joshua saw the movie, Karate Kid, he wanted to take karate lessons. I immediately signed him up, knowing full well that he'd likely get turned on by something else in two weeks and gradually lose interest in karate. But I want him to try it when he's excited about it. I try to affirm him in his choice of activities. For example, recently, we were throwing the football in the hallway, and he said, "Notice how good I am at football." He doesn't doubt his ability to do many different things well.

When we detect real talent in our children, we encourage them to develop it. For example, I could see Sean's athletic ability long before he participated in competitive athletics. When he was in grade school, I could sense the flexibility, coordination, quickness and balance in his body. I'd encourage him, "Why don't you compete? Why don't you enter the races?" But he was always a little hesitant for fear that if he tried, he might fail, and it would be better not to try than to experience failure. One day, he finally consented to compete in some races at school. He won all of them, and once he got a sense of what he could do, he started competing in several sports.

Fourth, we try to create an enjoyable family culture. We want our children to get more fun and satisfaction from the family than from the school or from their peers or from any other outside influence. Basically, we don't want them to have anything to rebel against because the family culture is so fun and so affirming, and there are so many opportunities associated with it. There's no feeling of limitation, no feeling that you can't do something. We cultivate the attitude, "You can do things, even great things if you plan ahead and work for it."

We try to have regular dates, at least one a month, with each child and do something that is special to them. We also have frequent one-on-one personal visits or interviews with them. We also have a lot of fun with birthdays. We call them birthweeks and dedicate the whole week to that person. Goings and comings are highlighted. We also have home evenings and family devotionals. We try to keep these positive and encourage everyone to express why they love or appreciate each other.

Fifth, we plan ahead. Right now, we have planned several major family events that we're going to do in the next six months. Our son Stephen and his wife Jeri said that a major hesitancy of moving first to Dallas, where he worked for Trammell Crow, and then to Boston, where he attended Harvard Business School, was that they didn't want to miss the fun things we had planned.

I think many parents fail to make champions of their children by not planning fun family events — events that become traditional. Part of the fun of any activity is in planning it; in fact, there's often as much satisfaction in the anticipation as there is in the realization of the event. Money is often an excuse, a cop out, for not planning or doing anything. What you do doesn't have to be expensive to be fun. What's important is that you have fun family times, that your children participate in planning them, that you all get excited anticipating them, that everybody feels part of it and thinks it was fun when they look back on it.

Of course, the extended family is a very important part of this planning. Our children keep close to their cousins and are concerned about their welfare and success. We often involve four generations in our family activities, and we all take great interest in each other. We don't want to miss family things, even the teenagers. That attitude is so important to building champions because it gives children identity, builds their self-esteem, provides them with a caring support system, and offers them service opportunities.

Sixth, we try to set an example of excellence. We all try to excel in what we do so that excellence becomes an unspoken, unwritten norm. We have never had to tell our kids to study and to do their homework, perhaps because they constantly sense the value of reading and learning. It's part of the family culture as well as the expectation at school. We'll help them with homework if they ask, but we try to empower them to be independent of us. In fact, our problem has been to get the kids not to study so much. They're sometimes too conscientious.

Seventh, we teach them to visualize to help them realize their own potential. When Sean was playing quarterback in high school, for example, I had many one-on-one visualization experiences with him, particularly on nights before games.

Visualization is based on the principle that all things are created twice: first mentally and then physically. Most training in athletics is physical. Coaches may talk about mental toughness and concentration, but very few have any sort of consistent system for mental rehearsal or visualization. However, world-class athletes are almost all visualizers; they literally experience their victories in their minds long before they experience them in fact.

When I started working with Sean in this area, I taught him how to relax and then described in vivid detail different situations in a football game. Sean would see himself performing ideally in each situation.

Such mental preparation has its payoffs. In a state championship game, for example, his team (Provo High School) fell behind by two touchdowns, and the momentum was with the other team. Provo was way back near their own end zone after having been thrown for a loss. I "saw" Sean make up his mind. "I'm not just going to take assignments. I'll consider the plays sent in, but we're going to have to make this thing happen." I could both see and feel it, and the team could feel it. That's when the momentum shifted. It all started in his head. They drove all the way down the field and scored a touchdown, and then another one, and another one and won the game. I think they won largely because Sean and others had already handled such situations time and time again in their minds.

As he prepared for each football season at BYU, he spent some time every day in visualization. He's also watched films of former great BYU quarterbacks — Robbi Bosco, Steve Young, Jim McMahan, Marc Wilson, and Gifford Nielson — and they became on-the-field mentors and models.

Eighth, we adopt their friends. For instance, we adopted several of Stephen's, Sean's and David's football teammates. We video taped all of the games and invited everyone to our home after each game to see those films. This helped create a kind of family/team culture.

Individual champions are often part of championship teams. That's why we invest so much in the teams and clubs, schools and classes our children belong to. When family, friends, school and church are all aligned, it makes a powerful training system. Any time something gets out of alignment — when there's a problem with a peer, for example — we just adopt the peer. It's better than trying to get them to drop the peer.

Ninth, we teach them to have faith, to believe and trust others, and to affirm, build, bless and serve others. Cynthia, Maria and Catherine all learned on their missions that empathy is the key to influence — that you've got to be very sensitive to the feelings and perceptions of others. If you're going to build champions, you've got to take an interest in people, especially the downcast and outcast. The key to the 99 is the one.

In football, Sean takes an active interest in people that no one will take an interest in, such as walk-on freshmen, and it's genuine interest. It's not feigned. He's convinced that the main reason people don't reach their potential is because they doubt themselves. He affirms them. People become great if you treat them in terms of their potential. The key to success with people is to believe in them, affirm them.

Goethe wisely taught, "Treat a person as he is, and he will remain as he is; treat him as he can and should be, and he'll become as he can and should be."

Tenth, we provide support, resources, and feedback. With all of our children, we exchange letters and phone calls to affirm each other. Such constant affirmations have a cumulative effect. It becomes a strong emotional support to people.

We also rely on each other for honest feedback, as good feedback is essential to growth. Sean has always welcomed it. For instance, he said to his football coaches, "I want you to know I want feedback. You're not going to offend me. Just tell me whatever you feel at any time." He's constantly willing to learn from those who have the knowledge and the skill. He's very open and teachable, even when some of the lessons are extremely tough to take.

Building champions requires constant effort. We strive endlessly and find the need to return to basics again and again.

Chapter 8

The Circle of Influence

One way to become more aware of our own degree of proactivity is to look at where we focus our time and energy.

We each have a wide range of things we're concerned about —our health, our children, problems at work, the national debt, nuclear war. We could separate those from things in which we have no particular mental or emotional involvement by creating a *Circle of Concern.*

As we look at those things within our Circle of Concern, it becomes apparent that there are some things over which we have no real control and others that we can do something about. We could identify those concerns in the latter group by circumscribing them within a smaller *Circle of Influence.*

No Concern

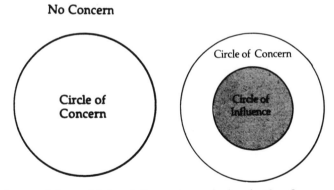

By determining which of these two circles is the focus of most of our time and energy, we can discover much about the degree of our proactivity.

Proactive people focus their efforts in the Circle of Influence. They work on the things they can do something about. The nature of their energy is positive, enlarging and magnifying, causing their Circle of Influence to increase.

Reactive people, on the other hand, focus their efforts in the Circle of Concern. They focus on the weakness of other people, the problems in the environment, and circumstances over which they have no control. Their focus results in blaming and accusing attitudes, reactive language, and increased feelings of victimization. The negative energy generated by that focus, combined with neglect in areas they could do something about, causes their Circle of Influence to shrink.

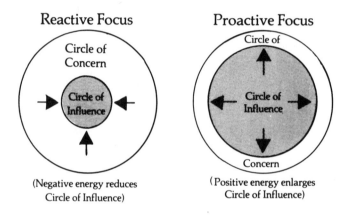

Reactive Focus — Circle of Concern / Circle of Influence
(Negative energy reduces Circle of Influence)

Proactive Focus — Circle of Concern / Circle of Influence
(Positive energy enlarges Circle of Influence)

As long as we are working in our Circle of Concern, we empower the things within it to control us. We aren't taking the proactive initiative necessary to affect positive change.

Direct, Indirect and No Control

The problems we face fall in one of three areas: direct control (problems involving our own behavior); indirect control (problems involving other people's behavior); or no control (problems we can do nothing about, such as our past or situational realities we cannot change).

The proactive approach to life puts the first step in the solution of all three kinds of problems within our present Circle of Influence:

• *Direct control problems* are solved by working on our habits. They are obviously within our Circle of Influence.

• *Indirect control problems* are solved by changing our methods of influence (I have personally identified over 30 different methods of influence, as different as empathy is from confrontation, or example is from persuasion).

• *No control problems* involve taking responsibility to genuinely and peacefully accept these problems and learn to live with them, even though we don't like them. In this way, we do not empower these problems to control us. We share in the spirit embodied in the Alcoholics Anonymous prayer, "Lord, give me the courage to change the things which can and ought to be changed, the serenity to accept the things which cannot be changed, and the wisdom to know the difference."

Whether a problem is direct, indirect or no control, we have the first step to the solution. Changing our habits, changing our methods of influence and changing the way we see our no control problems are all within our Circle of Influence.

Anytime we think the problem is "out there," we exacerbate the problem. We empower what's out there to control us.

Reactive people have an "outside in" paradigm — they think that what's "out there" has to change before they can change. Proactive people bring about change from the "inside out;" in fact, they often change what's "out there" by *being* different — by being more resourceful, diligent, creative or cooperative.

One of my favorite stories is the Bible story of Joseph, who at age 17 was sold into slavery in Egypt by his brothers. Rather than languish in self-pity as a servant of Potiphar or focus on the weaknesses of his brothers and his captors, Joseph was proactive. Within a short time, he was put in charge of Potiphar's household and all that Potiphar had because he was so highly trusted. Even when he was unjustly imprisoned for 13 years because he ran from Potiphar's wife, he continued to work proactively on the inner Circle of Influence, and soon he was running the prison and eventually the entire nation of Egypt, second only to the Pharaoh.

If you really want to improve your situation, work on the one thing over which you have control — yourself. Stop trying to shape up your spouse, your kids, your colleagues and your boss, and work on your own weaknesses and your own stewardship.

There are so many ways to work in the Circle of Influence — to be a better listener, to be a more loving marriage partner, to be a better student, to be a more cooperative and dedicated employee. Sometimes the most proactive thing we can do is to "grin and bear it," to be happy and accept those things that at present we can't control, while we focus our efforts on the things that we can.

The Other End of the Stick

While we are free to choose our actions, we are not free to choose the consequences of those actions. Consequences are governed by natural law; therefore, they are in the Circle of Concern. We can decide to step in front of a fast-moving train, but we cannot decide what will happen when the train hits us. The consequences of our action are governed by natural law.

We can decide to be dishonest in our business dealings. While the social consequences of that decision may vary depending on whether or not we are found out, the natural consequences to our basic character are a fixed result of natural law.

Living in harmony with correct principles brings positive consequences; violating them brings negative consequences. We are free to choose our response in any situation, but in doing so, we choose the attendant consequence. "When we pick up one end of the stick, we pick up the other."

Undoubtedly, there are times when we pick up what we later know was the wrong stick. Our choices bring consequences we would rather live without. If we could make the choice over again, we would make it differently.

We all make mistakes. What's important is that we learn from them and move on. Past mistakes are also out there in the Circle of Concern. We can't recall them; we can't undo them; we can't control the consequences that come as a result; but we can learn from them and move on.

As a college quarterback, my son Sean has learned to snap his wrist band between plays whenever he or anyone else on the team makes a "setting back" mistake. He does it as a mental discipline so the last mistake won't affect the resolve and execution of the next play. The proactive approach to a mistake is to instantly acknowledge it, correct and learn from it. This literally turns a failure into a success. "Success," said IBM founder T.J. Watson, is "on the far side of failure." Not to acknowledge a mistake, not to correct it and learn from it, is a mistake of a different order. It usually puts a person on a self-condemning, self-justifying path, often involving rationalization (rational lies) to self and to others. This second mistake, this cover-up, empowers the first, giving it disproportionate importance, and causes far deeper injury to self.

It is not what others do or even our own mistakes that hurt us the most; it is our response to those things. Chasing after the poisonous snake that bites us will only drive the poison through our entire system. It is far better to immediately take measures to get the poison out.

Making and Keeping Commitments

At the very heart of our Circle of Influence is our ability to make and keep commitments. The commitments we make to ourselves and to others, and our integrity to those commitments is the essence of proactivity.

Here also is the essence of our growth. Through our human endowments of self-awareness and conscience, we can identify areas of weakness, areas for improvement, areas of latent talent, areas that need to be changed or eliminated from our lives. As we recognize and use our independent will to act on that awareness — making promises, setting goals, and being true to them — we build the strength of character that makes possible every other positive thing in our lives.

Within the Circle of Influence, we find two ways to immediately put ourselves in control of our lives: 1) we can make a promise and keep it, or 2) we can set a goal and work to achieve it. As we make and keep commitments, we begin to establish an inner integrity that gives us the awareness of self-control and the courage and strength to accept more of the responsibility for our own lives. By making and keeping promises to ourselves and others, little by little, our honor becomes greater than our moods. We gain the power and strength of character to break bad habits and create more effective habits.

The 30-Day Test

We develop the proactive capacity to handle effectively the extraordinary pressures of life in ordinary events of every day. It's how we make and keep commitments, how we handle a traffic jam, how we respond to an irate customer or a disobedient child. It's how we view our problems and where we focus our energies. It's the language we use.

I would challenge you for 30 days to work only in your Circle of Influence. Keep the commitments you make. Be a light, not a judge. Be a model, not a critic. Be part of the solution, not part of the problem.

As part of this 30-day test, identify an experience or circumstance when, based of past performance, you will probably behave reactively. Consider the situation in the context of your Circle of Influence. How could you respond proactively? Take a moment and create the situation vividly in your mind. See yourself responding in a proactive manner. Make a commitment to yourself to exercise your freedom to choose.

People who daily exercise their freedom to choose will gradually expand their influence. People who do not will find that it withers until they are literally "being lived," acting out the scripts written by parents, associates, bosses and society.

We are responsible for our own effectiveness, for our own happiness, and ultimately, for most of our circumstances. Fortunately, we can control these to a high degree by focusing on our Circle of Influence.

Chapter 9

Organize Weekly, Adapt Daily

Imagine a large building that looks like a bank but is not. A brass marker on the front door reads: "Time for Sale."

All day long, people rush in and out of the building to purchase time. A man says, "Now I will buy the five years I need to prepare for a big promotion." A woman says, "I wasted the last three years I had with my daughter; I will buy them back and make them more productive." Each person leaves the building with what they desperately wanted: time to do the many things they had failed to do, or that they wanted to do.

You stop one man, a business executive, and ask him, "What will you now do differently with your time than you have done before? How will you be more effective?" The man only returns a blank stare. He has no idea what he will do differently or how he will be more effective in the new year.

Time is the currency of your life. How will you invest it?

Four Generations of Time Management

To be wise investors of time, the currency of life, we need both a philosophy and a tool to implement it. Over the last four decades, we've seen four generations of time management tools. Each generation has moved us toward greater control of our lives.

• *The first generation* could be characterized by notes and "to do" checklists. These help us to identify tasks and to recognize the many demands placed on our time. However, many "planners" and "organizers" are nothing more than note pads in expensive binders.

71

In fact, they often provide a false sense of organization and planning.

First-generation managers often take the course of least resistance. They experience little pain or strain because they "go with the flow." Externally imposed disciplines and schedules give them the feeling that they aren't responsible for results. These managers, by definition, are not effective people. They produce very little, and their lifestyle does nothing to build their production capability. Buffeted by outside forces, they are often seen as undependable and irresponsible, and they have very little sense of control and self-esteem.

• *The second generation* includes calendars and appointment books, reflecting an attempt to look ahead and to schedule events and activities. These tools encourage "daily planning," and some unknowingly reinforce habits of crisis management and provide hundreds of special forms to give the illusion of productivity.

Second-generation managers assume a little more control. They plan and schedule in advance and generally are seen as more responsible because they "show up" when they're supposed to. But again, their activities have no priority or correlation to deeper values and goals. They have few significant achievements and tend to be schedule-oriented.

• *The third generation* adds the important ideas of prioritizing activities, clarifying values, and aligning activities with values and goals. These tools emphasize daily planning and goal setting to direct one's time and energy. Most third-generation planners focus us on completing daily tasks, on *efficiency*; however, they don't help us improve our *effectiveness*. They are ill-suited to an increasingly complex world of interconnected lives and interdependent responsibilities.

Third-generation managers clarify values, set goals, plan each day and work on what they consider to be top priorities. While they may take a step forward in productivity, they often lose perspective. Their "daily planning" focuses them on the urgent, the "now." Seldom do they question the importance of the activity in the first place, nor do they consider activities in the context of principles, personal mission, roles, and goals. Basically, they prioritize the pressing problems and crises of the day, making no provision for managing roles in a balanced way. Moreover, they tend to over-schedule the day, resulting in the desire to throw away the plan and escape to diversions.

  • *The fourth generation* focuses primarily on people, relationships and results, secondarily on time and methods.

Fourth-generation managers open new windows of effectiveness in their personal and professional lives. They are more efficient with things, more effective with people. They realize that contribution and achievement are often determined by the quality of their relationships and the overall balance of their lives. Their focus, therefore, is on effectiveness and results, not on efficiency and methods. Effective people don't just do things differently, they do different things. Recently, a major U.S. corporation sent a team of executives to Japan to study managers and leaders in Japan's best-run companies — firms that had received the coveted Deming Award for quality in products, service, people and financial performance.

The American executives found that managers in these Japanese firms were spending 50 percent of their time *doing* different things than their American counterparts. The Japanese focused more on long-range strategic issues; they invested more time communicating, delegating, listening and cultivating personal capacities. In other words, the Japanese managers worked on chronic problems and long-term solutions, as opposed to quick fixes and acute crises.

Avoiding the Activity Trap

The time management matrix (following page) defines activities in terms of "urgent" or "not urgent" and "important" or "not important."

I Urgent Important	**II** Not Urgent Important
ACTIVITIES: Crises Pressing problems	ACTIVITIES: Prevention Relationships PC Activities Opportunities Planning Recreation
III Urgent Not Important	**IV** Not Urgent Not Important
ACTIVITIES: Interruptions Some calls Mail, Reports Some meetings Proximate pressing matters	ACTIVITIES: Trivia Procrastination Busy work Some mail Some phone calls "Escape" reading and TV

The key to effectiveness is to keep crises and pressing problems (Quadrant I) to a minimum, and to eliminate as many urgent but not important activities (Quadrant III) as possible by placing priority on the important but not urgent (Quadrant II).

Effective people are not problem-minded; they're opportunity minded. They feed opportunities and starve problems. They think preventively. They have genuine Quadrant I emergencies that require their immediate attention, but with prevention and planning, they keep the number comparatively small. They maintain balance by focusing on the capacity-building activities of Quadrant II.

Quadrant II is at the heart of effective management and leadership. It deals with such things as writing a personal mission statement, long-range planning, exercising, preventative maintenance, preparation — all those things we know we need to do but seldom get around to doing, because they aren't urgent. Time spent in Quadrant II is time spent in the "general's tent." Here we map out our campaigns, do strategic planning, anticipate and reduce crises, and focus on high-leverage activities that pay such huge dividends in terms of desired results.

To lead your life and "leverage" your talents, devote more time to Quadrant II, less time to activities that are pressing, proximate, popular or pleasant. Say "no" to some things. If you're not saying "no" to the unimportant, you may not be able to say "yes" to the important. Even "the good" can keep you from better and best — keep you from making your unique contribution if you let it. Indeed, the good is often the enemy of the best.

The answer, then, to the activity trap is to learn to say "no" to those things in Quadrant III which are urgent but not important,and "yes" to those things in Quadrant II which are not urgent, but vitally important.

Since Quadrant II is the heart of effective self-management, you need an organizer that moves you into Quadrant II. My work with this concept has led to the creation of such a tool, the *Seven Habits Organizer: Personal Leadership System.* You may want to use this tool or adapt your present planner.

Features of Fourth-Generation Organizers

A fourth-generation organizer meets six important criteria.

• *Coherence.* Coherence suggests harmony, unity and integrity between your vision and mission, your roles and goals, your priorities and plans, and your desires and discipline. In your planner, there should be a place for your personal mission statement, your roles and both short- and long-term goals.

• *Balance.* True effectiveness requires balance, and your organizer should help you create and maintain it. Some people seem to think that success in one area can compensate for failure in other areas of life. But can it really? Can success in your profession compensate for a broken marriage, ruined health, or weakness in personal character?

• *Focus.* Your planner should encourage you to organize on a weekly basis and to spend more time in Quadrant II to achieve greater life balance. Most societies and cultures operate within the framework of the week, designating certain days for business and others for relaxation or inspiration. While most people think in terms of weeks, their planning tools focus them on days — on organizing crises and busy work.

• *Flexibility.* Your planning tool should be your servant, never your master. Since it has to work for you, it should be tailored to your style, your needs, your particular ways.

• *Portability.* Your tool should also be portable so that you have access to important data at all times. You may want to review your personal mission statement while riding the bus or measure the value of a new opportunity against something you already have planned.

• *People Dimension.* A fourth-generation tool enables you to be more efficient with things, more effective with people. You begin to manage your relationships around principles — not just manage your time around priorities. The Quadrant II lifestyle may require you to subordinate schedules to people. Your tool needs to reflect that value, to facilitate building and maintaining relationships, rather than create guilt when schedules aren't met.

At one point in his life, one of my sons was deeply into scheduling and efficiency. One day he had a very tight schedule with down-to-the-minute time allocations for every activity, including picking up some books, washing his car, and "dropping" Carol, his girl friend. Everything went according to schedule until it came to Carol. They had been dating for a long period of time, and he had finally concluded that the relationship would not work out. So, congruent with his efficiency model, he called her and scheduled a 10-minute visit at her home.

Needless to say, the news was traumatic to her. Two hours after the visit began, he was still involved in a very intense conversation with her. Even then, one visit was not enough.

Becoming an Effective Self-Manager

Effective organizing involves the following six activities.

• *Discovering your personal mission.* Real self-management begins with you, with your own personal vision of who you are. Your mission statement should deal with 1) what you want to do or accomplish, what contributions you want to make; and 2) what you want to be, what character traits, qualities and talents you want to have. It should cover three dimensions: personal, family, and professional.

As you "discover" what you want to be and do, write a first draft of your personal mission statement. Over time, refine it and put a copy in the front of your organizer, and review weekly as you go through the planning process.

• *Defining roles.* We live our lives in terms of roles — roles at work, in the family, the community, and in other areas of life. These roles give order to what we want to do and to be. For example, you may define your family role as "wife" and "mother" or "husband" and "father." Your profession may involve several roles — in administration, marketing, personnel and long-range planning. Record the key "roles" or functions you fill. Since research shows that it is ineffective to attempt to manage more than seven categories, limit your roles to seven, combining some functions if necessary.

• *Selecting goals.* As you review your roles, ask yourself, "This week, what are the two or three most important things I can do to move forward in that role?" Write as goals the two or three important things you feel you should accomplish in each role during the next seven days. Short-term goals should be tied to your longer-term goals and to your mission statement.

• *Scheduling events.* As you look at the week ahead with your goals in mind, consider the opportunities for implementation each day. For example, you may want to set a goal to work on your personal mission statement on Sunday or to exercise for one hour three mornings a week. There are some goals that you may only be able to accomplish during business hours, or some that you can only do in the evenings or on weekends.

• *Prioritizing activities.* As you organize your week and plan your day, focus on those activities that produce the greatest results. Determine that you will accomplish your highest priorities first, so that the things that matter most are never at the mercy of the things that matter least. Remember to make appointments with yourself to act upon your goals — and when you set an appointment with yourself, keep it. Also, schedule time for other important activities. Ask yourself: "What one activity, if done consistently and well, would greatly improve the quality of my life and my standard of living?" Since these activities invariably fall into Quadrant II, find ways to fit them into your schedule.

• *Living a Quadrant II lifestyle.* This is primarily a function of our independent will, our self-discipline, our integrity, and commitment — not to short-term goals and schedules or to the impulse of the moment, but to the correct principles and our own deepest values, which give meaning and context to our goals, our schedules, and our lives.

As you go through your week, your commitment will be tested. The popularity of reacting to the urgent but unimportant priorities of other people in Quadrant III or the pleasure of escaping to Quadrant IV will threaten to overpower the important Quadrant II activities you have planned.

The test is to focus on the priorities you have scheduled or subordinate your schedule to higher values; to rise above the limiting perspective of a single day and keep in touch with your deepest values; and to invest your time, the currency of your life, in activities that will balance your life, leverage your talents and make best use of your time and all of your other resources.

Part 2:

INTERPERSONAL EFFECTIVENESS

We do not live alone on islands, isolated from other people. We are born into families; we grow up in societies; we become students of schools, members of other organizations. And once into our professions, we find that our jobs require us to interact frequently and effectively with others. If we fail to learn and apply the principles of interpersonal effectiveness, we can expect our progress to slow or stop.

This section deals with the attitudes, skills and strategies for creating and maintaining trustful relationships with other people. In effect, once we become relatively independent, our challenge is to become effectively interdependent with others. To do this, we must practice empathy and synergy in our efforts to be proactive and productive.

Chapter 10

Seven Habits of Effective People

You are not your habits. You can make and break your habits. You need not be a victim of conditions or conditioning.

Habits are patterns of behavior composed of three overlapping components: knowledge, attitude, and skill. And since these are learned rather than inherited, our habits constitute our second nature, not our first.

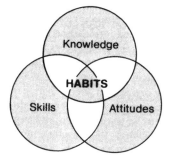

We are not our habits; hence, we should avoid defining ourselves in terms of our habits and characteristic tendencies. Habits of effectiveness can be learned, habits of ineffectiveness unlearned.

In his essay, "The Common Denominator of Success," Albert E. Gray says, "All successful people have the habit of doing the things failures don't like to do. They don't like doing them either, necessarily, but their dislike is subordinated to the strength of their purpose."

Successful people daily weave habits of effectiveness into their lives in order to achieve desired results. Often, they are internally motivated by a strong sense of mission. By subordinating their dislike for certain tasks to their goals, they commonly develop seven basic habits and discipline their lives in accordance with the underlying principles.

As illustrated in the following continuum, these seven habits are interrelated, interdependent, and sequential. The first three habits will lead you from a state of dependency to independency or self-mastery. The next three lead to interdependency and to mutual growth and benefit. And the seventh habit sustains the growth process.

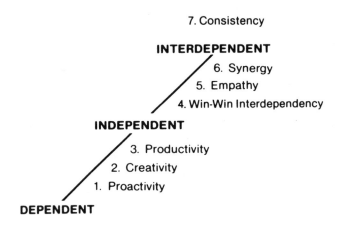

7. Consistency

INTERDEPENDENT

6. Synergy

5. Empathy

4. Win-Win Interdependency

INDEPENDENT

3. Productivity

2. Creativity

1. Proactivity

DEPENDENT

Habit 1: Proactivity -- Choose Your Course

The first habit, proactivity, means taking personal responsibility for our actions and attitudes. It's most instructive to break the word "responsibility" into two parts: response/ability. The proactive person develops the ability to choose his response — making him more a product of his decisions than his conditions, more a product of values than feelings.

Behavioral scientists have built reactive, stimulus-response models of human behavior based on their study of animals and neurotic people. Relatively little research has been conducted with healthy, creative, proactive people who exercise the freedom to choose their response to any given internal or external stimulus or condition.

The more we exercise this freedom, inherent in our agency, the more proactive we become. The key is to be a light, not a judge; a model, not a critic; to feed opportunities, starve problems; and to focus upon our immediate circle of influence, not upon our circle of concern.

We often see and hear inspiring accounts of proactivity in the media. For instance, I read the story of a young man who graduated from college in 1932, in the great depression, with a degree in social science. He had "not the slightest idea" what he wanted to do, and any job was hard to find. To earn a little money, he went back to an old job, lifeguarding at a local swimming pool. There the father of some children he had taught to swim told him to "look inside" himself and determine what he most wanted to do. After several days of soul searching, he decided he would like to be a radio announcer. The man next told him to start knocking on radio station doors, asking for any job just to break into the business. The young man hitch-hiked to Chicago and knocked on every door without success. He knocked on doors across Illinois and into Iowa. Finally, at WOC Davenport, he landed a job as a sports announcer. It was the first of several important steps in the career of former President Ronald Reagan.

Habit 2: Creativity — Begin with the End in Mind

All things are created twice: first mentally and then physically. The key to creativity is to begin with the end in mind, with a vision and a blueprint of the desired result.

The first creation requires us to clarify values and set priorities before selecting goals and going about the work. Effective people excel at this. They act rather than be acted upon. Ineffective people allow old habits, other people, and environmental conditions to dictate this first creation. They adopt values and goals from their culture and see themselves in the "social mirror." Often they will climb the proverbial ladder of success, only to find upon reaching the top rung that the ladder is leaning against the wrong wall. While they may achieve their goal, what they get is not what they expect or really want.

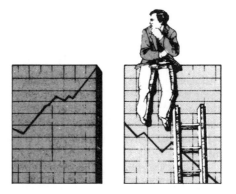

The second or physical creation follows from the first, as a building follows from a blueprint. If the first creation — the design — is done well, the second creation — the construction — is much faster and better. Quality, after all, cannot be inspected into a product; it must be designed and built into it from the beginning.

Habit 3: Productivity — Prioritize, Organize, Perform

Productivity is a measurement of production over time, and the key principle of time management is to put first things first. We can then organize and perform our activities around our priorities and goals.

The formula for increasing productivity may be simply coded P-O-P: prioritize, organize, perform. Studies have verified that about 80 percent of the desired results flow from a few (20 percent) "high leverage" activities. To "leverage" our time, we should devote less time to activities that are "urgent but unimportant" and more time to things that are important but not necessarily urgent.

If we don't know what's important, we are easily diverted into responding to what's urgent. Urgent matters are pressing; they're often popular with others; they're proximate, right in front of us; and they are pleasant. But they seldom lead toward desired results.

Habit 4: Interdependency — Think Win-Win or No Deal

In businesses and in families, effectiveness is largely achieved through the cooperative efforts of two or more people. Marriages and other partnerships are interdependent realities, and yet people often approach these relationships with an independent mentality, which is like trying to play golf with a tennis racket — the tool is not suited to the sport.

"Win-win" is only one of six "tools" or mental attitudes commonly used in everyday negotiation and problem solving. Other options include "win-lose," "lose-win," "win," "lose-lose," and "win-win or no deal."

To develop the habit of interdependency, we must think "win-win" or mutual benefit. Win-win thinking begins with a commitment to explore all options until a mutually satisfactory solution is reached or to make no deal at all. It is based on the belief that "there is more than enough for all" (the abundance mentality). People with scarcity mentalities—who think "there is only enough for the best" — will seek "win-lose" solutions. Great people and excellent companies model the win-win principle in their relationships, agreements, systems, and processes.

And models are so important to implementation; in fact, after 20 years of teaching the win-win principle, I have concluded that unless people have models and mentors of this principle, they will never practice win-win. Particularly in the American society, win-lose is powerfully reinforced in our systems and institutions.

Habit 5: Empathy — Seek First to Understand

The fifth habit, empathy, is the master skill for building win-win relationships. It is based on the principle, seek first to understand, then to be understood.

None of us see the world as it is but as we are, as our frames of references or "maps" define the territory. To make this point in my seminars, I often divide an audience in half and show one half a drawing of a young girl and the other half a drawing of an old lady. I then show everyone a composite illustration. Invariably, those who are conditioned to see the young girl see her in the composite drawing, and those conditioned otherwise see the old woman. As people from both sides interact, they sometimes question the credibility (or sanity) of those who see it differently.

Most credibility problems begin with perception differences. To resolve these differences and to restore credibility, one must exercise empathy, seeking first to understand the point of view of the other person. Hammering problems by probing is usually counter-productive. Evaluation, sympathy, and advisement are also ineffective as means of gaining understanding and influence.

I like Abraham Maslow's observation: "He who is good with a hammer tends to think everything is a nail." We are all experts at probing, evaluating, and advising, but these techniques are flawed as a means of understanding the mind and heart of another person.

Habit 6: Synergy — Value the Difference

Insecure people tend to make others over in their own image, and surround themselves with people who think similarly. They mistake uniformity for unity, sameness for oneness.

Synergy results from valuing differences, from bringing different perspectives together in the spirit of mutual respect. People then feel free to seek the best possible alternative, often the "third alternative," one that is better than either of the original proposals. It's a human resource approach to problem solving as opposed to a "please or appease" human relations approach.

Using the principle of synergy, a person may multiply his individual talents and abilities, thus making the whole greater than the sum of the parts: one plus one may equal more than two!

Habit 7: Consistency — Sharpen the Saw Regularly

Success has two sides: production capability (PC), and production (P) of desired results.

It's wise to keep both sides in balance. And yet when people get busy producing or "sawing," they rarely take time to "sharpen the saw" because maintenance seldom pays dramatic immediate dividends. Suppose that while walking through the woods one day, you see a man sawing down a tall tree. Your stop to ask him, "What are you doing?"

"Can't you see? I'm cutting down this tree."

You see exhaustion in his face and hear it in his voice; perspiration soaks his clothes. You inquire, "How long have you been sawing?"

"Oh, I don't know. Maybe four or five hours."

"I'll bet you're tired."

"I'm beat, really beat."

"How's the saw?"

"It's getting rather dull."

"Why don't you stop for a minute to sharpen it?"

"I can't. I'm too busy sawing!"

This habit of sharpening the saw regularly means having a balanced, systematic program for self-renewal in four areas: physical, mental, emotional-social, and moral. If we fail to develop this habit, the body becomes weak, the mind mechanical, the emotions raw, the spirit insensitive.

It's the law of the harvest: we reap as we sow. We will enjoy a successful harvest if we cultivate these seven habits of effectiveness and live in accordance with the underlying principles.

Chapter 11

The Proactive Person

While we are strongly influenced by our genes, our parents and our living conditions, we are not determined by them: the proactive person exercises agency, chooses his response and seeks continuous improvement in spite of opposition and odds.

The philosophy of determinism postulates that every event, act, and decision of our lives occurs independent of the human will as the inevitable consequence of physical, psychological, or environmental antecedents and conditions.

Free will philosophy assumes that we are responsible and accountable — that we are the programmers, not the programs. Once again, our genes, our childhood experiences, and environmental conditions may influence us powerfully, but they do not determine us.

There's a vast difference between being influenced and being determined. As we exercise our free will, our volition becomes stronger until the conditioning experiences of our heritage and environment influence us less and less.

In his book, *Man's Search for Meaning,* Viktor Frankl shares his experience in the death camps of Nazi Germany. Here is a moving and inspirational account of how a psychiatrist, raised in the deterministic tradition, discovered for himself "our last ultimate freedom" or our power to choose our response or attitude in any given set of circumstances. When he was stripped naked, put under white lights, and exposed to the most cruel indignities imaginable, he discovered that he had the power within himself to benefit from that experience and pass it along as an object lesson for those of us who feel controlled or victimized or simply sorry for ourselves. The lesson is this: We can choose our response and gradually acquire more and more personal power or freedom, even though outside circumstances may confine us.

Frankl eventually developed more freedom than his Nazi captors, even though they possessed more liberty. Liberty is a condition of the environment, a reflection of the number of options available to us. Freedom is a condition of the person, a reflection of the power to choose among available options. Many people have great freedom but have very little liberty. To some degree, the external conditions of our lives are subject to the internal conditions. Our inner environment creates our outer environment. Our head creates our world.

Proactivity: The Power to Choose

The power, freedom, and ability to choose one's response might be called "proactivity." This word isn't defined in the dictionary; however, it connotes man's free will or agency, our inherent freedom to choose.

The word, "responsibility," of course, is found in the dictionary. It denotes the quality of being responsible and accountable and connotes the ability to choose our response — response/ability. Highly responsible people have a highly developed ability to choose their response. Irresponsible people have a low ability or power or capacity to choose responses.

If we accept the fact that we are responsible, we must then accept that we may be judged as to whether we act responsibly or irresponsibly. Often this judgment comes as a natural consequence of our behavior, for while we are free to choose our response, we are not free to choose the consequence. Thus, we see that in the last analysis, our agency is the antecedent to the conditions of our lives. Agency is the basis of both our growth and our happiness and also our destruction and unhappiness. Psychologically, reactive behavior frees us from feeling responsible and gives us a false sense of security, but in reality, reactive behavior breeds insecurity and cheats us of true growth and happiness.

The following simple diagram helps to explain the difference between proactive and reactive behavior or between deterministic and free-will philosophy. The reactive model looks likes this:

This is clear determinism: the stimulus (from whatever source) directly produces the response.

The proactive model implies that regardless of the origin of the stimulus — whether it be genetic, psychic, environmental, or a combination of the three — or the strength of the stimulus, we still possess the freedom to choose the response.

Here is the proactive model:

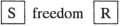

A proactive person's behavior is a product of decisions. A reactive person's behavior is a product of conditions.

Our very use of language, our words, reinforce our belief system and reflect proactivity or reactivity. The reactive person says, "I have to"; the proactive person says, "I choose to." The reactive person says, "I can't"; the proactive person says, "I prefer not." The reactive person says, "I must"; the proactive person says, "I want to." Reactive people transfer responsibility to some antecedent, some condition, something "out there" which makes them do something, or keeps them from doing something. On the other hand, proactive people develop responsibility, the power or the ability to choose the response, regardless of conditions.

Proactive people reject labels of others and of themselves. Internally, they say, "I can do it if I choose to or if conditions preclude my doing it, I can choose my response, even my attitude to those conditions." Proactive people recognize the power of predispositions and habits, but separate these "scripts" from themselves. Such a separation, however small, is the foundation of proactivity. Freedom is born of this self-awareness, this realization that we are not our bodies, our feelings, or our thoughts.

Focus on the Circle of Influence

The Circle of Influence is the focus of the proactive person. Within the Circle of Influence are those things we can control or do something about, such as our own behaviors and attitudes. The outer Circle of Concern represents things we can't control or change directly, such as international politics, the national deficit, the wars between nations, past events and certain fixed conditions.

Proactive people focus on the inner Circle of Influence; reactive people on the outer Circle of Concern. Proactive people do something about things they can control or influence. They generate positive energy, which feeds upon itself. As things get accomplished within the inner Circle of Influence, the circle gradually enlarges until it begins to encompass many of the concerns in the outer circle.

Reactive people generate negative energy, which also feeds upon itself. They neglect the inner Circle of Influence and worry pointlessly about things over which they have no control.

When we worry about things we can do nothing about, the worry itself becomes part of the problem; opportunity is lost, day by day, because it's either not seen or not used. When we go to work on things we can do something about, our industry becomes part of the solution. As the popular saying goes, "If we are not part of the solution, we are part of the problem."

For example, in one large organization, the top man was very dynamic, visionary, talented, and intelligent. But he also had some glaring personal weaknesses, which were manifest in his authoritarian style. His entire executive team essentially absolved themselves of responsibility for certain kinds of results in the name of the president's weaknesses. They would stand around in the executive corridors and validate each other's perceptions and articulate descriptions of these weaknesses.

They were all reactive, except for one member of the executive team who was very proactive. Instead of focusing upon the weaknesses of the president, he focused upon the president's strengths and attempted to complement them and thus make his weaknesses irrelevant. At first he was unable to do this in many areas of concern, but he was able to do it within his own circle of influence by exercising more initiative, more positive energy.

Hence, when the president treated these men like "go-fers," asking them to send messages or run errands or do his bidding, all but the proactive executive felt insulted and completely under-utilized: they would do their go-fer work begrudgingly, because of the extrinsic compensation, without feeling any intrinsic satisfaction. The proactive executive was not only most diligent in doing his go-fer work and bringing the desired information and data to the president's attention, but he was also diligent at adding his own analysis and judgment.

Little by little, over a period of a few years, the president developed enormous respect for this man's analytical powers and confidence in his judgments and stopped treating him like a go-fer. Instead, he would ask for his opinion, knowing from experience that the man's judgment was excellent − often better than his own − since the man was closer to the problems and had more time to deal with them.

Eventually, this proactive executive's Circle of Influence expanded and grew until the president would not make any significant moves or changes without first consulting this man. Now, the rest of the executive team had new ammunition for their reactive guns: favoritism! "He treats us like go-fers, and he asks him for his opinion," they said. But the proactive man chose to respond positively to reactive and vindictive review from the rest of the executive team. He also built up their strengths and made their weaknesses irrelevant by exercising his positive energy or proactive capacity, until they, too, developed increasing confidence in his competency.

Alcoholics Anonymous, one of the most successful self-help organizations in the world, stresses this principle of working on the inner circle, even to the point of admitting at the outset, "I cannot do it by myself. I choose to go for help." Their famous prayer is, "Oh Lord, give me the courage to change the things which ought to be changed, the serenity to accept the things which cannot be changed, and the wisdom to know the difference."

It certainly takes a great deal of wisdom. We may think something we cannot do a lot about right now is in the outer Circle of Concern when it really lies within our Circle of Influence. Conversely, we may think some things are in our control when really they are not.

Whether we have direct, indirect, or no control over conditions, we can still have influence with people and arrive at desirable solutions if we work first on ourselves. If we have direct control, we can change our habits; if we have indirect control, we can change our methods of influence; and even when we have no control, we can change our attitudes.

On Becoming Proactive

We become proactive through natural processes — through patient, persistent, diligent practice. It is one of the great illusions of life to think that there is a simple formula, a quick fix. If we want to improve our tennis game, we take lessons from a professional and then practice; get feedback and keep practicing;

take the next lesson and practice some more. Likewise, to increase our level of proactivity, we must exercise our patience and diligence, self-control and skill, improve our methods of influence, make deposits into other people's emotional bank accounts, listen with empathy, and, most importantly, fully accept the fact that we are responsible.

Once we have emotionally accepted that we are truly responsible, that we are the programmers, we can then begin the process of writing the program. We can learn to write the program in our heart and in our mind as well as on paper. We can sit down and clarify our values and prioritize them and think so clearly and deeply and consistently on them that they become governing principles in our lives. We can then write out our goals based on those values and our action plans to achieve those goals. We write all these things in full awareness of things over which we have no influence or control. We accept situational realities, but we also accept our power to choose our responses to them.

Samuel Johnson said, "The fountain of content must spring up in the mind, and he who hath so little knowledge of human nature as to seek happiness by changing anything but his own disposition, will waste his life in fruitless efforts and multiply the grief he proposes to remove." And Abraham Lincoln once said, "A person is as happy as he makes up his mind to be." When applied to this subject of proactivity, these statements take on additional meaning.

At the height of the recession I conducted a three-day business conference for CEO's in the home improvement industry. After spending a day discussing what was happening in the economy, people were depressed; and after discussing the future trends the second day, they became even more depressed. On the third day we shifted our attention to the inner Circle of Influence and discussed proactive issues in the context of the current economy and future trends — particularly, we addressed the question, "How can we better manage and reduce our costs and increase our market share?" Creative, synergistic minds began to interact and by the end of the day there was a fresh enthusiasm, an excitement, and sense of hope.

At the end of the three-day conference, we concluded our experience together by rehearsing a three-part response to the question, "How's business?" Part 1: "What's happening to us is not good, and trends suggest that it will get worse before it will get better." Part 2: "But what we are causing to happen is very good, for we are better managing and controlling our costs and increasing our market share." Part 3: "Therefore, my friend, business is better than ever."

To become more proactive, start now — plan to take control and make business better than ever. Take time to clearly write out your blueprint for life. You might start by writing your own eulogy or by thinking carefully about what things you are proud of and what things you want to be known for. Recognize, too, that "when we pick up one end of the stick, we pick up the other." In other words, we have the power to choose our response but not the consequence.

You might test this principle of proactivity during this coming month in your professional or personal life. My challenge is to be a light, not a judge; to focus on the inner Circle of Influence; to give energy to those things; to be a constructive producer, not a wasteful consumer; a model, not a critic.

Some people may feel threatened by your proactive behavior, sensing that their option is either to "shape up or ship out," but simply persist. Little by little your persistence will pay off — you will develop new habits, new capabilities for bringing about changes in the circumstances of your life. By focusing on things over which you have some influence or control, in constructive and positive ways, you will increase your Circle of Influence and begin to work on some of your concerns in equally positive and constructive ways.

Chapter 12

Begin With the End in Mind

All things are created twice: first mentally and then physically. The creative manager will begin the first creation with the end of the second creation in mind to ensure that values and visions, goals and plans are all aligned.

Perhaps nothing is more important right now in the United States than the development of creative power in people and in organizations, especially in light of Arnold Toynbee's definition of creativity as "the history-making talent."

The job of the chief executive is to exercise this talent: to make history by managing a company's course of events — by making things happen. This is the essence of the proactivity principle: the executive is the programmer.

The creativity principle, then, is to *write the program*, to create the "software" that will drive the "hardware" of the company toward desired results.

In this sense, every executive is a creative writer or performing artist. A study conducted by Calvin Taylor at the Institute of Behavioral Research in Creativity suggests that every person is a creative genius in at least one of six talent areas: academic, productive, evaluative, planning, forecasting, communication.

At his Institute, Taylor can measure a person's "talent quotient" — a more reliable indicator of potential, he says, than the intelligence quotient. Nine out of ten people, regardless of their IQ limitation or cultural background, could become very proficient in their own field.

The problem is that a vast amount of creative talent is wasted. Too many of America's institutions have become lifeless, tired organizations, living off the legacy of the past. Moreover, their presidents may be depicted not as dynamic leaders or decision makers who move creative ideas into constructive action but as cogs in a big machine. In such environments, people stop thinking freely, new ideas are snuffed out, and a sense of powerlessness sets in.

Restoring Creative Power

Effective executives work in their minds before they work with their hands. If they have two hours to a complete job, they may spend the first half hour planning, organizing and delegating to get the most out of the remaining hour and a half.

All things are created twice: first mentally and then physically. Buildings are created in every detail, in blueprint, before any earth is moved.

The First Creation. I once took my family to visit an architect who had designed a new shopping mall. At the time, the ground had not been broken, and yet the entire project was completed in every detail. Pointing to the vacant lot, I told my children to "see" the new shopping mall. One of my girls responded, "I can't see anything. Where is it?"

I then showed her the architectural drawings, artistic renderings and blueprints and asked her to "look" again at the land, with her eyes closed. "In your mind's eye, you will see it," I promised her. "I see it. I see it," she exclaimed. She was excited to experience the creative process that begins with the end in mind.

As the master architect or creative director of the business, the chief executive should begin with the end in mind. That means beginning with a clear vision, a compelling purpose, and a strong commitment. It means seeing in your mind's eye the desired end. It means exercising "faith," your belief in what can be.

Most of us grossly neglect this creative power. We live too much out of our memories, too little out of our imaginations — too much on what is or has been, not enough on what can be. That's like trying to drive forward by looking in the rear-view mirror.

Most people fail, I'm convinced, because they have not carefully thought through their value system or their priority system as a basis for goal selection and planning. They begin to adopt certain values and goals from the culture without considering the ramifications.

The first creation involves four steps: 1) define mission: clarify values, purposes, motives; 2) visualize the mission and purify the motives; 3) set short and long-term goals; and 4) make plans for achieving those goals.

The long-range planning of most people is merely an extrapolation of present trends into the future. The creative manager asks deeper questions, such as, where do we really want to go and why? The desired ends may be expressed in terms of character, contribution, or organization.

Let me suggest the following three-part exercise.

• *Verbal*: Express your mission, and your values in writing. Select goals and make plans based on your mission and system of values. Write these down as well.

• *Visual*: After writing, visualize it; see it in the mind's eye. Get the big picture.

• *Emotional*: Feel it. Involve the emotions. Feel strongly about what you write and see and say. Write it, say it, see it, feel it.

Be in charge of your own values, goals and plans. Write your own program. Otherwise, you will be a slave to someone else's program, plan or creation — or to your own past, your habits and biases and tendencies. You will find yourself working toward goals and actualizing values that are programmed into you. Your plans should be the children of your goals; your goals the children of your values. And all of this should be tied to your mission statement.

Write a mission statement, for your company (or department) and for your private life. It becomes a kind of constitution, a statement of your values by which all goals and action plans are evaluated.

The Second Creation. The second creation means working the plan. It means the physical execution of the creative ideas. Here is where successful people excel.

Remember that success is not so much a matter of hard work, good luck, or a positive mental attitude as it is the *habit* of subordinating moods to mission, conditions to goals, schedules to people, dislike for certain things to the strength of your purpose.

To complete the creative process, then, we need a strong desire, a compelling purpose, and a deep commitment. We can then subordinate all the unpleasant, costly, sacrificial, and inconvenient means necessary to finish the job.

I like the biblical injunction to those who intend to build towers: first sit down and count the costs to see if you have sufficient means to finish it, lest you begin to build but are not able to finish.

Counting the costs and making commitments before beginning to build "towers" taps our ingenuity, resourcefulness, intuition, creativity and energy to do whatever is necessary. Nothing much happens until there is a commitment.

Failure in the second creation is often only an indication of failure in the first creation. The creative process requires both vision and execution.

Cultivating Creativity

The creative executive is a light, not a judge; a model, not a critic; a history-maker in the Arnold Toynbee sense.

Creative people are observant, often seeing and expressing parts usually unobserved by others and giving things a displaced accent. They have the ability to hold many ideas and compare them; their minds are vigorous; they often lead complex lives. And they explore the subconscious, reverie and fantasy, in spite of education. We live in a world where words and measurement and logic are enthroned, often at the expense of creativity, intuition and artistry. Men, particularly, have a rough time. Because of the "macho" cultural scripting and heavy academic focus, they often neglect, even drive out, the more creative, aesthetic, intuitive capabilities (often considered feminine).

Eastern cultures spoke of Yin and Yang. The ancient Greeks spoke of ethos, pathos and logos. Modern philosophers speak of left and right brain dominance. I think most modern executives have the whole-brain message, but the challenge, as James Newman writes, is to *Release Your Brakes*: "The best way to release your creative potential is to be open to ideas which seem to come from 'left field.' When a thought pops into your mind which does not seem to be grounded in any of your past experience, examine it carefully and see if it might be a practical solution to your puzzle."

One of the keys, then, to cultivating creativity and innovation — a culture of "tomorrow minds" — is removing the censors, withholding judgment, and being open to new ideas, no matter the source.

In my seminars, I sometimes divide people into two groups. I ask people in one group "to create as many ideas as possible to bring about a higher level of cooperation and harmony among individuals and departments in the company in order to increase business and reduce costs. Use your imagination and brainstorm. Don't judge any of these ideas. Just create. Let your minds flow. The wilder the ideas the better."

To the second group, I say, "Develop five good ideas to bring about a higher level of cooperation and harmony. You may be asked to share these ideas with the group."

Invariably, the first group comes up with the most and the best ideas, perhaps because they are so uninhibited.

Along with Tom Peters and Bob Waterman, I have found that excellent companies excel at fostering new ideas and bringing them to market. Their corporate culture values, treasures, nurtures and protects creativity — the history-making talent of beginning with the end in mind.

Chapter 13

Doing More in Less Time

Productivity is a measurement of production over time, and the key principle of life and time management is to manage relationships around principles, to organize around roles, and to execute around priorities and goals:

Prioritize, organize, and then perform.

To prioritize means to decide what is most important to do, what values to actualize, which goals to pursue. To organize means to either schedule ourselves or delegate tasks to others to achieve the goal. To perform means to discipline our activity according to our plan for getting desired results.

Prioritization: First Things First

Over the years, I have used a number of exercises to help people prioritize their lives and deal with questions of direction and purpose.

• I sometimes challenge them to think what they would do if they had but six months to live and then to organize those months accordingly.

• Or, I ask them to write their own eulogy and decide what contributions really matter.

• Or, I ask them to review their lives and record what is most gratifying to them, what contributions they consider most valuable, and then see themselves passing from this earth and looking back and asking, "What is most rewarding?"

Time Management is really a misnomer. All people have exactly the same amount of time, but some accomplish several times as much as others do with their time. *Self-Management* and *Life Leadership* are better terms, because they imply that we manage ourselves in the time allotted us.

Priority matters — activities that are important but not necessarily urgent — require more initiative: we must act on them. If we neglect taking the initiative or seizing the opportunity, crises and other pressing problems will grow ever larger until they consume most of the time once allotted for preventive maintenance, planning, preparation, and interpersonal communication.

Proactive people develop the discipline to do important but not necessarily "urgent" things. Reactive people get caught up in being busy, buried in "the thick of thin things," where "things that matter most are at the mercy of things that matter least."

Proactive people make important contributions by focusing on those activities that make a significant difference in results. Many famous political leaders, business executives, and performing artists serve as good examples of efficient "self-managers." Their ideas and works flow from carefully selected values and goals. They give their energies to top priorities and new opportunities. Studies have verified that most (about 80 percent) of the desired results flow from a few (20 percent) high priority or "high leverage" activities.

Every profession will have its own high-leverage tasks, but the common denominator of success is having an all-consuming purpose. That's why an hour spent prioritizing and planning may be worth ten in execution. One hour of executive time invested in high-leverage activity can greatly increase the productivity of an entire organization.

Once when training a group of shopping center managers, I first tried to help them clarify values and prioritize goals. I asked them to identify one management activity, which, if done superbly well, would have a tremendous effect upon desired results. Almost to a man, they mentioned deep, one-on-one communication with their tenants and their staff members. They said they were only spending about five percent of their time with these people because they were so busy with other problems, crises, meetings, interruptions, phone calls, and record keeping.

Each of them then set a goal, agreeing to spend at least one-third of their time in meaningful association with tenants over a period of several months. Those managers who did so achieved dramatic results. No longer were they being seen by tenants only when they had to negotiate and enforce contracts. Many of them soon became mentors, consultants, advisors, or advocates, helping tenants to cope with the host of business problems confronting them.

Organization: Schedule It or Delegate It.

After selecting priorities, we need to carefully organize; otherwise, we procrastinate, wasting time and talents, weakening resolve, and undermining confidence and self-esteem. Organization involves scheduling the activities that produce results and delegating some tasks to others. Proper delegation will increase our time for high-priority tasks.

Scheduling. Most managers know exactly what they want to do and why they want to do it, but they simply don't take the time to schedule the activities necessary to achieve their desired results. For instance, they fully intend to have a meaningful communication with employees, but they don't schedule it. They fully intend to write an annual report to stockholders, but they don't block out the time to do it. They fully intend to get back into shape, but they don't schedule their exercise program. They simply hope that somehow things will automatically fall into place.

Our schedules, of course, are our servants, not our masters. They are not as important as people, principles or values, which is why we must be flexible and mature enough to adapt to changing realities, to new perceptions, and to changing values and goals. Generally, however, it's wise to stay with planned activities and schedules unless there is an overriding reason to abandon or to change them.

Many people schedule their activities using an obsolete tool, one for scheduling only, never for clarifying values or selecting goals.

I strongly recommend using a self-management or planning tool that has ample space for stating your mission, defining your roles, listing long-range goals and planning the activities necessary to achieve them.

In his brilliant book, *The Effective Executive*, Peter Drucker recommends that executives occasionally keep a time log in 15-minute segments for a period of two weeks and then use the information to assess their effectiveness. It's revealing to honestly document our activities in 15-minute segments and then compare our use of time with our priorities and goals. Invariably, people are shocked to see how much time is being spent in low-priority, low-leverage activities that don't produce desired results.

Delegating. William Oncken, Jr., tells the story of the harried executive who is caught in an activity trap and buried in the thick of thin things. He frantically tries to get through it all, but each time he meets someone he gets another assignment or "monkey."

He says to himself, "I can't take this anymore." He tries to sneak out the back door to take a break from all the monkeys in his office. But halfway down the hall, he meets a subordinate with a problem. After learning of the problem, the already overburdened executive agrees to check into it — and in the process, another hairy monkey leaps onto his back.

After spending a miserable Saturday morning in his office, he decides to study up on the nature of the monkeys. So he goes to the encyclopedia and looks under "M" for monkeys. "Monkeys climb as high as they can go," he reads, "and they have no reverse faculties." The light breaks. He reads on, "They each have a home room where they rightfully belong." He puts the monkeys back in their cages, goes home, and takes his boys fishing.

Monday morning, the subordinates come in to inquire about their monkeys. "What do you recommend be done with them?" asks the executive.

"We don't know," say the subordinates. "You said you'd handle them."

"But you're all so close to the problem," exclaims the executive. "I have great confidence in your abilities to analyze the situation and make a recommendation on the problem you spoke to me about. You study it, make your best recommendation, and then we'll deal with it."

Each subordinate left the executive's office carrying his own monkey, as the executive had finally learned to delegate.

Delegation makes the difference between the independent producer and the interdependent manager or leader. Properly done, delegation enables one to accomplish much more work in the same amount of time by multiplying one's strengths through others and by relieving oneself of "monkeys." Ultimately, much more work will get done in much less time. In fact, time spent delegating, in the long run, is our greatest time saved.

Delegation may take more time in the beginning, and many who feel they are now pushed to the hilt simply won't take this time to explain, to train, to commit. Instead, they will say to themselves, "Every time I delegate it, either it doesn't get done or it gets done poorly, and I have to redo it myself. So why delegate? It just takes more time." But they end up leading harassed lives, putting in 14-hour days, neglecting their family and their health, and undermining the vitality of the entire organization.

If delegation is done correctly — if it is based on high trust, considerable training, and mutual understanding of and commitment to desired results, guidelines, resources, accountabilities, and consequences — both parties will benefit.

The delegation agreement, of course, is flexible. If you have little confidence in a person, make the desired results very clear, measurable, and quantifiable; establish stringent guidelines; specify resources; have frequent progress reports; and make sure consequences soon follow the behavior. If you have great confidence in a person, involve him in setting the performance criteria and then allow him to evaluate himself. In their hearts, people know how they're doing, but if the trust level is low, they will not be honest with themselves or others. The performance appraisal then becomes a meaningless game.

Performance: Working the Plan

As Charles Garfield has discovered, peak performers have a habit of doing first things first. They plan their work and work their plan, exercising discipline and concentration and not submitting to moods and circumstances.

They schedule blocks of time for important planning and project work and for creative activity and do this work when they are most refreshed. They bunch less important and less demanding activities — appointments, phone calls, correspondence, detail matters — and work on them when the fatigue level is higher. Also, they avoid handling paper more than once, because shuffling through stacks of bills, letters, literature, and notices breeds procrastination. Avoid touching paperwork unless you intend to take specific action on it.

Our ability to do more and perform better will increase as we exercise the discipline of doing important and difficult work first, when we are fresh, and deferring routine jobs to other times. Emerson wrote: "That which we persist in doing becomes easier, not that the nature of the task has changed but that our ability to do has increased."

It is this critical action step where most people falter and fail, usually because they do not first set clear objectives and make careful plans. Hence, they bog down in details, mirror their moods and feelings, and react to the circumstances of the moment.

Poor performance can often be attributed to poor prioritization and organization. Weak resolve is easily uprooted by mood or circumstance, but deep resolve and good organization get results. If our priorities and plans are well internalized and visualized, we will find the ways and means to realize them.

Chapter 14

Think Win-Win or No Deal

At the Olympic Games, we witness the "agony and the ecstasy" of athletic competition. Etched into faces at the finish lines and victory stands are the joys of winning, the sorrows of losing. In most events, there can only be one winner, one gold medal. And yet the spirit of the Olympic Games suggests that all who participate are winners — that victory is not the primary value of the games.

The principle of "win-win" was taught remarkably well in the games of the 1936 Olympiad in Berlin by an American athlete, Jesse Owens. As portrayed in "The Jesse Owens Story," Owens took time during practice at the Games to help a competitor from Mexico. "Why not," he said, "I want him to do his best and to benefit from the excellent training and coaching I have received." A German athlete was amazed by this act of human kindness in a competitive event. "Why do you help this man?" he asked. "He is your competitor. He may beat you because of the help you give him."

"I guess I never thought of that," said Owens.

Later, in the finals of the broad jump competition, Owens scratched on his first two attempts. He had only one jump left. At this point, his German friend gave him a tip. Placing his towel beside the runway a foot in front of the board, he told Owens to jump from that point to avoid a foul.

"You will have to jump one foot farther to win, but that's nothing to you."

"Why help me?" Owens asked, returning the question asked of him earlier.

"Because I want to compete against the best," replied the German with a warm smile.

That's the attitude of win-win. Jesse Owens gave that spirit to the Berlin Games of 1936. To his memory is the inscription: "He personified the sportsmanship ideal. He cared for people and challenged them to give their best. As long as athletes compete in sports, or people strive for excellence in any undertaking, the life and accomplishment of Jesse Owens will remain an enduring inspiration."

In a sense, Owens served as a model and inspiration for the man who equalled his feat of winning four gold medals in track and field at the 1984 Los Angeles Games, Carl Lewis. When compared to Owens, Lewis gracefully acknowledged the debt. "I will never replace him. Jesse Owens is still the same to me, a legend."

At his management seminars, another win-win thinker, the indomitable Edwards Deming, tells people, "Let's work together. Let's help each other, even our competitors. Nobody can survive alone. Let's meet in groups and get our ideas criticized. Let's not be 'sold down river' for ideas and slogans that sound great but don't work."

While many people are conditioned to think in the competitive terms of "I win-you lose," effective managers and their companies think more in the cooperative terms of "I win-you win." Paradoxically, the win-win attitude and agreement provide a powerful competitive advantage.

One company that operates on this win-win principle is Trammell Crow in Dallas, named as one of the ten best of *The 100 Best Companies to Work for in America*, the book by Levering, Moskowitz, and Katz. I suspect that the other nine companies listed in the top ten — Bell Labs, Delta Airlines, Goldman Sachs, Hallmark Cards, Hewlett-Packard, IBM, Northwestern Mutual Life, Pitney Bowes, and Time Inc. — also operate on the win-win principle.

Behind the thinking of great athletes like Jesse Owens and Carl Lewis, great achievers like Edwards Deming, and great companies like Trammell Crow is an attitude of win-win.

What is Win-Win?

I see *win-win* as one of six fundamental attitudes in life. The five alternatives to win-win are win-lose, lose-win, lose-lose, win, and win-win or no deal.

Win-win is a frame of mind and heart that constantly seeks mutual benefit in all human interactions. Win-win means that everyone wins because agreements or solutions are mutually beneficial, mutually satisfying. With a win-win solution, all parties feel good about the decision and feel committed to the action plan.

A primary alternative is *win-lose*, which is a more self-seeking or selfish attitude. A win-lose leader is authoritarian, prone to use position power as a method of influence to get his or her own way. In a win-lose system, the boss thinks, "I win, you lose. I feel good about it, you don't; but I'm the boss and can't care too much about what you think or feel. If I think you should do something and if I feel good about it, that's all that matters. If you don't think you should do it, or you don't think you can do it, or you don't want to do it, that won't change a thing."

The opposite of win-lose is *lose-win*. Lose-win means, "I lose, you win. Have your way with me. Step on me again. Everyone else does." In negotiation, it is seen as capitulation — giving in or giving up. In leadership style, it's permissiveness or indulgence. It makes no demands, establishes no standards, draws upon no vision. It means being "a nice guy," even if "nice guys finish last."

Once the president of a large chain of retail stores said to me, "Stephen, while win-win sounds good, I think it's very idealistic. It's really not the way the business world works. Sometimes the competition is really vicious, and if you're not out there fighting for what you want, you'll lose everything."

From the depth and intensity of his expression, I sensed that he had a recent bad experience, and I asked him if he would share it with me. He said he had recently renegotiated his lease arrangements with mall owners and operators. "We went in with a win-win attitude," he said. "We were open, reasonable, conciliatory and anxious to seek mutual benefit. But the other side saw that position as being soft and weak, and they took us to the cleaners."

I asked him, "Why did you go for lose-win?"

He said, "We didn't. We went for win-win."

"I thought you said that they took you to the cleaners."

"They did."

"In other words, you lost."

"That's right," he answered.
"And the other party won?"
"That's right."
"What's that called?"

He reflected a minute and said, "Oh my. . ." He realized that what he called "win-win" was really "lose-win."

Win-lose/lose-win relationships — "Dominant Dan, Dorothy Doormat" — may appear harmonious on the surface, but they are usually mutually dissatisfying. The problem is this:

> *Unexpressed feelings don't die.*
> *They are buried alive and come forth later in uglier ways.*

People who think lose-win are usually quick to please or appease. They have little courage or strength of their own to express their own feelings and convictions. They are easily intimidated by the ego strength of others or by the forceful expression of their feelings and convictions. So they tend to give in. But over time they build internal resentments and hostilities. These eventually surface in many different ways, including psychosomatic illnesses, disproportionate rage or anger, overreaction to minor provocation, and cynicism.

Many executives, managers and parents swing back and forth, as if on a pendulum, from win-lose inconsideration to lose-win indulgence. When they can't stand confusion and lack of structure, direction, expectation and discipline any longer, they swing back to win-lose — until guilt undermines their resolve and drives them back to lose-win. . .until anger drives them back to win-lose again.

If both people, in a human transaction, think win-lose, the result will be *lose-lose* — as manifest in war, conflict, or adversarial activity. When two win-lose people get together — that is, when two determined, stubborn, ego-invested individuals interact — the result will be *lose-lose*. Both will lose. Both will become vindictive and want to "get back" or to "get even," blinded to the fact that murder is suicide, that revenge is a two-edged sword. In the last analysis, no one or no thing can hurt us without our consent. Vengeance is that consent: "An angry man digs two graves."

Nevertheless, the tendency is often to think in dichotomies: strong or weak, win or lose, hardball or softball. But that thinking is fundamentally flawed. It's based upon power and position rather than upon principle. People who think in terms of dichotomies, tend to define winning as defeating someone. And when all parties have this win-lose attitude, lose-lose is almost inevitable. If one of the parties feels overpowered or intimidated, he may adopt a lose-win position. This may result in temporary peace, but it is no long-term resolution of the problem.

The illuminating book, *Getting to Yes*, beautifully describes the weakness of the positional approach and strength of the principled approach to negotiation. This book was written by two Harvard law professors, Roger Fisher and William Ury, who were attempting to redress the adversarial imbalance in the legal profession by cultivating the gentler peacemaking approach to negotiation. They felt it would have greater long-term benefits for both parties than either hard-position bargaining or soft-position bargaining.

> *"It suggests that you look for mutual gains wherever possible, and that where your interests conflict, you should insist that the result be based on some fair standards independent of the will of either side. The method of principled negotiation is hard on the merits, soft on the people. It employs no tricks and no posturing. Principled negotiation shows you how to obtain what you are entitled to and still be decent. It enables you to be fair while protecting you against those who would take advantage of your fairness."*

A fifth common alternative is simply to think *win*, to think just of getting what you want. It's not that you want the other person to lose necessarily. That's irrelevant. What matters is that you get what you want — that you win.

The sixth alternative is superior in some respects to win-win. I call it, *win-win or no deal*. This means that if we can't come up with a win-win agreement or deal, we simply agree not to deal. We agree to disagree agreeably. If we both can't feel good about it, let's not enter into any agreement.

When you go into negotiation with a clear, up-front awareness and commitment to "win-win or no deal," you can balance your strong desire to get what you want with consideration for the feelings and convictions of others. You can work toward a synergistic solution, creating alternatives which are better than any of those originally proposed. You can also be very open, candid, as well as empathic toward each other. Both parties could sincerely say, "I would not be happy with this deal if you are not genuinely happy, because we are going to be associated for a long time."

What Works Best?

We might now ask, "Of these six different attitudes — win-win, win-lose, lose-win, lose-lose, win, and win-win or no deal — which is the most appropriate?" My answer is, "It depends." It depends on the circumstance, whether it is an independent or an interdependent circumstance.

For instance, in an independent athletic contest, win-lose competitive thinking is certainly appropriate. Competition is also appropriate in many legal, political, business, and academic circles. Competition can be a powerful motivator. But it must be used in a system of checks and balances and kept within a framework of rules, guidelines or laws. Competition or win-lose thinking may then produce incredible results.

However, in interdependent circumstances, desired results are achieved through the cooperative efforts of two or more people. In an interdependent circumstance, it would be foolish to talk win-win or cooperation and then set up a competitive system among those who should cooperate to get desired results.

One time, I was invited to discuss the win-win principle with the management and employees of a business organization. It was obvious to the president that more cooperation would benefit everyone. He told me that if the sales people would cooperate, support each other, and draw upon the unique strengths and talents of each member of the group, each one of them would earn far more than they would earn by persisting in a selfish pattern — each person protecting his own turf, withholding his support and keeping his unique strengths and talents to himself.

As he was talking to me about this, I saw on his wall a large chart with the names of all sales people written on the left side. Horses — representing their different sales records — showed the progress each was making toward the grand prize, a trip to Bermuda for the salesman and his wife. Here the president was talking cooperation or win-win but setting up a competitive win-lose system to achieve it. This is analogous to telling one flower to grow but then watering another. The point is this:

> *Win-lose compensation systems*
> *inevitably override win-win rhetoric.*

A Total Philosophy

"Win-win" is a total philosophy and manifests itself in at least five interdependent areas. It begins with *character* and moves toward *relationships* out of which flow *agreements,* and it is nurtured by *environment* where the structure and the systems and the strategies are also based upon the win-win principle. The last dimension is *process.* We cannot achieve "win-win" ends with "win-lose" or "lose-win" means. Character, relationships, agreements and systems must be established through a "win-win" process.

The following diagram shows how these five dimensions relate to each other.

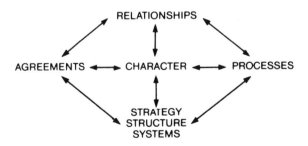

Everything else builds on the foundation of character.   A win-win character consists of three traits: integrity, maturity and the abundance mentality.

We gain and maintain integrity by educating and obeying our conscience, by keeping our habits in harmony with our value system, by keeping our commitments. We have control over our commitments and promises. If we make them carefully and keep them faithfully, it will build trust by giving others the feeling that we are dependable.

I define maturity as courage balanced with consideration. Mature people have the courage to express their feelings and convictions but balance their courage with consideration for the feelings and convictions of others. Most of the psychological tests devised for the purposes of hiring, training, and promoting people basically probe for this mature balance between courage and consideration, ego and empathy, toughness and kindness.

An abundance mentality basically means that we don't see life as a big competition, and that most of our psychic satisfactions don't come from competitions or comparisons. Most people develop the opposite of the abundance mentality − the scarcity mentality. They see life as a "zero sum" game and think that when someone else wins, in some way they lose.

A person with an abundance mentality sees life as having "plenty for everybody" and attempts to create many options to help others make the most of every situation. In management, the abundance mind would think in terms of releasing human potential instead of controlling it. Faith would be put in the potential of another person rather than in one's technique to get another to do what one wants.

Out of character, flows trust. And trust is the foundation of healthy human *relationships*. Without trust, there will be no basis for win-win negotiation or action, no medium for the expression of an abundance mentality.   In a low-trust culture, people act to protect and to defend themselves. Relationships then deteriorate.

If character and trust levels are high, people can then work out win-win *agreements* and *decisions*. However, these can only be implemented in a win-win *environment*. If the win-win principle is to govern human behavior, it must be built into the strategy, structure and systems of organizations. The executive who talks co-operation but rewards competition sets up a contradictory and self-defeating system. If he talks of human resource development but only audits financial and physical resources, he will undermine trust and breed conflict and cynicism in the culture. The process must be consistent with the principle. Otherwise, it's like the saying, "Firings will continue until morale improves!"

I'm convinced that the win-win principle can effectively govern human behavior in any organization, large or small. But it takes the modeling of win-win executives and managers, as well as the support of win-win relationships, processes, systems, and agreements.

Chapter 15

Clearing Communication Lines

Almost 30 years ago, in an administrative practices class at the Harvard Graduate School of Business, I was first introduced to an illuminating exercise in perception. It taught me that none of us sees the world as it is, but as we are, as our frames of reference or "maps" define the territory.

To make this point, my professor divided the class in half and showed one half a drawing of a young girl (A) and the other half a drawing of an old woman (C). Everyone was then shown a composite illustration (B).

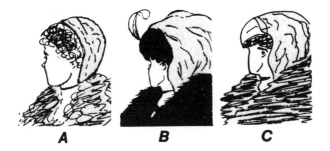

A   **B**   **C**

Invariably, those who were conditioned to see the young girl saw her in the composite drawing, and those conditioned otherwise saw the old woman. As people from both sides of the class interacted, they questioned the credibility (or sanity) of those who saw it differently.

Since that time, I have used these pictures scores of times in various contexts all over the world to teach people that our experience-induced perceptions greatly influence our feelings, our beliefs, and our behavior.

Perception and Credibility

Both perception and credibility problems may ultimately result in complicated knots, what we often call "personality conflicts" or "communication breakdowns." Credibility problems are far more difficult to resolve, primarily because each of the people involved thinks he sees the world as it is rather than as he is. Unaware of the distortion in his own perception, his attitude is this: "If you disagree with me, in my eyes you are automatically wrong, simply because I am sure that I'm right."

Whenever we are "so right" as to make everyone who sees and thinks differently feel wrong, their best protection from further injury from us is to label us, to peg us, to put us behind mental and emotional bars for an indeterminate jail sentence, and we will not be released until we pay "the uttermost farthing." Most credibility problems can be resolved if one or both of the parties involved will realize that, at the root, is a perception problem.

Attitudes and Behaviors

Certain attitudes and behaviors are essential to clearing communication lines.

Attitudes:

- I assume good faith; I do not question your sincerity or your sanity.

- I care about our relationship and want to resolve this difference in perception. Please help me to see it from your point of view.

- I am open to influence and am prepared to change.

Behaviors:

- Listen to understand.

- Speak to be understood.

- Start dialogue from a common point of reference or point of agreement and move slowly into areas of disagreement.

When these three attitudes and behaviors are acquired, almost any perception or credibility problem can be solved.

Often, once a person understands this, he will change his manner of speech. Instead of saying, "This is the way it is," he will say, "this is how I see it." Instead of saying, "Here it is," he will say, "In my view" or "In my opinion" or "As I see it." Such language admits other people to the human race by telling them: "You matter, too. Like mine, your view and feelings are legitimate and respectable."

When others judge us or disagree with us, our reply will be similar to the following in tone, if not in content: "Good, you see it differently. I would like to understand how you see it." When we disagree with another, instead of saying, "I'm right and you're wrong," we will say, "I see it differently. Let me share with you how I see it."

Words and Relationships

The crucial dimension in communication is the relationship. Many troublesome knots develop in communication lines because of poor interpersonal relations. When relationships are strained, we must be very careful about the words we use or risk giving offense, causing a scene, or being misunderstood. When relationships are poor, people become suspicious and distrustful, making a man "an offender for a word" instead of attempting to interpret the meaning and the intent of his words.

On the other hand, when the relationship is unified and harmonious, we can almost communicate without words. Where there is high trust and good feeling, we don't have to "watch our words" at all. We can smile or not and still communicate meaning and achieve understanding. When the relationship is not well established, a chapter of words won't be sufficient to communicate meaning because meanings are not found in words — they are found in people.

The key to effective communication is the one-on-one relationship. The moment we enter into this special relationship with another person, we begin to change the very nature of our communication with them. We begin to build trust and confidence in each other. In this context, consider the value of a private visit with each employee, a private lunch with a business associate, a private chat with a client or customer — a time when your attention is focused upon that person, upon his or her interests, concerns, needs, hopes, fears, and doubts.

There is a compelling mountain scene poster with this invitation at the bottom: "Let the mountain have you for a day." Let's change the slogan to, "Let your customer have you for an hour" or "Let your spouse have you for an evening." Try to be completely present with the other person, and to transcend your own personal interests, concerns, fears, and needs. Be fully with your manager, client, or spouse. Allow them to express their interests and goals, and subordinate your own feelings to theirs.

Map and Territory

Building harmonious relationships and achieving mutual understanding can be difficult. We all live in two worlds: 1) the private, subjective world inside our heads, and 2) the real, objective world outside. We could call the former, personal "maps," and the latter, the "territory."

None of us has an absolutely complete and perfect map of the territory, or of the real objective world. While scientists constantly attempt to make better and better maps, only the creator of the territory has the complete, perfect map. All true scientists hesitate to speak of their latest theory as fact, merely as the best explanation developed to that point.

To the degree that our map fails to match the territory they are inaccurate. If we use an inaccurate map of a city to search for a certain location, we will be lost and frustrated. If someone counsels us to "try harder" or "go faster" or "think positively," we will only become more frustrated because the problem has nothing to do with either diligence or attitude. The real problem is the inaccuracy of the map.

From time to time, we have experiences that change our pair of glasses, our frame of reference or the map through which we view the territory, the objective world. When this happens our behavior often changes to reflect the new frame of reference; in fact, the fastest way to change a person's behavior is to change his map or frame of reference by calling him a different name, giving him a different role or responsibility, or placing him in a different situation.

Skill and Security

We might look at the communication skill as we would at an iceberg — at two levels. The small, visible part of the iceberg is the skill level of communication. The great mass of the iceberg, silent and unseen beneath the surface, represents the deeper level — the attitudinal, motivational level. Let's call it one's security base. To make any significant long-term improvement in our communication abilities requires us to work at both levels, skill and security.

To listen deeply and genuinely to another on issues that affect our lives takes an enormous amount of internal personal security. It exposes our vulnerabilities. We may be changed. And if down deep we are feeling fairly insecure, we can't afford to risk being changed. We need to sense predictability and certainty. That is the anatomy of prejudice or prejudgment: we judge beforehand so that we don't have to deal with the possibility of a new thing happening. The specter of change frightens most people.

If we are changed or influenced as a result of empathic listening, we need to be able to say, "That's okay — it makes no real difference," because down deep we are changeless. At the core is a set of values and feelings which represent the real self, a sense of intrinsic worth which is independent of how others treat us. This is our inviolate self, our true identity.

Logic and Emotion

Effective, two-way communication demands that we capture both content and intent and learn to speak the language of logic and emotion.

The language of logic and the language of sentiment are simply two different languages, and of the two the language of sentiment or emotion is far more motivational and powerful. This is why it is so important to listen primarily with our eyes and heart, and secondarily with our ears. We must seek to understand the intent of the communication without prejudging or rejecting the content. We can do this by giving time, being patient, seeking first to understand, and openly expressing feelings.

To be effective in presenting your point of view, start by demonstrating a clear understanding of the alternative points of view. Articulate them better than their advocates can. Effective presentations begin with preassessment.

Sympathy and Empathy

Giving full attention, being completely present, striving to transcend one's autobiography and seeking to see things from another's point of view takes courage, patience, and inner sources of security. It means being open to new learning and to change. It means moving into the mind and heart of others to see the world as they see it. It does not mean that you feel as they feel. That is sympathy. Rather, it means that you understand how they feel, based on how they see the world. That is empathy.

An attitude of empathy is enormously attractive because it keeps you open, and others feel that you are learning, that you are influenceable. Remember that the key to your having influence with them is their perceiving that they have influence with you. When we finally learn to listen, seeking first to understand, we will learn more about communication. We will learn about the absolute futility of using the mind to dominate the heart. We will learn that there are two languages — the language of logic and the language of emotion — and that people behave more on the basis of how they feel than how they think. We will learn that unless there are good feelings between people, they will find it almost impossible to reason together because of emotional barriers. We will learn that fear is a knot of the heart and that to untie this knot, we must improve our relationship.

Communication, after all, is not so much a matter of intellect as it is of acceptance — acceptance of others, of their ideas and feelings, acceptance of the fact that they're different and from their point of view they are right.

Chapter 16

Empathy:
Key to Influencing Others

Once I was invited to Palm Springs, California, by a group of managers and executives representing Metropolitan Life Insurance Company. They asked me to give them a short presentation on developing what I consider to be the most valuable professional skill, empathy.

I defined empathy as the key to both understanding and influencing others. And, to train them in the basic steps and to help them assess their current level of development, I led them in a role play. I often use role play because it stimulates real situations and involves people in the problem. It also gives me a chance to teach the underlying principle:

Seek First to Understand, Then to be Understood.

Throughout the role play, I stressed the importance of valuing differences. "Strength lies in differences," I said. "The tendency of most people is to make others over in their own image. That's why it takes so much personal maturity and inner security to gain empathy."

I sensed that some of these insurance executives were incredulous, until they tried to exercise the skill in role play. Only then did many discover that they lacked both the right attitude and proper technique to understand the mind and heart of another person.

Why do I consider empathy to be the most valuable professional skill? Consider the cost of misunderstanding as it registers in such areas as executive turnover, poor product quality, reduced employee productivity, customer complaints, union grievances, and adversarial relationships.

The business media are filled with testimonials to the value of empathy. One example is this comment by William Murphy, founder of Cordis Corp., a leading medical technology company:

"My prime contribution is my sensitivity, not to what a doctor thinks he wants but to what he really does want. Most engineers don't understand the difference. Even after 25 years in the company, many don't yet understand that if it's good for the engineer, it isn't necessarily good for the physician."

The engineer or the executive who develops the skill of empathy will have the advantage in the company and in the marketplace. That is one of the main themes of the book, *In Search of Excellence*: "Excellent companies are better listeners. They benefit from market closeness. Most of their innovation comes from the market. From listening. From inviting customers into the company and paying attention to what they want."

Technique of Empathy

In essence, the technique of empathy is to capture and to reflect meaning and feeling. It is no easy matter. To listen with the eyes and heart to feelings takes more energy and skill than listening only with the ears to sayings.

I have identified five sequential steps in learning how to reflect our understanding of what another person attempts to communicate.

• *Mimic the content of the communication.* Simply repeat exactly what is said. If one says, "I like my job, but I don't feel challenged," you would say, "You like your job, but you don't feel challenged." To mimic, you must listen and repeat verbatim what is said.

• *Rephrase content.* Put their meaning into your own words. This takes thought or mental processing. For instance, one might say, "I'm terribly worried about the effect of the national deficit on our economy in the long run." And to rephrase the content, you might respond, "You're very concerned about the long-term effect of the national debt." When we rephrase, we must think as well as listen.

• *Reflect feeling.* When we reflect feeling, we listen with our eyes to capture the nature and the intensity of the emotion behind the communication. In fact, the communicator may say nothing with his lips, but a great deal with his face; or, the tone of his voice may say much more than the words alone. For instance, someone might say, "I talked to my supervisor about how I could get a raise. Mind you, I wasn't asking for a raise; I just wanted to know the criteria used by management in giving raises. And he got mad and jumped all over me. I can't work for a guy like that at all!" Reflecting the feeling, you might say, "You're upset and angry and feel completely misunderstood."

• *Combine rephrasing content and reflecting feelings.* For example, with regard to the last expression, you might say, "It hurts when you get reprimanded for seeking information." You are not agreeing or disagreeing with the person, only attempting to reflect your understanding of what the other person says and feels. If you sense the person would interpret your response as agreement, make it very clear what you're doing. You might say, "I sense you feel terribly upset, not so much by what he said, but by how he treated you." Or you might even become even more explicit. "Correct me if I'm wrong. I'm trying to understand. You feel really hurt and insulted and misunderstood by how he treated you."

• *Learn when and when not to rephrase and reflect verbally.* Sometimes it is obvious to both parties that understanding has taken place. There is simply no need to reflect or rephrase anything. Words would be out of place, perhaps even condescending or insulting.

Four Deadly Tendencies

Empathy requires us to transcend our own "autobiographies," to rise above seeing the world always through our own frames of reference. Again, this is no simple matter. Autobiographical responses are deeply imbedded into our natures. They produce the following four tendencies, each deadly to empathy.

• *Evaluating.* This is perhaps the strongest autobiographical tendency. It emerges without any conscious effort whatsoever in most of us, unless we work to stay in the "faithful translator" role. The translator faithfully captures and conveys what is communicated without evaluating the content. Too often we evaluate as we listen. We may even punish honest, open expressions or questions, causing others to cover up, to protect themselves. The greatest single barrier to open, honest communication is the tendency to criticize and evaluate.

•   *Probing.*   This common technique for seeking new information and gaining understanding has four fundamental weaknesses. First, it controls or directs the conversation. Second, it is autobiographical, since the questions come out of our own background, our own frame of reference. Third, it is logical, and therefore keeps sentiment from surfacing. And fourth, it is invasive. When probing, we seek to disclose another person's heart and mind at our own pace and speed.

Abraham Maslow's statement is appropriate here. "He that is good with a hammer tends to think everything is a nail." Most people are experts at probing (hammering). However, it's the wrong tool for gaining understanding of the internal, subjective world and emotional content of another person's mind and heart.

•   *Advising.* The urge to tell another person what he or she should do, think, or say comes very easily to a listener who means well and generally wants to help. Advice certainly has its place but not until understanding has been achieved.

Suppose that your vision is blurred. You think you need glasses. You call on your friend, Stan, an optometrist. He briefly listens to your complaint and replies, "Yes, I'm sure you need glasses. Here, I've worn this pair now for ten years, and they've really helped me. They'll do the same for you. Take this pair — I've got an extra one at home." You try them on. "But Stan, I can't even see as well as before," you report. He assures you, "That's okay; it's just a matter of getting used to them. Before long you'll see as well as I do."

The foolishness here is apparent. And yet, every day many executives prescribe (give advice) before they diagnose (get understanding).

•   *Interpreting.* We often try to explain other people's behavior and guess their intention. We tend to project our motives on the behavior of others and to play amateur shrink with their heads, reading into their present behavior the psychic dynamics from their earlier history or perhaps our earlier history. Also, we tend to judge others by their behaviors and ourselves by our intentions.

Good and Bad Attitudes

Often the major obstacle to understanding is a poor attitude. Here are four.

• *"I don't have time."* Perhaps this is the most common obstacle to empathy. It takes time and effort to understand another, and people simply "don't have all day to sit and listen" to other people. But, in fact, it takes far more time to deal with misunderstandings than to get that understanding initially. As the expression goes, "We always have time to do it over, but never time to do it right the first time."

When we take the time to understand and stay with the empathic process until the other person feels that we do understand, we have communicated many things: we care; we want to understand; we respect their ideas; we value their friendship; we accept them for who and what they are. People spend a great deal of effort and energy fighting for the feeling of being accepted and respected, for a sense of their own worth. If you grant them this by sincerely seeking to understand, you'll find that almost all of their fight will be gone.

• *"I already understand."* A friend of mine was heartsick over his relationship with his teenage son. "When I come into the room where he is reading or watching TV, he gets up and goes out — that's how bad the relationship is," he reported.

I encouraged him to try first to understand his son rather than to try first to get his son to understand him and his advice. He answered, "I already understand him! What he needs is to learn respect for his parents and to show appreciation for all we're trying to do for him."

"If you want your son to really open up, you must work on the assumption that you don't understand him and perhaps never fully will, but that you want to and will try."

Eventually, the father agreed to work on this assumption. As he listened, something marvelous began to happen. His son started to drop his defenses and open up with some of his real problems and deeper feelings. The father also opened up and shared some of his deep feelings and concerns as well as understandings regarding what had happened in the past. For the first time in years they weren't attacking and defending but were genuinely trying to understand each other.

We need to constantly be reminded of the prayer of St. Francis of Assisi: "Help me, oh God, to realize that it is in understanding another that I will be understood."

• *"I lack the skill, emotional discipline, or patience."* Most of us have never been trained how to listen, although we've had extensive training in how to read, write, and speak. Others of us may lack the discipline. Full and active listening takes discipline to supply the commitment, energy, and patience needed to stay in the process.

• *"I lack the desire to open up because of the emotional risk."* Empathy makes us open to influence. When we really listen to another, we are vulnerable; and if down deep we are insecure and self-doubting, we can't afford to be vulnerable in our interpersonal relations. Unless we continually cultivate the sources of intrinsic security, we can't afford the risk of genuinely opening up to another, being influenced by another, seeking to understand another.

Empathy means moving into the mind and heart of others to see the world as they see it. It does not mean that you feel as they feel. That is sympathy. Rather, it means that you understand how they feel, based on how they see the world, Strictly speaking, you will never fully see it as others see it, but you try.

Your attitude is: "I will try to understand. I may never understand, but I am going to try."

Such an attitude is enormously attractive because it keeps you open, and others feel that you are learning, that you are influenceable. Remember, the key to your having influence with them is their perceiving that they have influence with you.

Now, Seek to Be Understood

When seeking to be understood, follow these five principles of effective presentation.

• *Empathy.* We can influence or persuade others only to the degree they feel we understand and appreciate them and are seeking their interests as well as our own. That's why empathy is the first principle of effective presentations. The key to influence is first to be influenced.

• *Simplicity.* After seeking to understand another's point of view, then we need to express how we see it and how we feel about it in simple ways. I like the "KISS" formula: Keep it simple and straight-forward or "Keep it simple, stupid."

• *Imagery.* It is very helpful to make our presentation visual. The common expression — "a picture is worth a thousand words" — is very true. A "picture" can be a story, a parable, a metaphor or diagram. Help your audience "see" your point by using familiar imagery.

• *Objectivity.* Be objective in going through problem-solving steps, particularly when articulating their point of view. Express their position better than they can themselves. They will feel deeply understood and see you as impartial, objective, and open to influence.

• *Authenticity.* Be authentic — say what you mean. Be in touch with your feelings and opinions and express them simply. "I feel..." "In my opinion..." "As I see it..." Giving "you" messages - "Why are you so stubborn?" "You're so insensitive" - only stirs up defenses and ties knots in communication lines.

I emphasize again, in conclusion, that if you want to be effective and persuasive in presenting your point of view, start by demonstrating your understanding of the alternative points of view. Articulate them better than their advocates can. Then share your message clearly, simply, visually.

Chapter 17

Making Deposits in Emotional Bank Accounts

In every key relationship of our lives, we must daily build reserves of trust and love.

Some time ago, while conducting a training seminar at a beautiful site on the Oregon coast, I was approached by a man who asked if he might speak with me privately about his marriage.

"Look at this wonderful coastline," he began, as we both gazed out on the ocean. "I should be having a great time, and yet I really don't enjoy coming to these seminars."

He had my attention. "All I can think about is the grilling I'm going to get from my wife on the phone tonight. She gives me the third degree every time I'm away from home. She asks, Who did I have breakfast with? What did we talk about? What did I do for entertainment? Who was with me? And the tone of her interrogation is always, 'Who can I call to confirm all this?'"

He looked miserable. We continued to talk for a while, and then he made a very interesting comment. "I guess she knows all the questions to ask," he said rather sheepishly, "because it was on a trip like this that I met her...when I was married to someone else."

I considered the implications of his statement for a moment and then said, "You're really into quick-fix, aren't you?"

"What do you mean," he replied.

"Well, you'd like to somehow open your wife's head and rewire her and be done with the problem, wouldn't you?"

"Sure, I'd like her to change," he exclaimed. "I'd like her to stop grilling me and start trusting me." "My friend," I replied, *"you can't talk yourself out of a problem you behave yourself into."*

"So, what do I do," he asked.

"The best way to change her attitude and win her trust is to open an *emotional bank account* with her and start making deposits. And don't expect quick results. You'll need to make a thousand and one deposits in that account over time before you see significant change."

While he didn't want to hear that sort of advice, he acknowledged it was correct and agreed to open an account.

Daily Deposits

With each new relationship, we open an emotional bank account. Much like a financial bank account, it receives deposits and from it come withdrawals. When withdrawals exceed deposits, the account is overdrawn. One main difference between the two kinds of accounts is that the human relationship usually requires daily small deposits to maintain the balance and to build equity.

Deposits are made through courtesy, kindness, honesty and keeping commitments. Withdrawals are made through discourtesy, disrespect, threats and overreactions.

If I keep making deposits in your emotional bank account, my reserve builds up. Your trust in me becomes greater, and I can call on that trust often if I need to. I can even make mistakes and other forms of withdrawals and be forgiven.

But if I continually make withdrawals from the account without making deposits, the reserve is diminished. If I keep making withdrawals, the emotional bank account becomes overdrawn. At that point I have no trust with you. I'm walking on mine fields. I have to watch every step and measure every word to cover my backside.

Sadly, many managers who are wizards at making financial deposits (and therefore are the very people who tend to be promoted) are woefully inept at making emotional deposits.

A certain manager once bragged to me about his tough management style in dealing with "problem employees." He said that he told them to "either shape up or ship out."

When I asked him why he didn't tell his customers that if they weren't prepared to buy the goods and services at the prices requested, they too should "either shape up or ship out," he replied that he didn't have the same right to do this with customers as he had with his employees. I agreed that he could run his business as he chose, but he could not choose the consequences of his attitudes and actions.

We can pay for warm bodies, but we can't buy employee's hearts and minds with money. That's why managers should treat their employees like volunteers, because in a sense, that's what they are.

When the employees of this same manager elected to form a union, he expressed his disappointment to me. He felt that he had been fair and consistent with them. "I can't believe that they are so ungrateful, after all I have done for them."

What he viewed as benevolence, his employees viewed as a kind of paternalism that could be arbitrarily withdrawn. Moreover, they saw his "rewards" as basic rights, reflecting the wider democratic and egalitarian values of society. Whenever a state of collusion evolves, each party feels completely self-justified. They interpret each other's behavior as ungrateful or disloyal. And as the level of trust lowers, the communication process becomes exhausting, time-consuming, and ineffective. Each party is made an offender for a word, and so words are chosen carefully and used sparingly in face-to-face conversation. It's like negotiating in a mine field.

In contrast, when the trust level is high, communication is simple, effortless, instantaneous and effective. People can communicate intended meanings with few words. Mistakes are covered up with charity, and meaning is transferred with subtlety, nuance, good will, and humor.

Unions are usually symptomatic of a low emotional bank account with employees — and that's bad for business because generally it means that people in the same company are involved in adversarial relationships.

It's hard to imagine how a company can produce quality products when its management thinks that employees are trying to get as much as they can with as little work as possible. Meanwhile, employees are equally sure that management is trying to exploit them by getting more from them than they are being paid to do. In this sort of psychological armed camp, it's amazing that anything produced actually works.

The high costs of low emotional bank accounts are perhaps best seen in strained or broken marriage and family relationships. If marriage is viewed by both husband and wife as a courtship into which they must make continual deposits in the form of courtesies, respect, kindness, fidelity and loyalty, then the relationship will blossom and become tremendously fruitful in every way. If it is seen in a baser way, withdrawals will be made in some form of selfishness, a root cause of marital discord and divorce. In a sense, selfishness is a symptom for heavy focus on what we want — the results we desire.

For instance, a husband who is selfish and inconsiderate for a period of time, cajoles and manipulates and intimidates to get what he wants, but eventually the relationship deteriorates from one of a rich, spontaneous understanding to one of accommodation, to one of toleration, to one of hostility, and finally ends up in the legal courts or in a cold war at home. When he discovers he is not getting what he wants, all he'll want is out.

The same is true with parents in relation to their children. If parents focus on what they want and threaten and intimidate, yell and scream, wield the carrot and the stick, or go the other way and indulge the kids or simply leave them alone, relationships will deteriorate; discipline will be non-existent; vision, standards, and expectations will be unclear.

When the children are young and susceptible to threats and manipulation, parents often get what they want in spite of their methods. But by the time the child becomes a teenager, a parent's threats no longer have the same immediate force to bring about desired results. Unless there is a high trust level and a lot of mutual respect, they have virtually no control over their children. There are simply no reserve funds in the account. A lack of deposits in the formative years leads to an overdrawn emotional bank account in the teen years, a breakdown of the relationship, and a lack of influence.

Dramatic Dividends

Emotional bank accounts are very fragile, yet very resilient at the same time. If we have a large emotional bank account, say $200,000 of emotional reserve capacity with another, we can make small withdrawals of $5,000 and $10,000 from time to time, and others will understand and accommodate us.

For instance, we may need to make a very unpopular, authoritarian decision because of certain time pressures without even involving others or explaining it to them. If we have a $200,000 bank account and make a $10,000 withdrawal in this manner, we would still have $190,000 left. Perhaps the next day we could explain what we did and why we did it, thus redepositing the $10,000.

The practice of making daily deposits in the emotional bank accounts of others often pays dramatic dividends.

Personal Example. Once, I explained the principle of the emotional bank account to a friend of mine who felt as though he was $150,000 overdrawn in his relationship with his son.

I encouraged him to be patient in making deposits into the emotional bank account and not to expect too much too soon. He admitted that he had made some small deposits from time to time, but because he expected more immediate results, he grew impatient and overreacted, making a huge withdrawal that put him further back than when he started making his small deposits. I explained that when others sense that we are making deposits into the relationship primarily to get what we want, they feel manipulated and grow cynical and distrustful of new deposits.

A service orientation flows directly out of the character and integrity and the sincerity of a person. If one is insincere, and uses manipulative technology, his motives undoubtedly will be revealed for what they are, the net effect being a huge withdrawal.

My friend caught this vision and began to do this kind of personal-computer work on himself which enabled him to sincerely do personal-computer work with his son. Then when his sincerity was tested, it was not found wanting, and the small deposits made consistently over a period of time accumulated until he had a huge reserve and the quality of the relationship was such that they enjoyed thinking out loud in each other's presence without fear of ridicule or embarrassment.

These small deposits were made in the form of patience, courtesies, empathy, kindnesses, services, sacrifices, honesty, and sincere apologies for past mistakes, overreactions, ego trips, and other forms of withdrawal. The father began to "waste" time with his son. When the son saw consistent actions behind these kind words, the deposit process accelerated without effort or straining, and within a few weeks the relationship had turned 180 degrees.

Business Example. When in 1983 Lawrence H. Lee was elected CEO of Western Airlines (since acquired by Delta Airlines), his company faced a number of serious problems. There was no strong, unified senior management team in place to deal with the fare wars, an imposing near-term land debt load, and a frustrated employee group. Soon after taking office, Lee had a strong management team in place; successfully completed a $155 million public offering; initiated the Western Partnership, an employee stock plan born out of a labor-management cooperation; started a new marketing thrust; launched a new hub operation out of Salt Lake City; and persuaded the pilots to take a 30 percent cut in pay. Within a year, Western had turned a $16.8 million, six-month operating loss into a quarterly operating profit of $23.2 million.

Duane "Dewey" Gerard, then vice-president of flight operations, explains the turnaround in terms of Lee's enormous credibility, earned over a 40-year period with the company. "He had the complete confidence and trust of the employees," said Gerard. "Over the years, he had worked in baggage, ticket sales, marketing, training, personnel, services, and operations. Everybody knew he had their best interests at heart. He asked nothing of us that he didn't ask of himself. He himself took a 100 percent cut in pay for the same period."

For four decades, Lee had made several small deposits in people. "He has a genuine concern for people, and that comes across as he visits with pilots in the cockpits, baggage loaders in the bays, or stockholders in the boardrooms. He knows every job and every person in the company. That's how he gets the most from his human resources."

Human resource development is fundamentally the management of human relationships.

Laws of Love & Laws of Life

When we live the primary laws of love, we encourage others to live the primary laws of life.

In other words, when we love without condition, without strings, we help people feel secure, safe, validated and affirmed in their intrinsic worth, identity and integrity. Their natural growth is encouraged. We make it easy for them to live the laws of life — cooperation, contribution, discipline, integrity — and to discover and to live true to the highest and best within them. We give them the freedom to act on their own inner imperatives rather than react to conditions, comparisons or limitations.

Now, this doesn't mean that we become soft and permissive. That, in itself, is a massive withdrawal. We counsel; we coach; we motivate; we set guidelines; we define roles; we have goals. But regardless of outcomes, we show love.

When we violate the primary law of love and start attaching strings and conditions, we actually encourage others to violate the laws of life and become defensive. They may feel they have to prove "I matter" or "I count." They become more concerned with defending their "rights" and proving their individuality than they are about honoring their own inner imperatives. Rebellion and ignorance are both knots of the heart, not of the mind. And the key to untying them is to make many deposits of unconditional love.

For instance, I once had a friend who was the dean of a very prestigious school. He planned and saved for years to provide his son the opportunity to attend that institution. But when the time came, the son refused to go.

The father knew what graduating from that school would mean to the boy; besides, it was a family tradition — for three generations! He urged his son to change his mind. But the only message the boy heard was that his father's desire for him to attend that school outweighed the value he placed on him as a person and as a son, which was terribly threatening. Naturally, the boy resisted.

After some intense soul searching, the father, along with his wife, resolved to love and support their son regardless of his choice and to express their love sincerely. It was a difficult process, but they reached the point where they could honestly say, "Son, your decision — whatever it is — will not affect the love we feel for you." Let me emphasize that they did not do this to manipulate their son. They did it as the logical extension of their growth and character.

The boy made no immediate response, but about a week later, he told his parents that he had decided, once and for all, not to go. They were prepared for this and again expressed their love.

Some time later an interesting thing happened. Now that the boy no longer had to defend his position, he searched within himself and found that he really did want to go to that school. He began the admission process at once.

What Are Deposits?

An important part of making deposits into other people's emotional bank accounts is an awareness of what deposits are to them: *What may be a deposit in your eyes may be perceived as a withdrawal in the eyes of others.*

The tendency is to project our own desires and preferences onto others. This is why most people judge others by their behavior and themselves by their intentions — when they see someone else's particular behavior, they project what their intention would be with that behavior. Consequently, they do not understand that other person at all, but they act as if they did and they end up feeling terribly misunderstood themselves.

We tend to deposit what we esteem to be of value. But what we esteem to be of great worth, others may think worthless; they may, in fact, despise it. To know what a deposit is to another person, you will need to employ the skill of empathy. In some cases, you will need "leave the 99 and seek after the one."

The key to the 99 is the one. As we are loyal to those who are absent — as we defend the rights of the defenseless, as we seek the opinion of the outcast, as we show respect to the customer who complains, as we give unconditional love to a confused teenager — we make a major deposit with every individual within our Circle of Influence. Remember, everyone is a "one" at some time.

Since every situation is different and unique, we simply must "read" what would amount to a deposit or a withdrawal to the other person and cultivate patience for accounts that are significantly overdrawn.

Six Ways to Make Deposits

Here are six ways you can make major deposits that build emotional bank accounts.

• *Empathize.* Until you understand another from within his or her frame of reference, you don't know what a deposit or withdrawal is.

• *Remember the little things.* In relationships, the little things are big. Perform kindnesses and courtesies. Small discourtesies, little unkindnesses and small forms of disrespect make large withdrawals.

• *Keep commitments.* People build their hopes around promises — particularly promises about their rice bowl and their livelihood. If you make and keep promises over time, that integrity builds a large reserve of trust.

• *Clarify and fulfill expectations.* Many expectations are explicit, but many are implicit. People bring both types of expectations to relationships. Fulfilling expectations is a major deposit — that's why it is so important to begin new endeavors or employments with a clarification of expectations.

• *Be loyal.* Your many daily deposits can be destroyed by a single act of disloyalty. For example, if I hear you sweet-talking someone to his face, yet bad-mouthing him to his back, what can I expect when you and I have a falling out? The same treatment! I will recognize your duplicity and distrust you. If, on the other hand, you are constant and loyal, even when it costs you, you will build big reserves among all your associates. To retain those present, defend those absent.

• *Sincerely apologize.* You make a great deposit when you can sincerely say, "I was wrong. I'm sorry. That was my fault. What I said was unkind." Words such as "I'll say I'm sorry if you'll say you're sorry," or "I'll tell you why I did what I did" only make withdrawals.

One final word: the only real deposits are those that are *sincere*; in Latin, that word means, "without wax." Remembering the little things, keeping commitments, clarifying and fulfilling expectations, apologizing, and being loyal all add up to trust reserves if they are sincere.

Chapter 18

Synergy: Value the Differences

Most people think of differences as weaknesses. But the effective executive will value them as strengths and use them in meetings and projects to bring about synergy, the natural fruit of the creative problem-solving, decision-making process.

Just as each of us has a unique set of fingerprints, we each have our own unique perception of the world, which is both an asset and a liability. Through our perception, we see the world as we are, not as it is. Therefore, unless we have access to the perceptions in other people's minds, we will always be limited by the perceptions in our own. Perhaps the word "limited" is too moderate; the stronger word "enslaved" may be more appropriate.

We may even reach the point where we think our perception represents the world as it truly is and condemn all other views as being wrong. Our stance might then become, "All decent, level-headed, rational people see what I see! I don't see the world as I am; I see the world as it is. And anyone who sees it differently is a fool!"

This is the position of the closed-minded person, the one who refuses to communicate openly in respectful ways with others. Such a prideful posture would cause the individual to become increasingly insulated and isolated from others, to reject the culture in which he lives, and to become a law unto himself. His efforts in associating and working with others will be essentially to clone them, to make them over in his own image. He will surround himself with people who think as he thinks and see as he sees. Since differences are not appreciated or tolerated, he will experience no synergy.

Synergy means that the whole is greater than the sum of its parts, that one plus one equals more than two. Synergy is a natural phenomenon, common to all of life, and it produces incredible results.

For example, University of Maryland researchers have discovered what observant gardeners have known for a long time: that growing tomatoes and asparagus together benefits both crops. The asparagus roots exude a chemical that kills many of the nematodes that either feed on tomato roots or carry diseases to the plant. Tomatoes, in turn, repel the asparagus beetle. Both plants do better when planted together than either does alone.

But in my mind, the most powerful example of synergy is the interaction between two creative people who, while harboring different perceptions, nevertheless work together to produce remarkable results that neither person alone could achieve. Moreover, both parties are somehow influenced in the process and often changed.

An interesting example of synergy evolved out of the post-World War II establishment of the Atomic Energy Commission. This commission was given the charge of developing atomic energy and directing its use. David Lilienthal, former director of the Tennessee Valley Authority and, therefore, no novice to the demands of leadership, was appointed chairman. He did something very significant to create synergy.

His first step was to bring together a group of talented, highly influential people, including the cream of America's scientific crop. Some might almost say they were prima donnas — celebrities in their own right, each with his own discipline and frame of reference. This group had a heavy agenda with demanding deadlines: to make peaceful atomic energy a reality, to make it part of the American mainstream of life, and to do it fast; or, as President Truman said, to "make it a blessing." In addition, the military was pressing for immediate A-bomb tests for the quite legitimate reasons of planning, research, and product testing.

Notwithstanding these pressures, Lilienthal devoted valuable weeks developing the esprit de corps of his group, believing deeply that the success of his organization depended upon the evolution of what he termed a "fraternal spirit."

He, of course, was criticized for doing this, for taking precious time and producing no visible results with it. The powers-that-be were impatient to get right at the agenda itself. But Lilienthal, no newcomer to criticism, proceeded determinedly with his plan. He encouraged his commission to get to know each other — to understand the varying interests, hopes, goals, concerns, backgrounds, and paradigms. Through this process, they developed deep respect for each other. The spirit of reverence and respect, they found, is the essence of synergy.

Synergy results from valuing differences, from bringing different perspectives together in a spirit of mutual trust. Mistaking uniformity for unity, sameness for oneness, insecure people surround themselves with others who think similarly. Secure people, on the other hand, realize that the strength of their relationships with others lies as much in their differences as in their similarities. They not only respect individuals with different views, but they actively seek them out.

When you look on a difference between you and your spouse, between you and your children, between you and your associates as being a strength, not a weakness, then you reflect the spirit of synergy. You begin to seek objective feedback, both internal and external, on your performance, your products and your services, knowing that without feedback, you develop significant blind spots. You look for ways to build a complementary team, where the strengths of one compensate for the weaknesses of another. You realize that the strength of a relationship lies in its differences.

Frequently an independent-thinking leader, one who minimizes the importance of feedback, feels he must maintain the posture of invincible leader. Hesitant to appear wrong, yet nonetheless afraid that he might be in error, this leader assumes the self-sufficient stance which says, "I don't need your opinions, only your corroboration." His basic insecurity forces him to define oneness as sameness, not complementariness, and thus he foregoes the benefits of synergy.

Negative Synergy

In many marriages, groups, and organizations, relationships are such that rather than having one plus one equal more than two, one plus one equals something less than two. This negative synergy occurs whenever people put some of their creative energy into politicking, masterminding, manipulating, disparaging, or condemning — resulting in interpersonal rivalries, defensive communication, and protective communication.

Negative synergy may also result when one or more members of the group has not developed an internal or individual synergy. If one does not value the two sides of his nature — the logical, analytical, verbal left side and the creative, emotional, visual right side — or if one side continually overpowers the other, there's no basis for internal synergy. If the emotional, more intuitive side completely overpowers the verbal and analytical side, or visa versa, there will be little chance to communicate effectively.

Intrapersonal synergy is a fruit of internal unity and balance, not just between the right and left sides of our brains, but between our values and our habits. From this base we can progress to interpersonal synergy, whereby we can contribute more to a relationship, a conflict resolution, a communication.

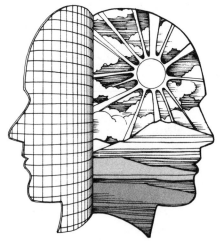

Without internal synergy, interpersonal synergy cannot exist. Interpersonal synergy results from respecting the fact that you see something differently, that you think differently, that other people have a different frame of reference, a different viewpoint, and that it, too, is valid and valuable.

Differences: Strengths or Weaknesses?

You may be rationally convinced of the need to value differences and yet unable to truly appreciate the perceptual, temperamental, and conceptual differences in your key relationships. Think about a difference you have with your spouse or with any other individual with whom you have a significant relationship. How do you handle the difference on this important issue? Are you grateful for it? Do you see it as a strength or as a weakness?

Many people, perhaps even a majority of married people, cannot talk through a difference on an important issue in a respectful way. It's uncommon to see a couple sit down and talk through a difference with respect and demonstrate that they value their differences. It requires unusual maturity, security, self-esteem, and great respect for the other person.

How can such strength be developed? I suggest that you start in small ways, learning how to discuss differences on relatively safe, peripheral, unimportant topics — developing ways of talking through differences and cultivating the attitude of appreciating differences, of valuing them, of seeing them as strengths rather than weaknesses.

Continue by making synergy the underlying goal of almost all meetings. Compromise, a frequent outcome of meetings, deals in tradeoffs, while synergy optimizes available resources — trades an old idea for a better, higher one. Therefore, an executive management team may arrive at the most effective decision not by intimidating or pressing for unanimity but by bringing different points of view together, sharing perceptions respectfully, valuing differences and diversity.

Synergistic decision-making refines thinking. It's a human resource approach to problem solving, not just a human relations approach. The human resources leader fully and courageously shares his vision and perception but balances his courage with consideration and empathy for the feelings and convictions of others. He values their opinions, not to placate them or to enlist their blind support, as a human relations advocate might, but to involve them meaningfully. An effective human resources leader knows that synergy both unifies an organization and gives it better and higher quality decisions because the decisions reflect the wisdom and commitment of the entire group.

The Japanese society readily characterizes collective decision making, or decision making by consensus. Nearly everyone in a Japanese business has some voice in running the company, which equates with running their society and even their very lives. For example, if the issue at hand is the maximum allowable time for a new employee to reside in company-provided housing, work will literally grind to a halt until the people involved reach consensus.

This is called nemawashi, "root binding," a metaphor derived from an experience common to the Oriental culture — a careful gardener transplanting a tree. Just as a gardener meticulously wraps all the roots of a tree together before he transplants it, Japanese leaders bring all members of society together before an important decision is made. This process is often tedious, and sometimes interminable. But in the end, the group as a whole benefits because all members are aligned behind the same goal. It may take forever to get a decision, but once made, the whole culture moves.

Another way strong leaders use the power of synergy to their advantage is to ask several mature, proactive people who disagree on how to solve difficult problems to serve on an ad hoc committee and then to challenge them to reach a consensus around synergistic recommendations.

The synergistic model magnifies the individual. Using the principle of synergy, a person, through interaction with others, can multiply his individual talents and abilities, thus making the whole greater than the sum of its parts. Counterfeit models of compromise, public relations, and intimidation divide people, destroy unity, and impede progress.

Part 3:

MANAGERIAL EFFECTIVENESS

Very early in my life, at age 21, I was assigned to manage the work of others and to train men more than twice my age in the principles and skills of effective management. It was a humbling, frightening experience.

Like me, most people — once on their own — soon find themselves in some sort of "management" position. Often these responsibilities come before we are ready for them. But we learn by doing and by making mistakes and over time we gain some degree of competence and confidence.

In this section, I focus on issues and challenges that face all managers — supervision, delegation, participation, expectations and performance agreements.

Chapter 19

The Two Sides of Success

Wise management will take a lesson from an old Aesop fable: only a fool would kill the productive goose that lays the daily golden egg in an attempt to have it all now. Many business failures suggest, however, that some executives have not yet learned the lesson.

Aesop's fable about the goose and the golden egg is the story of a poor farmer who one day visits the nest of his goose and finds at her side a glittering yellow egg. Suspecting it to be a trick, he is about to throw it away but on second thought takes it home where he discovers, to his delight, that it is an egg of pure gold. Every morning thereafter the farmer gathers one golden egg from the nest of the dear goose, and soon he becomes fabulously rich. As he grows rich, however, he also grows greedy and impatient. Hoping to get at once all the gold in the goose, he kills it and opens it, only to find nothing.

The moral of this old fable has a modern ring to it. Much is being written about our current economic malaise. Some commentators suggest that like the foolish farmer, we often emphasize short-term profits (golden eggs) at the expense of long-term prosperity (the goose).

For example, in his book, *Megatrends*, John Naisbitt writes about the consequences of "golden-egg" thinking among managers. "We hear a lot of alibis, but their preoccupation with short-term results in quantitative measurements of performance was responsible for the neglect of the kinds of investments and innovations necessary to increase the nation's capacity to create wealth.

"The criticism about short-term management," Naisbitt continues, "is becoming widely accepted by the business community itself. Of nearly one thousand top executives surveyed in 1981 by the Chicago management firm, Hendrick and Struggles, 76 percent said there has been a damaging overemphasis on immediate financial goals."

It seems that most managers, like the farmer, are methods-minded, concerned with efficiency or doing things right. Effective executives, on the other hand, are results-minded, concerned with doing the right things.

The wisdom of this orientation is illustrated in the fable. In his efforts to be efficient, the farmer became grossly ineffective; he could not sustain his success or be effective over the long run because he destroyed his capacity to get desired results.

The farmer learned from sad experience that success has two sides: the goose, which represents performance capability (PC), and the golden egg, the production (P) of desired results.

In this chapter, I consider the importance of keeping both sides in balance.

No Goose, No Egg

Managers who are determined to make a good showing in the short-term often neglect to maintain the performance capability of the "goose."

Consider the case of an ambitious foreman who is newly appointed to supervise a production machine in a strong-growth company. Anxious to receive another promotion as soon as possible, he runs the machine night and day at high speeds and postpones scheduled maintenance to reduce costs and boost profits. Indeed, he makes an impressive showing and receives a promotion into the junior executive ranks of the company.

When another man is appointed foreman, the machine starts to break down. As the new foreman shuts it down for repairs and maintenance, his production drops and costs increase; in less than three months, charts show that his department has moved from a profit to a loss. And in the executive corridors, people talk to his predecessor about his outstanding track record and about the loser that succeeded him, even though the first foreman had increased productivity and profits by liquidating the asset itself!

Although this lesson may be fairly evident when applied to physical resources, it seems less obvious when applied to human resources. Many executives give lip service to the importance of their people, but few actually audit the condition of their human resources. Instead, they audit all other resources, using accounting as the primary information system.

Unfortunately, financial statements and balance sheets tell us little about people. Using accounting alone, we have no way of quantifying the worth of people (as we can the worth of other assets) or the long-term benefits of research and development, quality control, advertising, human resource development, or preventive maintenance. Just as short-term "P" tends to push out long-term "PC," hard data tends to push out soft data, and the net effect is that we don't look upon people as our primary resource.

If every business executive would audit the human assets of the organization — beginning with self and continuing with customers, employees, managers, suppliers, distributors, owners and the general public — he or she could detect and correct a "P/PC" imbalance in any single category before it negatively affects every other category.

"PC" on self requires a regimen of regular exercise, proper nutrition, rest, stress management, and recreation. If we follow a preventive maintenance health program of proper diet, exercise and stress management, we will improve the quality of our waking and sleeping hours and increase longevity, energy level and performance capacity. Conversely, if we don't maintain balance, we tend to become too production-minded, omit exercise and maintenance from our schedules, dissipate our energies and capacities, endanger our health, and eventually ruin the quality of our sleep and the efficiency of our activities.

Likewise, if we fail to safeguard customer opinion of our goods and services, we stand to lose their business. For example, a small restaurant in my community once served great clam chowder. Customers crowded into the place between 11 a.m. and 2 p.m. and again in the evening, and they also supported a huge take-home business. The owners were so successful that several other businesses tried to buy them out. Eventually one did at a very high price. The new owners immediately began to cut the quality of the clam chowder by adding fewer clams and more water. For a period of time, business remained high and, with reduced costs, profits soared. But within a few weeks, people got smart and went elsewhere. Business dropped to a fourth of what it was, as most customers never came back.

How we regard our employees will influence how they, in turn, regard our customers. In most instances, the customer gets treated exactly as the employee who deals with the customer is treated. Study your own business carefully and see if this is not the case: employees tend to treat customers exactly as they are being treated by management. The principle, then, is always, "treat your own people, your employees, exactly as you want them to treat your best customers" — and they will.

And, too, with managers, suppliers, distributors, owners and the general public, we can see how "P/PC" principle applies. Whenever "PC" is neglected, people begin to mistrust the motives of the producers of the goods or service. If they are perceived as exploitive, controls will be put in place. And the people, the unions, the legislature are not to blame. Business only has itself — its short-sighted, "P"-oriented, golden-egg appetite — to blame.

Balance is the Key

Business must work continuously to maintain a proper ecological "P/PC" balance with all eight categories. In the physical world, when the ecological elements are out of balance, every aspect of the environment suffers. So, also, is this true with business.

Consider, for example, that of the top 100 companies in the nation in 1917, only 40 remain in the top 100 today. Of those in the top 100 in 1933, 50 remain; and of the top 100 in 1967, 75 remain. The reasons why so many companies drop from the top are many, but basically all business failure may be attributed to an imbalance between production and performance capability.

It's interesting to note that the big winners, and losers, among Fortune 500 companies in any given year follow the P/PC formula.

For example, one year Weirton Steel showed the highest return on stockholders' equity — 100 percent! Weirton is entirely owned by its workers under an Employee Stock Ownership Plan, which grants stock to employees and gets tax benefits that help pay off loans or finance capital expenditures. Weirton earned $60.6 million on sales of $1 billion in its first year as an employee-owned enterprise.

One year, the Fortune 500 company showing the highest total return to investors (118 percent) was Tyson Foods, a family-run Alabama-based purveyor of poultry. It's stock, traded over the counter, went from $16.50 a share to $36 during the year. And the company plows its profits back into the business. With such "PC," Tyson became a major supplier of McDonald's Chicken McNuggets and controlled about 7 percent of the U.S. poultry market.

Another year, the biggest money loser among the Fortune 500 was A.H. Robins Co. The Richmond, Virginia, pharmaceutical company was plagued with lawsuits. They settled about 8,300 damage claims for $314.6 million. (Another 4,000 cases were still pending, and new claims were being filed at the rate of about 300 per month.) Robins had a negative net worth and limited resources to satisfy claims. They needed a "PC" transfusion.

And yet too much "PC" or the wrong kind of "PC" may be worse than no "PC" at all. We can't afford "PC" very long if we don't have

"P." The business that commits too much of its time and energy to tomorrow to the neglect of today won't be around tomorrow. In all things, balance is the key. And balance comes by effectively cultivating and nurturing production capacity while efficiently producing desired results. The farmer may yet be gathering a golden egg a day if he had only taken care of the goose.

The moral for modern-day managers is clear. Success has two sides: the goose and the golden egg.

Chapter 20

Abundance Management

Executives who are expert at handling "hot potatoes" keep cool by concentrating more on creating markets for their products and less on protecting their "turf," promoting their "thing," and getting their "piece of the pie."

Two potato farmers from Idaho made it big in business by cultivating an abundance mentality. J.R. Simplot and Nephi Grigg both built successful frozen-food companies (J.R. Simplot Company and Ore-Ida Foods) on the idea that one can create a market, not just steal shares from others.

Simplot, the major spud supplier to McDonald's, and Grigg, who founded Ore-Ida and later sold it to Heinz, found that creating new wealth doesn't always mean taking it away from other players in the market. Like other legends of their time, Ray A. Kroc and J. Willard Marriott, Simplot and Grigg built their own markets for their products.

They did it with an *abundance mentality* — a bone-deep belief that "there are enough natural and human resources to realize my dream" and that "my success does not necessarily mean failure for others, just as their success does not preclude my own."

Over the past 25 years of working with organizations and with individuals, I have observed that the abundance mentality often makes the difference between excellence and mediocrity, particularly because it virtually eliminates small thinking and adversarial relations.

I often ask managers at my seminars, "How much time is spent by your people in interpersonal conflict, interdepartmental rivalries, defensive or protective communication, politicking, second-guessing, back-biting, criticizing, and attacking the competition?" I ask people to put down a figure on their paper. Then, I ask for a tally. Usually, about half the people acknowledge that they spend more than 25 percent of their time in such activities. Many believe it but won't acknowledge it because their bosses are present.

There is so much negative energy in organizations and in our society. People think of taking the legal approach to problem solving, often at the very first blush of a problem. Everyone is looking out for number one, anxious to get their "piece of the pie" and protect their "turf". Such self-centered activity springs from a belief that resources are limited. I call it the *scarcity mentality.*

The normal distribution curve, embedded deep in the bowels of academia, tends to spawn the scarcity mentality because of the perceived "zero sum" situation. If people somehow avoid being "scripted" into a scarcity mentality by their schooling, they may acquire it from an athletic or social experience.

People with a scarcity mentality tend to see everything in terms of "win-lose." They believe, "There is only so much; and if someone else has it, that means there will be less for me." They have a very hard time, for instance, being genuinely happy for the successes of other people — particularly, if these people are from their own company, household or neighborhood — because, in some way, it may cause them to feel that something is being taken from them.

If you see life as a "zero sum" game, you tend to think in adversarial or competitive ways, since anyone else's "win" implies your loss. And, if you were brought up on conditional love and constant comparisons, you adopt a scarcity script, thinking in dichotomies — either "haves" or "have nots," either "I'm okay, you're not okay" or "I'm not okay, you're okay."

In my life, I've gone through many cycles of abundance and scarcity thinking. When I have an abundance mentality, I am trusting, open, giving, willing to live and let live and able to value differences. I realize that strength lies in differences. I define unity not as sameness but as complementary oneness where one's weakness is compensated by the strength of another.

People with an abundance mentality employ the negotiation principle of win-win and the communication principle of seeking first to understand before seeking to be understood. Their psychic satisfactions don't come from winning through beating others or from being compared to others, either positively or negatively. They are not possessive. They don't force and push natural processes by requiring other people to tell them where they stand all the time. They don't get their security from someone else's opinion.

An abundance mentality springs from an *internal security*, not from external rankings, comparisons, opinions, possessions, or associations. People who derive their security from such sources become dependent on them. Their lives are affected by whatever happens to the sources of their security.

Seven Characteristics of Abundance Managers

What characteristics distinguish abundance thinkers such as Simplot, Grigg, Kroc, and Marriott from scarcity thinkers? Consider the following seven.

• *They return often to the right sources.* In my book, *The Divine Center*, I suggest that the most fundamental source, and the root of all the rest, is the divine source. If our lives are centered on other sources — spouse, work, money, possession, pleasure, leader, friend, enemy, self — distortions and dependencies develop.

Abundance thinkers drink deeply from sources of internal security — sources that keep them gentle, open, trusting, and genuinely happy for the successes of other people...that renew and recreate them...that nurture and nourish abundance feelings, enabling them to grow and develop and giving them comfort, insight, inspiration, guidance, protection, direction, peace of mind. They look forward to returning to these springs. To go for any length of time — even a few hours — and not seek this refreshment would cause them genuine withdrawal pains, similar in the physical sense to going without food and water.

   •   *They seek solitude and enjoy nature.*   People with an abundance mentality practice private meditation and contemplation. They reserve time for solitude. People with a scarcity mentality are often bored when they are alone because of the merry-go-round nature of their lives. Cultivate the ability to be alone and to think deeply, to enjoy silence and solitude. Reflect, write, listen, plan, prepare, visualize, ponder, relax.

   Let nature filter its quiet beauty and strength into your soul. It is almost like being given a fresh tank of oxygen. Nature can teach us many valuable lessons and replenish our spiritual reserves. Vacations or outings that get us into serene natural settings make us more contemplative and peaceful and better prepared to return to the fast pace of our careers. Vacations filled with rush and travel, socials and carnivals can leave us exhausted and frazzled.

   •   *They sharpen the saw regularly.*   Cultivate the habit of "sharpening your saw" every day by exercising mind and body. Weekend exercise isn't enough; in fact, some studies show it hurts us more than helps us, because of overdoing it. And our bodies, particularly as we grow older, haven't the flexibility and resiliency to deal with those weekend stresses. Regular, vigorous exercise is vital to radiant health and unquestionably influences not just the quantity of our years but the quality of the life in those years.

   For mental exercise, I suggest cultivating the habit of reading widely and deeply. Take an executive development course now and then to add discipline and accountability. When we continue our education, our economic security is not as dependent upon our jobs, our boss's opinion, or human institutions, but rather upon our ability to produce. The great unseen job market is called "unsolved problems," and there are always many vacancies for those who exercise initiative and learn how to create value for themselves by showing how they essentially represent solutions to these problems.

In the book *Executive Jobs Unlimited*, Carl Boll basically suggests that people who fail to sharpen the saw regularly not only find that their saw becomes dull but also that they become obsolete and increasingly dependent upon playing it safe. They become protective, politically minded, or security minded, and start wearing the golden handcuffs.

• *They serve others anonymously.* By returning often to nurturing sources of internal security, they restore their willingness and ability to serve others effectively. They take particular delight in anonymous service, feeling that service is the rent we pay to live in this world.

Paradoxically, we will find our life when we lose it in service. If our intent is to serve others without self-concern, we are rewarded with increased internal security and an abundance mentality.

• *They maintain a long-term intimate relationship with another person.* This is a person (or persons) — usually a spouse or close friend — who loves us and believes in us even when we don't believe in ourselves ... people who are true and faithful and are so inwardly anchored and secured and rooted that we can depend upon them, not in the ultimate sense, but perhaps in the more proximate sense. They know us; they care about us; their love is unconditional; and they will stay with us when everyone else deserts us, particularly when we desert ourselves. But they are not permissive; they neither give in nor give up. Such people can make all the difference in our lives.

Often people who have an abundance mentality serve this role in relationship to many other people. Whenever they sense someone is at the crossroads, they go the second mile in communicating their belief in that person.

• *They forgive themselves and others.* They don't condemn themselves for every foolish mistake or social blunder. They forgive others of their tresspasses. They don't brood about yesterday or daydream about tomorrow. They live sensibly in the present, carefully plan the future, and flexibly adapt to changing circumstances. Their self-honesty is revealed by their sense of humor, their willingness to admit then forget mistakes, and to cheerfully do the things ahead which lie within their power.

• *They are problem solvers.* They are part of the solution. They learn to separate the people from the problem being discussed. They focus on people's interests and concerns rather than fight over positions. Gradually others discover their sincerity and become part of a creative problem-solving process, and the synergistic solutions coming out of these interactions are usually far better than those originally proposed because they are not compromise solutions.

In the context of the "potato farmer," the abundance mentality ultimately means "more pounds with less peel." And in plain "John Wayne" English, that's the bottom line.

Chapter 21

Managing Expectations

Each of us enters situations with certain implicit expectations. And one of the major causes of "people problems" is unclear, ambiguous or unfulfilled expectations. Conflicting expectations regarding roles and goals cause many people pain and problems in organizations and in relationships.

Examples of Conflicting Expectations

Illustrations or examples of conflicting expectations include the following.

• *Company mergers.* Look at what happened with Roger Smith at General Motors and Ross Perot at Electronic Data Systems. When these two cultures came together, the executives clashed in their attempts to deal with tough problems and mesh two different social wills.

We saw, on one hand, Ross Perot advocating the rights of the common worker — trying to do away with layers of management and special executive privileges, seemingly unaware that certain features of the GM culture are intergenerational and simply can't be done away with overnight.

Consultants can't mandate changes like that. It takes more education and a lot of communication. But most people in acquisitions and mergers don't get into communication. They play either hard ball or soft ball, win-lose or lose-win.

• *Marriage relations.* Today, many of the once hidden issues and expectations of marriage are out in the open. But there is still much debate over the role of the man and the woman.

For example, if a young man from a more traditional family approaches marriage with the implicit expectation, "I'm the breadwinner, and you take care of the kids," he may be in for a rude awakening. It's evident that young and old couples alike are struggling with conflicting role expectations. Many women are unfulfilled without a professional career outside the home — a phenomenon fueled by a society that doesn't provide much appreciation, validation and reinforcement for women as homemakers.

• *Parent-child relations.* Parents often experience conflicting expectations in their relationships with their children, especially as these children enter teenage years. Parent and child have different ideas about their roles, and these ideas change as they go through various stages of growth and development.

• *Government relations.* Is the role of government to do good or is the role of government to keep people from doing harm? If I am working with someone who believes that the government's role is to do good, we may have totally different expectations, which leads to conflict, disappointment, and cynicism.

• *Hiring and promoting.* What a new person expects of the job and the company is often something very different from what his or her employer expects.

During the "honeymoon" period, these expectations are soft and negotiable. It's a good time to clarify them while people are open and willing to talk things through.

If the system is unfair, it shows when people are hired or promoted. For example, if the new hires are paid more, the people in place will say, "How come you pay them this when I've been working here this long and make less?" When managers violate such expectations, they must live with the consequences: trust goes down; people start moonlighting; they come up with other agendas; they wonder what's going on; or they become almost paranoid and begin to see things in the worst possible light.

• *Interdepartmental and entrepreneurial projects.* Any time you have interface among different departments or among people from different disciplines, you can expect conflicting expectations. In fact, at the outset of any interdepartmental or entrepreneurial project, you will likely find several examples of violated expectations.

- *Client relationships.* Seasoned managers of product and service companies know how hazardous it is to have clients that expect more than the company can possibly deliver. Therefore, they monitor and manage client expectations through empathy and through customer information systems.

They try to identify people's feelings and expectations: "What are they thinking?" "What are they expecting us to do?" "What service do they expect after the sale?" "What kind of a social relationship do they expect?" If these expectations are not clarified, clients will be disappointed and disillusioned — and later lost.

The Problem: Implicit Expectations

An expectation is a human hope, the embodiment of a person's desires — what he or she wants out of a situation such as a marriage or a family or a business relationship. Each of us comes into a situation with certain implicit expectations. These come from our previous experiences, from earlier roles, from other relationships. Some of these expectations may be quite romantic, meaning they aren't based on reality. They're picked up from media or from some fantasy.

There's a difference between an expectation and reality. An expectation is an imaginary map, a "should" map rather than an "is" map. But a lot of people think that their maps are accurate, that "This is the way it is — your map is wrong."

Implicit expectations — these human wants, wishes and desires — are the baggage we carry with us into a relationship, into a company, or into a business as customers. For example, if we go shopping, we may implicitly expect courteous and competent service. If a certain store violates those expectations, we are usually quick to change to one that is more customer-oriented and fulfills our psychological wants and needs.

Wise managers make things very explicit, spelling out "what we do and don't do" so that the client can say, "Okay, we understand and feel good about that" or "We feel good about one area but would suggest another approach to serving our needs in this other area." They explicitly state what their mission is, what their resources are, and what they have chosen to do and not do with their resources.

The Solution: The Performance Agreement

The performance agreement is the solution to the problem of conflicting expectations. It is the tool for managing expectations. It makes all expectations explicit.

The performance agreement is a clear, mutual understanding and commitment regarding expectations surrounding roles and goals. If management can get a performance agreement between people and groups of people, management has solved many of its problems.

That's because the performance agreement embodies all of the expectations of all the parties involved. And if these parties trust each other and are willing to listen and speak authentically, and to synergize and learn from each other's expression — then usually they can create a win-win performance agreement. Then they can create a situation where everybody has the same understanding regarding expectations.

There are three parts to a performance agreement: the two preconditions (trust and communication); the five content elements; and the reinforcement of the systems and structure of the organization.

Trust. Coming in, people carry many implicit expectations and some hidden agendas. Often real agendas and feelings are hidden because the trust level isn't high enough to share them. Trust, then, is one precondition of a good performance agreement, and the foundation of trust is the character of trustworthiness—the feeling in others that you will honor your commitments.

If trust has been eroded and respect lost, it's difficult to form win-win performance agreements because there's no foundation for it. Companies or departments within companies can still work out acceptable performance agreements, however, by starting small and letting the process of making and keeping agreements gradually develop or rebuild the trust. Construct the best performance agreement you can under the circumstances — even if it's a compromise — and then work toward a synergistic win-win deal next time around.

The performance agreement should always be open and negotiable — open by either party at any time. If the situation changes, either party can initiate the communication process and change the agreement. While there may be certain inviolate principles, parts that would not be negotiable, much of it is open for discussion.

Communication. The second precondition, then, is communication, a reality-testing process: "Oh, I didn't realize you felt that way. You mean, you expected me to take the first step? I see. Now, let me tell you what I thought."

It's horizontal communication, an authentic sharing between people as prized contributors — as equals, not as superiors and subordinates.

"I expected you to exercise more initiative. I was waiting on you...and you were waiting on me? Now that I understand what you expect, next time I'll study it out and make recommendations."

That's the dialogue of people trying to clarify the expectations of a working relationship.

Such communication is easier when the culture supports it. Unfortunately, in many companies, formally talking about expectations almost seems illegitimate, and yet it's a big part of the informal office talk — "What is your agenda? What are you really concerned about?"

I highly recommend the communication process outlined by Roger Fisher and William Ury in their book, *Getting to Yes*. It's a sensible process for making expectations explicit and arriving at a mutually rewarding agreement. Consider again the four basic principles:

- Separate the people from the problem
- Focus on interests not positions
- Invent options for mutual gain
- Insist on using objective criteria.

This win-win negotiation process requires the skill of empathy, seeking first to understand. People have a lot of front-burner concerns they want to express, and they want first to be understood.

"Seeking first the interest of another" means finding out what his interests are, what is good for him, his growth and happiness. You can't assume you know what's best for the person. Find out through empathy, and then build that into the agreement.

Clarifying expectations about roles and goals is the essence of team building. The idea is to get different groups together — salespeople with manufacturing or purchasing people, for example — and sharing expectations regarding roles and goals in an atmosphere that isn't emotionally charged.

Once people go through this interaction and make their implicit expectations explicit, it is just amazing what happens. People begin to say, "I didn't realize that. I thought you meant something else. No wonder you felt that way! I see, then, you probably interpreted what I did the next week in this way."

"Yeah, exactly that's what I thought."

It's amazingly therapeutic. People are relieved. "Gosh it's good to finally get this out on the table." By getting agendas on the table, we know where each other stands. We can then enter the negotiation process.

Principles of Win-Win Performance

I'll explore the five parts to the win-win performance agreement in detail in the next chapter. I first want to establish a few guiding principles of win-win performance.

- *Specify desired results but don't supervise methods and means* — otherwise, you'll be buried in management minutiae, and your span of control will be severely restricted.

- *Go heavy on guidelines, light on procedures*, so that as circumstances change, people have the flexibility to function, exercising their own initiative.

- *Mention all available resources* within the organizations as well as outside networks.

- *Involve people in setting the standards* or criteria of acceptable and exceptional performance.

- *Maintain trust and use discernment*, more than so-called "objective" or quantitative measurements, to assess results.

- *Reach an understanding of what positive and negative consequences might follow* achieving or failing to achieve desired results.

- *Make sure the performance agreement is reinforced by organizational structure and systems* to stand the test of time.

From Control to Release Management

A win-win performance agreement is much more than a job description. Most companies already have job descriptions that define what the job is and what is expected of the person in the position. Most of that's very clear and explicit. But the performance agreement goes beyond the job description by making the implicit expectations part of a win-win contract, established through a process of synergistic communication.

Most job descriptions have very little sense of what constitutes a "win" for the employee. The only win for them is they've got the job and make the money. The job description doesn't address other needs — psychological, spiritual, social needs. They're not being expressed at all.

Moreover, a job description is usually focused on methods and based on external control. The performance agreement moves us from external control to internal control, from a situation where someone or something in the environment controls someone to a situation where a person can say, "I understand, and I am committed because it's a win for me too."

The performance agreement shifts the whole approach from control to release management. The reason why most companies don't use release management is because they don't manage people by win-win performance agreements.

If managing expectations by performance agreements is not something that is now done in a company, individual managers can still initiate this and do it on their own. But they should be aware that they are dealing with social will, and they had better not be naive to think they can just hammer out some psychological performance agreement, because that performance agreement is interwoven with all social contracts, the unspoken culture of the organization.

A smart manager would say, "We have to be aware of the culture, of the nature of the situation, of the social will." More powerful than a psychological contract is a social contract, and culture is nothing more than a composite social contract. And what we call "shared values" are merely making implicit kind of norms, explicit — "This is how we do things around here."

Managing expectations by performance agreement is one of the things that "ought to be done around here."

Chapter 22

Managing by Win-Win Performance Agreements

The win-win agreement clarifies expectations, unleashes human potential and leads to enlightened self-management.

To improve organizational effectiveness and individual productivity, establish win-win performance agreements with your employees in high incentive areas where organizational needs and goals overlap individual needs, goals, and capabilities.

Essentially, the win-win agreement is a psychological contract between manager and subordinate. It represents a clear mutual understanding and commitment regarding expectations in five areas: first, desired results; second, guidelines; third, resources; fourth, accountability; and fifth, consequences.

How to Set Up the Agreement

To better understand how to set up and manage the win-win agreement, let's review each of these five steps and then look at an application of the principle in the banking business.

First, specify desired results. Discuss what results you expect to achieve. Be specific about the quantity and quality. Set budget and schedule. Commit people to getting the results but then let them determine the best methods and means. Set target dates or time lines, when objectives are to be accomplished. These objectives essentially represent the overlap between the organizational strategy, goals, and job design and the personal values, goals, needs and capabilities. The concept of win-win suggests that managers and

177

employees clarify expectations and mutually commit themselves to getting desired results.

Second, set some guidelines. Communicate whatever principles, policies and procedures are considered essential to getting desired results. Mention as few procedures as possible to allow as much freedom and flexibility as possible. Organizational policy and procedure manuals should be brief, focusing primarily on the principles behind the policy and procedures. Then, as the circumstances change, people are not frozen — they can still function, using their own initiative and good judgment and doing what's necessary to get desired results within the value framework of the company.

Guidelines should also identify "no-no's" or failure paths which experience has identified as being inimical to accomplishing organizational goals or maintaining organizational values. Many a management-by-objective (MBO) program goes down in flames because these failure paths or organizational no-no's are not clearly identified.

People are given the feeling that they have almost unlimited flexibility and freedom to do whatever is necessary to accomplish agreed-upon results and end up reinventing the wheel, encountering certain organizational sacred cows, upsetting apple carts, getting blown out of the saddle, and becoming increasingly gun-shy about ever exercising initiative again.

The general attitude of employees then becomes, "Let's forget about this MBO crap. Just tell us what you want us to do." Their expectations are blasted, and the scar tissue on their behinds is so thick that they begin to see the job purely as a means to an economic end and seek to satisfy their higher needs in other places off the job.

When identifying the "no-no's" or sacred cows, also identify what level of initiative a person has regarding different responsibilities: Is the person to   wait until told,   or ask whenever he has a question, or study it out and then make recommendations, or do it and report immediately, or do it and report routinely? In this way, expectations are clarified and limits set.

In some areas of responsibility, the initiative level would simply be to wait until told, while in other areas, higher levels could be exercised including, "Use your own good judgment and do what you think is appropriate; let us know routinely what you're doing and what the results are."

Third, identify available resources.   Identify the various financial, human, technical and organizational resources available to employees to assist them in getting desired results.   Mention the structural and systemic arrangements and processes. Such systems might include information, communication, and training.   You may want to identify yourself or other people as resources and indicate how these human resources could be used.   You may want to set some limits on access or merely share your experience and let the person decide how to benefit most from it.

Fourth, define accountability.   Holding people accountable for results puts teeth into the win-win agreement.   If there is no accountability, people gradually lose their sense of responsibility and start blaming circumstance or other people for poor performance. But when people participate in setting the exact standard of acceptable performance, they feel a deep sense of responsibility to get desired results.

Results can be evaluated in three ways: measurement, observation, and discernment. Specify how you will evaluate performance. Also, specify when and how progress reports are to be made and accountability sessions held.

When the trust level is high, people will be much tougher on themselves than an outside evaluator or manager would ever dare be. Also, when trust is high, discernment is often more accurate than so-called "objective" measurement. That's because people know in their hearts much more than the measurement system can reveal about their performance.

Fifth, determine the consequences. Reach an understanding of what follows both naturally and logically when the desired results are achieved or not achieved. Positive consequences might include financial and psychic rewards recognition, appreciation, advancement, new assignment, training, flexible schedule, leave of absence, enlarged scope of responsibilities, perks or promotion. Negative consequences might range from reprimand to retraining to termination.

Working Toward Self-Management

These five features of a win-win agreement basically cover what a person needs to understand before undertaking a job. We clarify the desired results, the guidelines to work within, and the resources to draw upon, the means of accountability, and the consequences of on-the-job performance. But we do not deal with methods. Win-Win is a human resource principle that recognizes people are capable of self-direction and self-control and can govern themselves to do whatever is necessary within the guidelines to achieve the desired results.

When more than two individuals are involved in the win-win agreement, the psychological contract becomes a social contract.We may set up the agreement with a team or a department or an entire division. Whatever the size of the group, all of the members should participate in developing the win-win agreement. This social contract then becomes even more powerful, more reinforcing, and more motivating than the psychological contract because it taps into the social nature and human need to belong and be part of a meaningful team project or effort.

One of the strengths of this psychological or social win-win contract is that it is almost infinitely flexible and adaptable to any set of circumstances or to any level of maturity or competence. If the ability or desire to do a job is small, then you would identify fewer and smaller results; perhaps have more guidelines, including procedures; make resources more available, attractive and visible; have more frequent accountability with tighter, clearer, more measurable criteria; have consequences follow immediately, making feedback powerfully reinforcing.

In another situation where there is a great deal of maturity, a great deal of ability and desire to do a job, the win-win agreement would have broader, longer range desired results with fewer guidelines, particularly regarding procedures and policy. You might make the resources available but not necessarily that visible; have less frequent accountability, using discernment as well as measurement to evaluate performance; and set longer-term consequences with particularly heavy emphasis on intrinsic psychological rewards rather than extrinsic rewards.

Once a win-win agreement is established, people can then supervise themselves in terms of that agreement. Managers may then serve as sources of help and establish helpful organizational structures and systems upon which these self-directing, self-controlling individuals can draw to fulfill the win-win agreement. Having participated in the formation of the agreement, employees feel good about giving accountability on their responsibilities periodically; basically, they evaluate themselves against the specified criteria.

When the win-win agreement is set up properly, people will do whatever is necessary to accomplish the desired results within the guidelines.

Banking on the Results

To illustrate the power of this approach, let me recount one experience. I was one of a group of consultants involved in an organizational improvement project involving a large banking organization with hundreds of branch offices. This bank had budgeted three quarters of a million dollars for a six-month training program for junior executives.

The idea was to take college graduates and put them through a series of rotating positions. After spending two weeks in one department, they would shift to another for a period of two weeks. After the six-month program, they would then be assigned to a branch office in some kind of a junior executive position.

Top management wanted this whole program carefully analyzed and improved.

The first thing we did was press to understand what their objectives were. We wondered if there was an up-front understanding about expectations. There was not. We found that the expectations were very general, very vague, and that there was wide-spread disagreement among the top officers of the bank over what the objectives and priorities should be.

We continued to press them until finally they hammered out what they wanted a person to be able to do by the end of the training period, before being assigned to a junior executive position. They came up with more than 100 objectives for these trainees. We boiled these down to 39 objectives — the desired results.

The next step was to give these 39 objectives to the trainees. These people were excited about their jobs and about the chance to move into a junior executive position rather rapidly; they were entirely willing to identify with these objectives, internalize them, and do what was necessary to accomplish them.

They understood the objectives; they understood the criteria for evaluation. They had a complete list of resources that they could draw upon to accomplish those objectives, including visits with department managers, reading materials, outside educational agencies, etc. They realized that they could be assigned to a junior executive position as soon as they could demonstrate competency in those 39 areas.

This motivated them so much that they accomplished the objectives in three and a half weeks, on the average.

This performance totally astounded most of the top executives. Some of them could hardly believe it. They carefully reexamined the objectives and the criteria and reviewed the results to ensure that the criteria had been met. Many of them said that three and a half weeks simply was not enough time for these trainees to get the kind of seasoning and exposure which would give them mature judgment.

We basically said, "Fair enough. Write some tougher objectives, including the kinds of problems and challenges which would require seasoned judgment." Several more objectives were hammered out, and almost everyone agreed that if the trainees could accomplish those other things, along with the other 39, they would be better prepared than most of the trainees that had gone through the six-month program.

We next shared those additional objectives with the trainees. By this time, they were allowed to supervise themselves. We witnessed a tremendous release of human energy and talent.

Almost all the trainees accomplished these other objectives in a week and a half!

In other words, we found that the six-month program could be reduced to five weeks with even better results by setting up a win-win agreement with these young junior executives.

This has far-reaching implications in many areas of management, not just training. And some of the enlightened managers in this bank began to see them. Others were very threatened by the whole process, feeling that there is a certain amount of time that people have to put in to win their stripes. But no one could deny the results.

The win-win performance agreement is all about getting desired results.

Chapter 23

Keeping the House in Order

To briefly review, my idea of delegation is to establish a clear, up-front mutual understanding and commitment regarding expectations in five areas:

- *Desired results* — specify the quantity and quality;

- *Guidelines* — focus on principles, not on procedures, policies or practices;

- *Resources* — identify available human, financial and physical resources;

- *Accountability* — schedule progress reports and specify performance criteria;

- *Consequences* — state both positive and negative rewards; these should reflect the natural consequences of actions taken.

I often refer to this system of management as the "win-win performance agreement." Another term I use is "stewardship delegation," since in such agreements each person becomes a "steward" over certain resources and responsibilities.

Stewardship Delegation

To bridge the gap between the abstract theory and the concrete reality, I share the following true story about delegating a job to my son Stephen when he was a boy. As you read it, consider the management implications.

On a particular evening in June, we wrote down our family goals for the summer — identifying all the important activities that had to

185

be done to meet our objectives and to keep the house in order.

Each member of the family volunteered to do certain jobs.

My son Stephen volunteered for the yard. I defined the job in terms of green and clean. "Son, your job is green and clean."

Then we began a two-week training process. "Son, green is the color of our neighbor's yard." (Up to this time the yard job was mine; I hadn't done all that well, so I needed my son to see a standard.)

I taught him that green was a function of water. During the training period, as we watered the lawn, he could see a relationship between water and green. I also trained him what clean meant.

After defining what green and clean meant, I next told my son that it really didn't make any difference how he accomplished green and clean.

About the middle of the second week of training, I said to him, "Stephen, on Saturday I'm going to ask you if you will take the job. If you say yes, it will be yours from then on."

He said he was willing to take it right then.

I said, "No, son, I want you to think carefully what this means and what kind of work it involves. Let's keep working together, and you think about it, and then I'll ask you about it on Saturday morning." (It's important not to go too fast in establishing stewardships. There needs to be a process of understanding, of internalizing, and that involves more than just intellectual understanding.)

Three Things to Understand

I told him that there were three other things that he needed to understand about the job before deciding whether to take it.

First, "Who will be the boss?"

He shrugged and said nothing.

I said, "Son, you will be the boss. You are in charge; you boss yourself.

"Second, son, guess who your helper will be."

"Who, dad?"   "I will. I will be your helper. If you get into problems or have trouble, let me know and I will be happy to help.

But you must realize, son, that I am often away from home, and sometimes when I'm home I'm too busy doing other things and won't be able to help. But whenever I have the time and whenever you really need my help, you've got it."

"Third, guess who judges your work, son?"

He said, "Who?"

"You judge yourself. And how do you judge yourself, son?"

He answered, "Green and clean."

"That's right, Stephen."

We agreed that twice a week we would walk around the yard together, and he would show me how he was doing in his stewardship.

When Saturday morning came, I asked him if he was prepared to take the job. He said yes, so we rehearsed again exactly what this meant, what our agreement was.

He was committed and trained. All systems were "go."

Green Light But No Go

But he did nothing. He did nothing all that Saturday, Sunday, and Monday. The yard was becoming cluttered, and the grass was starting to yellow. I became concerned. By Tuesday evening when I returned from work, nothing had changed. The yard was still cluttered, grass very dry, and my son Stephen was playing in the park across the street.

Frankly, I was ready to either punish him or resort to gofer delegation. I was upset and disillusioned by his performance after two weeks of training and all those commitments.

But I faked it. I tried to be pleasant. I shouted across the street to Stephen, "Hi, son, how are you doing?"

He answered, "Fine."

By asking for an accountability in that way, I had just broken the mutual understanding we had achieved. We had agreed to walk around the yard together and see how he was doing. So he felt perfectly justified in his response. I bit my tongue and decided to say nothing until after dinner and then to walk around the yard with him. I had to reaffirm within myself that my primary purpose was his character development. The yard was only a means to that end: I was really raising children, not grass.

So after dinner I said, "Son, why don't we walk around the yard and see how things are going, just as we agreed?" When we got out in the middle of the front yard, he broke down and started to cry. His lip and chin started to quiver, and he whispered, "It's so hard."

What was hard? He hadn't done one single thing. (What was hard, of course, was the exercise of initiative or self-governance, the essence of growth. If I had nagged him, work would have become the course of least resistance, the easiest thing to do).

I responded, "Is there anything you would like me to do?"

He answered, "Would you?" He ran into the house and came out with two sacks. He handed me one and said, "Would you clean up over there?" He directed me in cleaning up the yard. I did exactly as he asked, then held the sack. He took it and emptied it.

Signing the Agreement

It was at that very moment that he signed the stewardship agreement deep within himself. It then became his yard. He asked for help only two or three more times that entire summer. It became a trust, a stewardship.

Stewardship delegation requires high trust, considerable training, and a clear mutual understanding of desired results, guidelines, resources, accountabilities and consequences.

Once people gain a sense of stewardship, of ownership in an area of responsibility, they will faithfully perform their jobs to the best of their abilities.

Chapter 24

Involve People in the Problem

Involvement is the key to implementing change and increasing commitment. We tend to be more interested in our own ideas than in those of others. If we are not involved, we will likely resist change.

Before you start involving people in the problems of your organization, however, you may want to learn a few new skills. Let me explain.

I once played racquetball with an older, overweight medical doctor. He told me that he had played a great deal when he was younger. Even so, because he was so far out of shape, I thought he would give me very little competition and, therefore, little exercise.

I was wrong. Even though I was in far better shape and had a great desire to win, he had more shots in his repertoire — his higher level of skill compensated for his physical condition. I barely won the first game, and he totally dominated the next two games.

I kept saying to myself, "If I'm going to win, I've got to change. And I tried to change, but for some reason I couldn't. He kept making me play his game. I tried to play my game and make my shots. I tried to be more aggressive, but I simply lacked the repertoire of shots and the skills. I tried to objectively assess the situation and make some adjustments. Nothing seemed to help.

The Management Dilemma

Business managers sometimes find themselves in a similar dilemma. They sense that they ought to be doing better in the competitive market but seem powerless to make necessary changes. Bringing about changes in people and in organizations is not simple; or if it is simple, it is not easy. We are dealing with momentum,

189

with attitudes, with skill levels, with perceptions, and with established patterns. People tend to cling to old views, old ways, old habits. And, old styles and habits are hard to change.

To make or break a habit takes great commitment, and commitment comes from involvement — it acts as a catalyst in the change process.

Of course, the downside of involvement is risk. Whenever you involve people in the problem, you risk losing control. It is so much easier, simpler, and safer — and seemingly so much more efficient — to not involve others, but simply to tell them, to direct them, to advise them.

In his book, *Managing*, former ITT president Harold Geneen writes: "Most chief executives slip into authoritarian roles without realizing that the process is going on. Subtly, they change (because) it's easier and less time-consuming to be authoritarian."

Most authoritarian managers and executives are not tyrants. Most are benevolent — using the principles of *human relations* to the fullest to direct behavior and get desired results.

To manage by the principles of *human resources* is to leave safe territory. Involvement is a ticket to adventure. The executive really never knows at the outset what will happen or where he or she will end up. Is the risk worth taking?

"One of the primary, fundamental faults with American management," responds Geneen, "is that over the years it has lost its *zest for adventure*, for taking a risk, for doing something that no one has done before. The reason behind this change is the mistaken belief that professional business managers are supposed to be sure of themselves and never make a mistake."

So, managers are caught between these two positions: the safer, easier, more efficient human relations position of directive, authoritative leadership and the far more risky, but infinitely more effective human resource principle of involvement.

Quality & Commitment

An effective decision has two dimensions: quality and commitment. By weighing these two dimensions and multiplying them, we can determine the effectiveness factor. For example, let's suppose that we make a quality decision — a perfect 10 on a 10-point scale; however, for some reason, the commitment to that decision is low — a 2 on a 10-point scale.

As a result, we have a relatively ineffective decision (by multiplying 10 and 2, we get an effectiveness factor of 20).

Now, let's assume that by involving others, we compromise the quality of the decision (it drops from 10 down to 7), but we increase the commitment to it (let's say, from 2 to 8).

In this case, we have an effectiveness factor of 56 (7 times 8). That means the decision may not be as good, but it is almost three times as effective!

Nonetheless, many young or new managers hesitate to involve people in decision making for fear of opening up other options, contaminating their own thinking, or compromising their position.

Eventually, through experience, most managers learn that the effectiveness of their decisions depends on quality and commitment, and that commitment comes through involvement. They are then willing to assume the risks and to develop the skills of involving people appropriately.

Driving & Restraining Forces

Kurt Lewin, one of the great social scientists, contributed enormously to our understanding of the change process. His Force Field Analysis theory, developed some 40 years ago, depicts the dynamics at play in a change process.

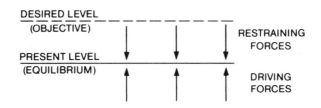

The lower line represents the present level of activity or performance. The dotted line above represents the desired level or what might be called the "objective" of the change effort. The arrows pushing down against the first line are the "restraining forces" and the arrows pushing up are the "driving forces." Sometimes the restraining forces are called "resisting forces" or "discouraging forces," and the driving force arrows are often called "encouraging forces." The present level of performance or the present behavior represents the state of equilibrium between the driving and the restraining forces.

One of Lewin's earliest and most significant studies came as a result of a commission from the United States government to see what he could do to change the buying, cooking and eating habits of American housewives during World War II. To help the war effort, government agents encouraged women to buy and use more of the visceral organs and less of the muscle cuts of beef.

They explained the facts and logically presented the driving forces — patriotism, availability, economy, and nutrition — to motivate and encourage housewives to buy, cook and serve the visceral cuts of beef to their families. But they underestimated the restraining forces. People simply were not used to eating tongue, heart and kidney. The women didn't know how to buy such products, how to serve them, how to cook them. They feared their families would respond negatively.

They resisted change until they started meeting together and gaining an understanding of the nature of the problem. When the housewives really got involved in the nature of the problem — the same problem which the government was facing — they gradually loosened up, "unfroze" their perceptions, broadened their thinking, and seriously considered alternatives. As these women came to understand how their change of diet could help the war effort and as they expressed themselves fully — without fear of being censored, embarrassed or ridiculed about their fears and doubts — many actually changed their buying and eating habits.

Lewin and the government learned an important lesson:

When people become involved in the problem,
they become significantly and sincerely committed
to coming up with solutions to the problem.

Solutions to Problems

I can personally attest to the power of involving people in the problem, even in family problems.

One night I was visiting with my oldest daughter about some of her feelings and concerns. After I listened for a while, she asked me if I had anything I wanted to talk about. I decided to involve her in a problem that had irritated my wife and me for sometime — that of getting the children down and in bed at an hour that gave them sufficient sleep and gave us some time to ourselves.

To my amazement, she came up with some ingenious ideas. Once involved, she felt responsible, and her responsible involvement greatly contributed to the solution.

On another occasion, I wanted to keep my cars in good running condition without having to invest an inordinate amount of time and money for maintenance. I went to the manager of a local service station and involved him in the problem. I expressed my trust in him and in his judgment. The moment he felt involved, he became responsible for results. He took care of my cars as if they were his own. He personally serviced them, made preventive checkups, and gave me the best deals on purchases.

Enlightened leaders and business managers throughout the world have used this simple principle in one way or another for many years. They know that when people are meaningfully involved, they willingly commit the best that is in them. Moreover, when people identify their personal goals with the goals of an organization, they release an enormous amount of energy, creativity, and loyalty.

Again, Harold Geneen writes: "The mental attitude of the executive when he faces a decision is most important. I wanted the ITT executive to be imaginative and creative, also objective about the facts of the situation at hand. The climate control is in the hands of the chief executive. To me, the most important element in establishing a happy, prosperous atmosphere was an insistence upon open, free, and honest communication up and down the ranks of our management structure."

If we use an authoritarian or benevolent authoritarian approach to problem solving, we slip into a kind of condescending or vertical communication pattern. If people sense that we are "talking down" to them or that our motive is to manipulate them into making a change, they will resist our efforts.

Increase Driving or Decrease Restraining Forces?

The question managers often ask when they learn about Force Field Analysis is, "Which is the best approach − to increase the driving forces or to decrease the restraining forces?"

Certainly the easiest and simplest approach is to increase the driving forces because we have control over them. Traditionally, this approach is used the most, even though it is less effective. What happens is that people put on a big push. That is, to use our diagram again, they add two or three more arrows of force or energy to get company performance or personal behavior up to the desired level. But they don't change the essential nature of the restraining forces. They only create new tensions at the higher level, and as soon as those are relaxed, performance springs back to the same old standard or level.

We see this happening in organizations when one new management principle after another comes and goes...when there is a big drive for cost-consciousness for a period of time − until everyone becomes so sensitive about costs that they forget about sales. Predictably, the next new drive focuses on marketing and sales. Everyone becomes more customer and service-oriented until, little by little, they get the sales back up − only to lose control of costs once again. When the work force becomes cynical, management then sponsors more socials, parties, and bowling leagues: they get into a country club atmosphere and forget about both sales and costs. An organization that goes through such cycles, one after another dealing with different crises, soon becomes cynical. The trust level gets very low. The communication processes deteriorate as the culture becomes polarized between "us and them." And then the next new drive or the next new technique, however beautifully packaged and powerfully endorsed by experts from the outside, has little, if any, effect. Cynicism is simply too thick. The trust level is too low, and the next new effort is just seen as the next new manipulation by management to get what they want.

The question of whether to increase driving or decrease restraining forces is analogous to the question, "If I'm driving a car and see the emergency brake is partly on, should I release the brake or put on more gas?" Accelerating may increase the speed, but it may also burn up the engine. Releasing the brake, on the other hand, would allow you to attain high speeds more efficiently.

Accordingly, I suggest that we spend our first energy, usually about two-thirds of our energy, on reducing the restraining forces and one-third on increasing the driving forces. However, since every situation is different, we should first study the nature of the restraining forces and work on those. Many of these forces will transform into driving forces.

By getting other people involved in the problem, we release some of the natural driving forces already in people. When our external driving forces are synchronized with their internal drives and motivations, we can create a synergistic problem-solving team.

Chapter 25

Diagnosing Strengths and Weaknesses

The major problem facing most executives is simply, "How do we get from where we are now to where we want to be?"

The solutions are basically always the same for any situation, any field. First, we gather complete and balanced data to get a clear picture of where we are now. We analyze it to diagnose our strengths and weaknesses. We select objectives; we identify and evaluate our options and make some decisions. We identify critical action steps, implement the plan, and then compare results against the objectives, which takes us back to the beginning of the process.

Over the years, my associates and I have seen the need for a simple diagnostic tool to help executives gather and organize data and make sense out of what's happening inside their organizations. We finally devised such a tool, which we call *Human Resource Accounting or a Stakeholder Information System.* Basically, it helps executives to monitor the condition of employees, customers, suppliers, etc., using some personal and organizational profiling surveys as well as their own diagnostic skills.

While it is simple, it does not yield simplistic solutions. It recognizes that the systems of human organizations can be complex. The human body is analogous to the human organization. The body is made up of rather complex systems. These systems are interdependent: a significant change in one may upset the equilibrium of the whole.

Organizations, like bodies, also have equilibrium states. When they are operating in a state of equilibrium, they are relatively free of distress and pain; they may be operating, however, at totally different levels of productivity. One organization might be highly creative; synergistic; filled with team spirit, a sense of mission, purpose, excitement and innovation; and be relatively free of painful handicaps. Another organization may be characterized by a strong adversarial climate, protective or defensive behaviors, low productivity, low profit. It, too, is in a state of equilibrium — all of the various systems are somewhat integrated and balanced but at a low level of performance.

Human resource accounting gives executives the right kind of data. It helps them assess the condition of their people. I'm confident that it will soon become commonplace as more executives experience tangible benefits.

Tangible Benefits

For instance, Novations, a human resource accounting firm, was once called in to work with the management of Howard Johnson Motels. The executives already knew they had problems: profits were down, productivity was down, morale was low. They could sense an undercurrent of dissatisfaction in the organization. They thought the major cause was low pay, but they had no concrete information on which to base a decision. They had considered bringing in a compensation specialist, hoping for a quick fix.

However, Novations' "Organizational Analysis Survey" showed that the real problem was that people were not trained; they were not sure what management expected them to do or how to do it. If the Howard Johnson executives had merely paid their people more, they would have only spent more for low performance. Novations identified several areas where the employees perceived a need for improvement: system effectiveness, leadership, organizational climate, human effectiveness, working environment, and interdepartmental relations. Executives found the data so valuable they decided to do this survey annually.

In another instance, the CEO of a company perceived himself and his company as being very people-oriented. But when we conducted human resource accounting, we found that people throughout his company had no sense of career development, no clear career path, no idea of what peak performance would mean to them. As a result, a majority of his managers and executives were actively looking for work in other firms or thinking about it. As he learned of their feelings, he was able to remedy the situation before it resulted in the loss of key people. For him, the survey revealed a dangerous "blind spot."

Four Systems

Human resource accounting and analysis examines the following four interdependent systems: first, the formal organization, made up of the physical environment, the technology, and the strategy, structure, policies and procedures; second, the people, including their perceptions and motivations, values, habits, skills and talents; third, the self, one's own perceptions, motivations, values, habits, skills and talents; and fourth, the informal organization or culture — the values and norms emerging from the interaction of the other three systems. The production and production capability of the organization could be seen as the output of culture. The background factors of the first three systems — the formal organization, the people, and the self — form the fourth system, the culture.

The following diagram shows this interrelationship.

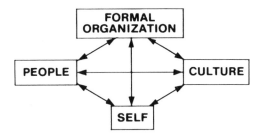

Human resource accounting involves gathering data around these four systems before diagnosing and prescribing. While this fact gathering may be time-consuming and tedious, if done correctly and completely, it will gradually give a fairly accurate picture of what is happening inside the human organization. Let's look at each of these four systems more carefully, starting with the people system.

The People System. The people system includes the self-system. People are real; their perceptions and feelings are facts, affecting the way they behave. The formal organization is abstract. It may appear concrete because we can chart it and measure it, account for its sales and costs. However, organization charts, job descriptions, chains of command, lines of authority, channels of communications are really just abstract descriptions of things.

When diagnosing the strengths and weaknesses of the people system, gather as much data as possible about your people. Personnel records can tell us much about the demographics of our people, about their backgrounds and track records, their interests and talents and profiles. But in addition to these records, managers should have one-on-one visits, group meetings, open-door briefings, suggestion systems, as well as the use of scientific instruments which give us a more objective picture of what's happening with our people.

Compared with traditional accounting of physical and financial resources, human resource accounting may be considered subjective and soft, but if we accept that feelings are facts to the people that hold them, and that those facts influence their behavior in our organizations, we must acknowledge that "soft" human data can be very "hard."

While many organizations have not yet sanctioned human resource accounting, those organizations using it should have an enormous competitive advantage as we increasingly move into the leadership-by-principles paradigm.

Formal Organization. When we begin to diagnose the strengths and weaknesses of the formal organization, we really get back to people, because all of the background factors ultimately rest in the values, motivations, and perceptions of people.

The external background factors are the economic, social, political, and cultural trends of society. People's perceptions, motivations, and values make up these trends. They tell us what's happening, and what people are thinking, and what they will likely be doing and thinking in the days to come. It's important to study the trends in our particular industry, and to relate our unique strengths, our distinctive competencies, to those industrial trends.

The internal factors basically represent the traditions underlying the organization and the values of the founders, owners, and directors of the enterprise. As we examine these external and internal background factors together, we can see how strategy is formed as well as organizational structure and the establishment of the many different kinds of systems, policies, and procedures which represent the muscle, nerves, and arteries of the organization.

Culture or the Informal Organization. Now, as we integrate the people, including self, with the formal organization — with the physical environment, technology, strategy, structure and systems — we get culture, the informal organization, with its values, norms, mores and unwritten expectations and assumptions.

When the norms of the informal organization conflict with the standards of the formal organization, we find adversarial relations between management and labor, between "us and them." In an adversarial culture, management inevitably thinks more in terms of controlling and directing human behavior rather than releasing human potential toward win-win goals, where people's needs and interests overlap the needs and interests of the organization.

Culture is difficult to define and even more difficult to measure, and yet we can all feel it. Often, we cannot directly change the culture, but we can change the self system, our own character and skill. We can do a number of things with the formal organization to change the way we put people together, define their jobs, and design their responsibilities.

If we're wise in the way we do these things, we can gradually help create a powerful win-win culture. But if we lack sincerity and integrity and only do things to please or appease people, we may well create a culture that is more cynical, protective, and defensive than the one we were trying to improve. Just as the body creates defensive mechanisms to safeguard its own welfare, so might a culture.

While we cannot directly and immediately improve our health, we can significantly improve it by obeying a number of natural

health laws over a period of time. Likewise, if we follow correct
principles — fairness, human relations, human resources and meaning
— and integrate those principles into structure and systems, we can
greatly influence the culture.

Risk & Reward

The more we take a slow, scientific approach in gathering and
diagnosing data about what is happening inside organizations, the
more hesitant we are to move in quickly and throw our weight
around to shape up everybody and everything. Instead, we begin to
pay the price to cultivate the kind of personal maturity, character
strength, and skills necessary to be a catalyst in improving our
culture. We realize that we can no longer supply and supervise
methods if we want to hold people responsible for results. We
begin to establish win-win agreements with people, motivating them
to cultivate certain desired skills and character traits, and allowing
them to supervise themselves under the terms of the agreement.
We set up helpful structures and systems; and we require people to
give an accounting regularly.

It all takes time, patience and self-discipline. And it will take
interaction with others to build teams and to identify overarching
goals which have meaning to all the people involved. The processes
may be hard and painful, but in the long run, these processes are
not as painful or risky or time-consuming as operating in the dark,
without accurate data on your most important resource — people.

Chapter 26

Completed Staff Work

When working with organizations that are mired in meetings and committee work, I counsel executives to use the tried and true principle of completed staff work.

Effective human resource management begins with effective delegation, with making the best possible use of the time and talents of people.

And in the process of delegation, effective managers set up a win-win performance agreement with each employee. One important guideline is the principle of completed staff work.

The Principle: No Cop Out

Completed staff work is one of the best ideas to come out of an otherwise militaristic, authoritarian model of management. The principle is that people are to think through the whole problem area, analyze the issue in depth, identify several alternatives, the consequences of those alternatives, and then finally recommend one of them.

It causes people to plumb their own resources and put together a specific, final recommendation which represents their best thinking. All a manager must then do is approve it or disapprove it. And if he or she decides to approve it, all that remains is to implement the decision or the recommended plan of action. Besides saving the manager's time, completed staff work stops people from copping out in the name of synergy or group-think or in the name of "let's get together and talk it over."

Decision making by groups may not tap the best resources because in meetings people sometimes take the course of least resistance and merely discuss ideas that they haven't really thought through.

The effective executive asks people to think through problems and issues and to bring a final recommendation. He or she is not likely to intercede and intervene in the process and provide people with quick and easy answers, even though they plead for them. He waits until their work is done; otherwise, he cheats people of growth — and they cheat him of time. Moreover, people cannot be held responsible for results if they are "bailed out" in the middle of the fact-finding or decision-making process.

In this the executive must exercise great wisdom. Completed staff work is not a panacea, nor is it applicable to all situations. There is a place for some early brainstorming, especially in the incubation period of a project. There is also a place for synergistic consensus.

But the principle of making people do their homework before coming to the table holds true in most situations. It guards against people bringing half-baked ideas to the table without paying the price to understand the issues and implications. It also guards against the common practice of coming together too early, before people can prepare well thought-through "white papers."

Now I'll Read It!

When Henry Kissinger was Secretary of State, he reportedly required his staff people to bring him their best recommendations. He would then take them, table them for 48 hours, and get back to them with the question, "Is this the very best you can do?"

And they said, "Well, no. We might think it through a little more; we might document it a little better; and we might present other alternatives and identify the consequences in the event that the people don't take our recommendation."

He said, "Well, then, continue to work on it."

And they would bring it back a second time. And the same thing happened. "Is this the very best you can do?" Kissinger would ask.

Now, most people know the flaws of their own presentation. And so the principle of completed staff work gives them the responsibility to identify their own flaws and correct them, or at least to identify them and suggest some measures for dealing with those flaws.

Invariably, Kissinger's staff would identify some minor flaws. He would then tell them to get back to work on it, to improve it, and to strengthen it, which they did.

And they brought it in the third time. And for the third time he said, "Is this the very best you can do? Is this your final recommendation? Is there anything that could be improved?"

And they said, "We really feel good about it, but maybe we could tighten the language a little; maybe we could make the presentation a little better."

They continued to work on it. And they brought it back yet another time and said, "This is the best we can do. We have thought it through thoroughly, and we have clearly identified the alternatives, the consequences, and the recommendations. We have also outlined the plan of action to carry it out in every detail, and we've got it in final shape. We're now convinced that you can present it in full confidence."

And Kissinger said, "Good, now I'll read it."

This story illustrates that staff people often want to save themselves time and effort, rather than the time and effort of the executive. And yet his time is worth so much more than their time – all the more reason to get the very best distilled thoughts from his staff.

Sony's Mini Compact Disc Player

Sony got off to a slow start in laser-operated compact disc players, only to beat the competition in bringing out the first successful product to sweep the market. The one man most directly responsible for Sony's success in this area is Kozo Ohsone, a consumer-oriented manager who had overseen the development of the Walkman cassette player.

Ohsone went to his lab one day and made a block of wood about five inches square – the size of a compact disc – and put it out in front of his engineers. To avoid unwanted advice from the top brass, Ohsone didn't tell anyone outside the lab what he was doing. He next brought in some product engineers to help with the design, since the disc players would be so small that researchers needed to know at each step whether their tightly packed circuitry could be mass-produced by robots.

Ohsone told his people that he would not accept the question, Why this size? "That was our size, and that was it." His design and production engineers grumbled, but they got to work and completed the project as charged. When Sony's mini version hit the market in 1984, it was one-twentieth the size of the original players, one-third the cost, and infinitely more attractive to consumers.

How to Get Completed Staff Work

Use the following five-step process for getting completed staff work.

First, provide a clear understanding of the desired results to set up the psychological contract. That's what Kissinger and Ohsone did so well. Once a person has that, then he or she can be set free to work independently or with others to meet a particular deadline for bringing in a final recommendation of what the decision should be, why, and what the alternatives are in the event that the executive wants to go for Plan B or C. But the plan of action should be spelled out. There should be no detail that has not been thoroughly digested and finalized.

Second, give a clear sense of what level of initiative people have: whether they are to wait until told, ask, make a recommendation, do it and report immediately, or do it and report periodically.

Third, clarify assumptions. If people want some feedback from the executive early to make sure they're not going in the wrong direction, they should bring in their understanding of the assumptions that the executive is making before they complete their work. If they do not clarify assumptions up front, they could go in an entirely different direction and bring in their final recommendations, only to have the chief executive say, "You didn't even understand the premises and the assumptions on which I was operating."

Fourth, provide those people charged to do completed staff work with as much time, resource and access as possible. Nothing is more frustrating to staff people than the expectation of doing completed work without the necessary information and resources. But if you face a genuine crisis and simply don't have much time to respond, clearly communicate these conditions to your staff.

Fifth, set a time and place for presenting and reviewing the completed staff work. Give your people the chance to make an effective presentation of their work.

Again, this principle is not a panacea. It is simply an effective means for motivating people to do their own thinking and to put their work in as finished form as possible before they give their final recommendations. My experience is that most staff people welcome the chance to study things out and to show what they are capable of doing. If executed well, completed staff work saves everybody's time in the long run and produces a much higher quality product. That's because the process plumbs the depths of the individual brilliance and talents of people.

Applications of the Principle

Speeches and Presentations. Spend as much time as necessary in getting the preliminaries all together so that the person that's to do the completed staff work knows what resources are available and understands fully what the expectations are. The executive might have to do some work up front to get the process started. Particularly with speeches and presentations, the executive would need to spell out some things. "These are the basic things I want to touch on in that meeting in two weeks," he might say; "in the meantime, I'm going to be gone on a trip. Let's review your recommendations when I get back."

Issue Development. An executive could say to a trusted staff person, "Please think this issue through and bring to me a specific recommendation as to what you think the charter should be and what you should do." In other words, "You do the issue development for me and then write your own contract."

I once did this with a company. I sat in and listened to those staff reports. They were excellent. The chief executive himself just sat back in amazement. He later told me, "I never realized the depth of their thinking."

Meeting Management. Completed staff work not only plumbs the genius and talents of good staff people but also makes for more effective meetings. When people have analyzed an issue in depth, carefully thought through the implications and the alternatives, and responsibly made their recommendations, they make a more powerful contribution to meetings.

Synergistic Problem Solving. Once you identify the key issues and prioritize them, you can then set up a small ad hoc committee and give them the challenge of completed staff work.

For instance, you may find that one of the major problems is communications or career development or compensation. Get three or four people from different levels in the organization into a viable working committee and ask them to study in depth that one issue and come up with a specific recommendation to bring back to the executive group: "We recommend this for these reasons. Here are the alternatives. Here are the consequences. And here are the problems we came to understand, along with the causes of the problems." If they have a synergy in their team, you get a strong recommendation representing different points of view. And seldom have I seen top executives turn down such a recommendation.

The process also moderates the extremists — the dissident and negative people who might be riding some hobby horse and pushing it. As soon as they've had a free forum, their day in court as it were, they get all of that negative energy out of them. It takes the sword out of their hand, and it moderates them. And it makes for a better win-win solution.

A final word of caution. If this principle is not integrated with others, it could create a perception, "Who does the boss think he is? We do his work, and all he has to do is put his name and stamp on it." Or some may say, "He doesn't care; he doesn't want to get involved in the process at all."

But done well, completed staff work develops people and saves the executive's time. It also gives much more responsibility to the staff people. In fact, it increases their response-ability, their ability to choose wise responses to different situations.

Chapter 27

Manage from the Left,
Lead from the Right

In organizations, people usually perform one of three essential roles: producer, manager, or leader. Each role is vital to the success of the organization.

For example, if there is no producer, great ideas and high resolves are not carried out. The work simply doesn't get done. Where there is no manager, there is role conflict and ambiguity; everyone attempts to be a producer, working independently, with few established systems or procedures. And if there is no leader, there is lack of vision and direction. People begin to lose sight of their mission.

While each role is important to the organization, the role of leader is most important. Without strategic leadership, people may dutifully climb the "ladder of success" but upon reaching the top rung discover that it is leaning against the wrong wall.

Consider the following examples:

Automobile Industry. Several years ago, in spite of the counsel of insightful forecasters, American automobile manufacturers continued to build big gas-guzzling cars. Their short-sightedness resulted in a widely-known disaster, from which they are only now recovering.

Steel Industry. The old-line big producers continue to operate our of archaic mills while trying to compete with high technology foreign companies and domestic mini-mills that can produce high quality steel at a much lower cost.

Semi-conductors. American companies virtually owned the world semi-conductor market until the mid-1970's. During the recessionary years that followed, they cut back production, and by 1979, the U.S.

suppliers were simply at a loss to meet the demand for 16K RAMs. The Japanese had since jumped into the market and by the end of that year had captured over 42 percent.

Banking.   Most major banks in the United States find their balance sheets held ransom by third-world countries.   Conventional wisdom regarded making big loans to developing countries as an excellent way to build a financial statement.   Bank executives failed to see that a combination of social unrest, high unemployment, and rapid inflation in most of these countries would make loan paybacks virtually impossible.

Transportation.   In the railroad industry, managers lost sight of their essential role − to provide transportation − and instead saw themselves in the railroading business.   Then, as they gave their energies to building better railroads, the pipelines, airlines, and truck lines took away most of their business.

Accounting.   Managers continue to account almost exclusively for financial and physical resources and neglect accounting for the most important resource of all − people.

We could look at every field of human endeavor, and find endless examples of people scrambling to the top of a ladder that is leaning against the wrong wall.   Peter Drucker teaches that within a few years of their establishment most organizations lose sight of their mission and essential role and become focused on methods or efficiency or doing things right rather than focusing on effectiveness or doing the right things.   It seems that people tend to codify past successful practices into rules for the future and give energy to preserving and enforcing these rules even after they no longer apply. Indeed, traditional procedures and practices die hard!

Management vs. Leadership

That's why the role of the leader is so crucial to continual success.   Leadership deals with direction − with making sure that the ladder is leaning against the right wall.   Management deals with speed.   To double one's speed in the wrong direction, however, is the very definition of foolishness.   Leadership deals with vision − with keeping the mission in sight − and with effectiveness and results. Management deals with establishing structure and systems to get those results. It focuses on efficiency, cost-benefit analyses, logistics, methods, procedures, and policies.

Leadership focuses on the top line. Management focuses on the bottom line. Leadership derives its power from values and correct principles. Management organizes resources to serve selected objectives to produce the bottom line.

Of course, management and leadership are not mutually exclusive; in fact, it might be said that leadership is the highest component of management. And leadership, itself, can be broken into two parts: one having to do with vision and direction, values and purposes, and the other with inspiring and motivating people to work together with a common vision and purpose. Some leaders have vision but lack team-building talents. Other leaders can inspire people and build teams but lack vision.

As a team builder, the leader attempts to reduce the dysfunctional friction, while recognizing that in a complementary team, strength lies in differences; hence, he need not attempt to clone people or to make everyone else over in his own image. As long as people have the same goals, it is not important that they have the same roles. When team members regard each other with mutual respect, differences are utilized and are considered strengths rather than weaknesses.

The basic role of the leader is to foster mutual respect and build a complementary team where each strength is made productive and each weakness made irrelevant. The essential role of a manager is to use leverage to multiply the work and role of the producer. A producer rolls up his sleeves and does what's necessary to solve problems and get results.

It is most interesting and instructive to study how well people's jobs fit their personal style or preference with regard to these three roles. For instance, some people may be in a job which requires little production but a lot of management and a little leadership, but their personal style or preference is to be a producer rather than a manager or a leader. Needless to say, a poor fit between job expectations and personal preference will be a source of great frustration as well as criticism from others. And if a holder of a job has a different perception than that of his boss or peers regarding the relative importance of these three roles in his particular position, his problems will be compounded.

Left Brain/Right Brain

Research on brain theory helps us to understand why some people are excellent producers but poor managers or great managers but weak leaders. The research basically indicates that the brain is divided into two hemispheres, the left and the right, and that each hemisphere specializes in different functions, processes different kinds of information, and deals with different kinds of problems.

While both hemispheres are involved in logical and creative processes, the left works more with logic, the right works more with emotions. The left deals with words, the right with pictures; the left with parts and specifics, the right with wholes and with relationships among the parts. The left deals with analysis, which means to break apart; the right with synthesis, which means to put together. The left deals with sequential thinking, the right with simultaneous and holistic thinking. The left is time-bound, meaning it has a sense of time and goals and one's position in relation to those goals; the right is time free, meaning it might lose a sense of time altogether. The left governs the right side of the body and the right, the left side of the body.

Using these terms, we might say that we live in a very left-brain-dominant world, where words and measurement and logic are enthroned and creativity, intuition, and artistry are often subordinated, even punished. This is particularly true with men: the masculine "macho" cultural stereotype, combined with the heavy academic focus on the left side, can often negate or even drive out the more creative, aesthetic, intuitive capacities (often considered feminine).

The Eastern cultures speak of the two parts of man's nature, the Yin and Yang. The Yin is the feminine part, and the Yang the masculine. Entire libraries have been written on this subject, including organizational books. Many organizations have great management systems and controls but lack heart. Others may have heart but lack mind, good systems, and controls.

The ancient Greek philosophers spoke of influence or persuasion processes in terms of ethos, pathos, and logos. Basically, ethos concerns one's credibility, or what I have called the emotional bank account; pathos deals with the emotions and motivation, which we would here call the right brain; and logos deals with the logical reasoning process, the left brain.

As we apply brain dominance theory to the three essential roles of organizations, we see that the manager's role would primarily be left brain and the leader's role right brain. The producer's role would depend upon the nature of the work. If it's verbal, logical, analytical work, that would be essentially left brain; it it's more intuitive, emotional, or creative work, it would be right brain.

People who are excellent managers but poor leaders may be extremely well organized and run a tight ship with superior systems and procedures and detailed job descriptions. But unless they are internally motivated, little gets done because there is no feeling, no heart; everything is too mechanical, too formal, too tight, too protective. A looser organization may work much better even though it may appear to an outside observer to be disorganized and confused. Truly significant accomplishments may result simply because people share a common vision, purpose or sense of mission.

Accordingly, my suggestion is this:

Lead from the right, manage from the left.

Of course, the ideal is to cultivate the ability to have crossover between the right and left sides of the brain; a person could then discern the situation and use the appropriate tool to deal with it. If someone were to ask regarding a game of chess, "What's the best move?" we'd first have to ask, "What's the situation?" Then we could decide what the best move would be. If someone were to ask, "What is the best club to use in golf?" again we'd first have to ask about the lay of the land, lie of the ball, placement of the pin, and so forth. The ability to correctly diagnose the situation comes first, and this itself may require a good combination of left and right brain skills. To acquire a functional balance, a person may need to exercise the weaker side of the brain. For example, a person who is left-brain dominant should purposely exercise right-brain muscles by learning to communicate through sensing and touching and visual imagery and to listen more with the eyes than the ears, getting involved in artistic endeavors and the creative side of problem-solving and so forth. Those who are right-brain dominant should exercise the latent left-brain muscles through analytical problem-solving processes, communication through words and logic, reading textbooks, studying scientific and technical material in computer science, law, business accounting, or any of the applied sciences.

Organizations devoted to short-term, bottom-line, hard-data orientations usually neglect such leadership development and therefore breed "half-brained" executives who seldom find time, for example, to communicate vision and direction, build teams, develop people or plan meetings, except in a kind of crisis way.

If leadership issues get on the agendas, they are usually at the bottom, under "other business." Executives seldom address leadership issues because they are so fatigued from putting out fires and dealing with the production and management issues at the top of the agenda.

No wonder many individuals and institutions are caught going in the wrong direction, being in the wrong jungle, or leaning against the wrong wall. Strategic leadership can eliminate such misdirection and make things right again.

A strategic leader can provide direction and vision, motivate through love, and build a complementary team based on mutual respect if he is more effectiveness-minded than efficiency-minded, more concerned with direction and results than with methods, systems, and procedures. While all of the producers are hacking their way though the jungle and while their managers are sharpening their machetes for them and setting up machete-wielding working schedules and putting on training programs for machete wielders, an enlightened and courageous leader must sometimes cry out, "Wrong jungle!" even though he can expect the answer back, "Be quiet! We're making progress."

Part 4:

ORGANIZATIONAL LEADERSHIP

When we become leaders of organizations, we encounter a whole new set of problems. Some of these are chronic, others acute. Many are as common to Fortune 500 companies as they are to families, small businesses and volunteer groups. The good news is that certain conditions of organizational effectiveness also apply across the board.

While in this section, I deal mostly with the mega-issues of structure, strategy, stream and systems, I maintain a strong individual character component in my PS model or paradigm. No leader can afford to forget that personal and organizational integrity are closely intertwined. Nor can any leader afford to lose sight of the mission and shared values – the constitution of the corporation.

Chapter 28

Six Conditions of Effectiveness

To motivate and manage people to peak performance, executives must identify areas where organizational needs and goals overlap individual needs, goals and capabilities; they can then set up win-win performance agreements in those common areas.

Once an agreement is established, people may govern or supervise themselves in terms of that agreement. They become more self-directing and self-controlling. Executives may then serve as a source of help — establishing systems that help people fulfill the specific terms of the win-win agreement and evaluate themselves periodically against the criteria of the agreement.

Central to these elements are two other conditions, character and skills. Character is what a person is; skills are what a person can do — the human competencies required to establish and maintain trusting relationships, win-win agreements, helpful systems, self-supervision and self-evaluation.

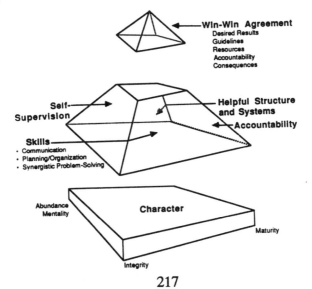

Condition #1: Win-Win Performance Agreements

Although I introduced win-win agreements in Chapter 22, I want to briefly review the concept here as part of my six conditions of organizational effectiveness. Win-win performance agreements are psychological contracts between managers and subordinates. The agreement clarifies expectations and represents a mutual commitment in five areas. To set up and manage win-win agreements, follow these five steps:

- *First, specify desired results.*

- *Second, set some guidelines.*

- *Third, identify available resources.*

- *Fourth, define accountability.*

- *Fifth, determine the consequences.*

Condition #2: Self-Management

In the win-win performance agreement, we do not deal with methods. Win-win is a human resource principle that recognizes people are capable of self-direction and self-control and can govern themselves to do whatever is necessary within the guidelines to achieve desired results.

When more than two individuals are involved in the win-win agreement, the psychological contract becomes a social contract. We may set up the agreement with a team, department, or an entire division. Whatever the size of the group, all members should participate in developing the win-win agreement. This social contract then becomes even more powerful, reinforcing, and motivating because it taps into the social nature and human need to belong and be part of a meaningful team project or effort.

One of the strengths of this win-win contract is that it is very flexible and adaptable to any set of circumstances or to any level of maturity or competence. If the ability or desire to do a job is small, identify fewer results and more guidelines and procedures; make resources more available, attractive and visible; have more frequent accountability with tighter, clearer, more measurable criteria; have consequences follow immediately, making feedback powerfully reinforcing.

If there is a great deal of maturity and ability and desire to do a job, the win-win agreement would have broader, longer range desired results with fewer guidelines, particularly regarding procedures and policy. You might make the resources available but not necessarily that visible; have less frequent accountability, using discernment as well as measurement to evaluate performance; and set longer-term consequences with particularly heavy emphasis on intrinsic psychological rewards rather than extrinsic rewards.

Once you have established win-win performance agreements and achieved a greater degree of self-management with your people, next focus on constructing helpful structures and systems. When people participate in the formation of the agreement, they feel better about participating in periodic accountability for results; basically, they evaluate themselves against the specified criteria. When the win-win agreement is set up properly, they will do whatever is necessary to accomplish the desired results within the guidelines.

Condition #3: Helpful Systems

Helpful organizational systems greatly facilitate the fulfillment of win-win agreements. These systems might include strategic planning, company structure, job design, communication, budgeting, compensation, information, recruitment, selection, placement, training, and development. In a helpful system, people receive information about their performance directly, and they use it to make necessary corrections. Less information passes over the desk of the manager, who in the past has felt responsible for that information.

If any of the so-called "helpful" systems are really harmful win-lose systems, they will override the win-win agreement. This is particularly the case with the compensation system. If management talks win-win cooperation but rewards win-lose competition, for example, they defeat their own system. It would be analogous to telling one flower, "Grow! Grow!" and then watering another flower.

All of the systems within the organization must be totally integrated with and supportive of the win-win agreement. Win-Win should be reflected in recruiting, hiring and training. It should be evident in professional development and compensation, job design and company structure, strategic planning and mission and goal selection, as well as in all the tactical activities done to accomplish those goals.

Condition #4: Personal Accountability

In a win-win agreement, people evaluate themselves. Since they have a clear, up-front understanding of what results are expected and what criteria are used to assess their performance, they are in the best position to evaluate themselves.

The old notion is that the manager evaluates the performance of his people, often rather subjectively. This, of course, is absolutely insulting to professional people, which is why some managers hate performance appraisals. Unless expectations are clarified and commitments made up front, people can expect performance appraisals to be difficult, embarrassing and sometimes downright insulting.

In this case, the manager's attitude is helpful, not judgmental. He may identify himself as a resource in the win-win agreement. He may serve as a trainer when his people undertake new tasks or new responsibilities or as a counselor in the areas of career planning and professional development. He involves his people in establishing the win-win agreement and allows them to evaluate their own performance. If the trust level is high, the employee's evaluation will be more accurate, more complete, more honest than the manager's evaluation ever could be, because the person knows more about the conditions and the details.

If the manager becomes aware of changing trends or other conditions which are not part of the original agreement, he would reopen the agreement for rethinking.

Condition #5: Character

In a low-trust culture, it is very difficult to establish a win-win agreement or to allow self-supervision and evaluation. There would be a need, instead, for control systems and for external supervision and evaluation. Before a manager could set up the first four conditions, he would need to begin making deposits into the "emotional bank account" and do whatever is necessary to build a trust relationship so that the win-win agreement could be established. And once the win-win agreement is in place, the other conditions will naturally follow.

The character traits most critical to establishing the win-win agreement are integrity (habits are congruent with values, words with deeds, expressions with feelings), maturity (courage balanced with consideration), and the abundance mentality (there is plenty out there for everyone). A person with these character traits can be genuinely happy for the success and accomplishments of others.

Condition #6: Skills

The three most critical skills are communication, planning and organization, and synergistic problem solving because these three personal skills enable an individual to establish the other four conditions of organizational effectiveness.

When individuals are duplicitous, when they say one thing but practice another or when they bad mouth people behind their backs but sweet talk them to their face, there is a subtle but eloquent, communication that undermines trust and, inevitably, leads to win-lose agreements and arrangements requiring external supervision, control and evaluation.

These six conditions are so interdependent that if any one of them is thrown out of balance, it will immediately affect the other five; in fact, changing just one character trait can affect all of the other conditions.

For instance, consider the character trait of maturity, defined as courage balanced with consideration. If a manager had a great deal of courage but lacked consideration, he would probably express himself aggressively but listen poorly, without true empathy. Consequently, the agreement would be win-lose. He would get his way, thinking that his way is best for everyone concerned. He would likely not encourage or allow his people to express their true feelings. He would fail to tap the internal motivation, requiring external motivation or supervision and the use of good control systems and performance appraisal procedures and compensation systems to reinforce desired behavior.

On the other hand, if a person lacks courage but is high on consideration, high in the need for acceptance and popularity, he will tend to develop a lose-win psychological contract where people do their own thing. Often these agreements lead to various forms of self-indulgence and organizational chaos. People may begin to blame others for poor performance or bad results. They may also get very demanding. Such behavior only reinforces the lose-win agreement, which eventually cannot be economically sustained, and leads to win-lose central control as management battles to survive and maintain some semblance of order.

Anarchy breeds dictatorship. As Patrick Henry put it, "If we don't govern ourselves wisely, we will be governed by despots."

Chapter 29

Seven Chronic Problems

Most organizations suffer from some serious chronic problems; and the long-term solutions often require surgery.

Every day we're bombarded with advertisements promising fast, easy and free results or relief. What we often forget is that most "wonder drugs" work only on acute symptoms, as opposed to chronic problems.

What is an acute illness? It is one that causes us immediate pain. Chronic illness is the persistent, continuing disease which underlies the acute pain.

Most people are into solving acute illnesses and problems. They want the sharp pain to be relieved now. They want broken relationships to be instantly repaired. They find, however, that the more they seek quick fixes and attempt to apply some gimmick, some technique that seems to work for someone else, or that seems to have instant appeal, the worse the chronic problem becomes.

For instance, if I am chronically fatigued — that is, if my reserve capacities are depleted; if my working style has put me into a situation of management by crisis; if I am always overexerting or pressing myself to do far more than I should do; if my emotional life is a function of other people's opinions of me to the point that I am always trying to become all things to all people; or if I am just stressed out — I could develop a chronic case of mononucleosis or some other disease. This would become manifest in certain symptoms, and I might try to treat these symptoms with some medicine that promises a quick solution.

But the promise is deceptive. There is no quick fix to chronic problems. To solve these, we must apply natural processes. The only way we can bring the harvest in the fall is to plant in the spring and to water, weed, cultivate and fertilize during the long summer.

We seem to understand that fact of life when working in a natural system; however, when it comes to social systems, we often practice quick fixes. For example, how many of us crammed in school? How many of us got good grades, even graduate degrees by cramming? Inwardly we know we didn't get the best education possible because we didn't pay the price day in and day out.   Rather, when we were hurting in one area, we worked on that immediate hurt.   Then, when another crisis broke out, we ran to that.

That lifestyle breaks people down and burns them out, and then their capacity to relate well with others, particularly under stress and pressure, is reduced to a minimum.   Their life becomes a function of what is happening to them.   They become victimized by it all.

I once visited a friend who is the head of surgery at a hospital. He allowed me to observe about 20 different operations.   I also assisted him in an open-heart surgery.   I held the instrument that kept the chest wall open while he replaced three blood vessels.   I felt those vessels; they were stiff and brittle because they were filled with plaque, a cholesterol substance.

And I asked, "Why don't you just clean them out?"

He said, "For a while, you can reverse the process, but over time, the plaque, the cholesterol, becomes the very content of the wall."

I then asked, "Now that you have corrected these three places, is the man clear?"

He said, "No, it's through his whole system.   He has a chronic vascular problem, a heart disease problem.   I can see that he exercises because some of the supplementary circulatory system has been developed, but he hasn't changed other aspects of his lifestyle. He's got a chronic problem.   I'm only working on the three most acute things that might cause a heart attack or stroke because of the lack of oxygen flow to those parts of the body."

The one thing people don't want to change is their lifestyle, but people generally must change their lifestyle if they want to deal with the chronic nature of their most serious problems.

Chronic Problems in Organizations

Individuals comprise organizations. Even though we try to exercise more discipline in our professional life, our personal tendencies are carried with us into our organizations. There we continue to look for a quick fix around the symptoms, the acute painful symptoms, rather than deal with the chronic habit patterns built into day-to-day operations.

Chronic individual problems become chronic organizational problems as a "critical mass" of people bring these problems with them through the gates each day and as social values encourage instant gratification and quick solutions to deep and difficult problems.

While this is particularly true in America, I would say, from my international experience, that to some degree, the following seven problems are universal — that they apply to many other cultures and organizations, even to departments and individuals within organizations.

Problem 1 — No shared vision and values: either the organization has no mission statement or there is no deep understanding of and commitment to the mission at all levels of the organization.

Most executives don't realize what's involved in creating a mission statement that truly represents deeply shared values and vision at all levels of the organization. It takes patience, a long-term perspective and meaningful involvement — and few organizations rank high in those virtues. Many organizations have a mission statement, but typically people aren't committed to it because they aren't involved in developing it; consequently, it's not part of the culture. Culture, by definition, assumes shared vision and values, as represented by a mission statement put together and understood and implemented by all levels of the organization.

My experience suggests that if you don't have a corporate constitution and govern everything else by that constitution, you will likely have the other six chronic problems in your organization, in spades.

To be most effective, your mission statement should deal with all four basic human needs: economic or money need; social or relationship need; psychological or growth need; and spiritual or contribution need. Most mission statements do not deal with all four needs. Many leave off the psychological, or the need for human growth and development. Some lack wording on win-win relationships, equity in economic compensation, and the commitment to a set of principles or values and to service and contribution to the community, suppliers and to customers.

This first chronic problem is like an unseen iceberg. If the company has a "mission" of sorts, the problem is not clearly evident —executives may not see that the mission is not deeply shared. But the lack of shared vision and values is the seed bed of almost all other problems.

Problem 2 — No strategic path: the strategy is not well developed or it ineffectively expresses the mission statement and fails to meet the wants and needs and realities of the stream.

In recent years, the best strategic thinking has changed from a "road map" to a "compass" model because we are in a wilderness —the stream, the environment is so unpredictable that road maps are worthless. People need compasses that are fixed on constitutions (the mission statement with its set of principles and values) so they can flexibly adapt to the environment.

The old strategic planning model was called Ends (where we are going), Ways (how we are going to get there), and Means (how we organize the resource). The new model calls for people to use a compass, a set of principles and values, and create ways to achieve the ends. The natural tendency of most organizations is to forecast by extrapolating trends and to call it strategic planning. The leaders of these organizations never really ask the question, "Where do we want to be in five years." "What kind of an organization do we want to have." Instead, they become very reactive to the environment, to the stream they operate in. So, while the strategic plan reflects the stream, it doesn't reflect the vision. Other organizations become so mission or vision-driven that their strategy does not reflect the stream.

Good strategic planning reflects both vision and stream. Make sure your strategic path leads from your mission statement and reflects its vision and values and also reflects the environmental realities, the stream, so that you are not producing obsolete products and services. It's tough to create and maintain that balance. It takes tremendous judgment and wisdom. It takes a social radar with regard to the stream.

It also takes a deep commitment and conscience with regard to the value system. If you don't have a deeply embedded and shared value system at the center of your organization, you will likely lack internal security, and so you will seek it from the outside. You then vacillate and become subject to all the fickle forces that are playing on the outside.

Problem 3 — Poor alignment: bad alignment between structure and shared values, between vision and systems; the structure and systems of the organization poorly serve and reinforce the strategic paths.

The alignment problem is prevalent everywhere. Ask yourself: "Is our mission statement a constitution? Is it the supreme law of the land? Does every person who comes into the organization make a commitment of allegiance to that constitution? Is every program, every system, even our organizational structure subject to the constitution?" If your answer is "no" — and it usually is — you have an alignment problem.

If you don't have a shared value system, you don't have an inner source of security. So, where do you get the security? In rigid structure and systems. Why? Because it gives you predictability, a sense that the sun will come up tomorrow. By having rigid structure and systems in place, you have a sense of predictability. But you have very little flexibility to adapt to the stream — and that can kill you in a hurry, as many American companies, and industries, can attest.

Many American companies are being managed on a span of control of one to six, one to seven, maybe up to one to 10. All of a sudden, they have competition out there with a span of control of one to 50 or more — and a totally different cost structure. They know that unless they restructure, they can't possibly compete; and yet, some companies keep the same old structure, simply because "that's the way things are done around here." Other organizations are downsizing because the stream is forcing them to simplify the structure and systems. And that is causing great consternation; people are fearful. They are looking for a new structure while they are still dependent on the old.

Many executives say they value capitalism but reward feudalism. They say they value democracy but reward autocracy. They say they value openness and "glasnost," but they behave in ways that value closeness, hidden agendas and politicking.

The acute symptoms of this chronic problem are interpersonal conflicts and poor interdepartmental relations (turf wars). And the "quick fix" is to come up with cosmetic solutions — a new temporary training program on communication skills — but the trust is shot so it means nothing. The next cosmetic solution might be to rearrange the compensation system in an attempt to get some temporary motivation. But then people feel ripped off because management is messing around with their rice bowl, and they no longer know what is going to happen tomorrow. The new compensation system may force them to increase productivity through competition, even if their governing values are teamwork and cooperation.

Problem 4 — Wrong style: the management style is either incongruent with shared vision and values or the style inconsistently embodies the vision and values of the mission statement.

In a sense, this chronic problem is even more fundamental than the other three — because most people get their style from their upbringing, from early mentors, either in their family or in their schools or business. Our early mentoring has an enormous impact on our style because our emotional and psychological need for acceptance is very strong when we are highly dependent. Whether we like it or not, an authoritarian father, even an abusive father, may be our only link to survival, and so his style becomes our style.

When we encounter a style that is different from our own — an abrasive, abusive or confrontive style, for example — we may be shocked. For example, my eight-year old son, Joshua, was shocked to hear in the news of a boy his same age who was abandoned by his parents. He was shocked for two days. He asked, "How could that happen?" He couldn't even see that to be an option — because the action was so foreign to him.

When people find themselves in a new stream with a new value system that is inconsistent with their particular style — be it authoritarian, permissive or democratic — they must have a new birthing. They must get so deeply involved in the new value system that they get reprogrammed by it. It must become the new constitution to their own personal life.

The style of staff people is strongly influenced by the style of senior executive mentors; and most people are mentored toward management, not toward leadership. Consequently, they think efficiency; they think things; they climb ladders leaning against the wrong wall. They don't think people; they don't think principles — because they weren't mentored that way.

With so much diversity and mobility in our society, it's often a challenge to make your style congruent with the vision and values of your organization. You may need to adapt your style to some degree. That's why principle-centered leadership is so vital. If you're principle-centered, you can be very flexible, very fluid on the surface of your life, as long as the style is congruent with those principles.

Some may wonder if it's possible for senior managers, old dogs, to learn a new style or trick? Some may contend that our styles — whether we be vocalists, comedians or managers — are so deeply imprinted that by the time we turn 10, 20 or 30, they're indelibly etched in stone. I think that while it is very difficult to adapt or change our style, it's not impossible. Our leadership style can be "situational," but before we're able to make a change, we may require new mentors and models.

One of the on-going debates is whether managers are made or born. I believe most are reborn, through some kind of mentoring — learning and applying correct principles. That's why great leaders serve as mentors and help bring about a whole new generation, a total transformation. But the personal price of doing it is tremendous — you may have to pay a "fourfold," that is, you may have to suffer tremendously to make significant changes.

An organization can tolerate many different styles as long as people are anchored in the same governing principles. Still, it's wise to try to find an environment that is compatible with your style. Your style will fit better in some organizations than in others. You need real wisdom in deciding where you best fit, and whether your style is congruent with the organizational style, recognizing how hard it is to change.

Problem 5 — Poor skills: style does not match skills, or managers lack the skills they need to use an appropriate vision.

Sometimes I find that people want to shift to a different style but that they simply lack the skills. They don't know, for example, how to set up a complete delegation; how to use empathy to get the other person's point of view; how to use synergy to create a third alternative; or how to work up a win-win performance agreement. Now, lacking knowledge and skills is not as deep a chronic problem because through education and training, we may solve those problems.

For instance, beginning skiers soon develop a certain style, skill level and comfort zone on the slopes; however, they lack the skills to effectively negotiate the hill under certain conditions. Their style and skills may be suited to only one kind of snow, terrain or weather condition; they would not be prepared for whatever comes. Even if they have the desire, motivation and physical ability, they still need improved skills to negotiate effectively.

By developing their skills, people may also develop their desire, even change their style. For example, when people get a new time management tool and the skill training to go with it, they often make some major changes in their lives. Or, when people start to learn and apply the skills of empathy, they may find that the development of these skills enhances their style. In fact, Carl Rogers claimed that if you really want to help people change, empathize with them. Gradually, they gain new insights and start to realize new potential; in a sense, the very process starts to change them.

Problem 6 — Low trust: staff has low trust, a depleted emotional bank account, and that low trust results in closed communication, little problem solving and poor cooperation and teamwork.

Trust determines the quality of the relationship between people. And in a sense, trust is a chicken-and-egg problem. If you attempt to work on building trust, at the exclusion of other chronic and acute problems, you will only exacerbate your situation. For example, one of the best ways to build trust is to work on the mission statement and to work on alignment issues. But then, if you try to do this while keeping a closed management style, your people will always be walking on eggs without much trust in your words.

Low trust spoils communication in spite of skill training. For example, in low-trust cultures, managers usually come up with performance agreements, job descriptions and mission statements that people don't buy into, and then when they don't buy into them, they don't use them as a constitution; instead, they try to set up policy and procedure manuals to preserve their jobs and build their pyramids.

The trust level — the sense that "I can trust you" or "you're a trustworthy person" or "you're a person who, if you make mistakes, you admit them" or "you're approachable" or "you're open and teachable" or "if you make a promise, you keep it" — that kind of gut-level sense really undergirds the rest. If you're fundamentally duplicitous, you can't solve the low-trust problem: you can't talk yourself out of problems you behave yourself into.

Trustworthiness is more than integrity: it also connotes competence. In other words, you may be an honest doctor, but before I trust you, I want to know that you're competent as well. We sometimes focus too much on integrity, not enough on personal competence and professional performance. Honest people who are incompetent in their area of professed expertise are not trustworthy.

Problem 7 — No self-integrity: values do not equal habits; there is no correlation between what I value and believe and what I do.

If a person lacks integrity, how is he going to build an emotional bank account? How is he going to be trustworthy? How is he going to adapt his style to match the demands of the new stream? How will he create a culture where there is genuine trust?

And if a company lacks integrity, how is it going to satisfy its customers? How is it going to keep its best employees? How is it going to stay in business?

A person who fails to live by his value system probably doesn't have a mission statement. Without a clear statement of values, our habits will be all over the place. Of course, we may have a mission statement but fail to live by it. We are then hypocritical or duplicitous.

Corporate duplicity is much the same, only compounded, since a corporation is made up of individuals. That's why, when we detect one or more of the seven chronic problems in an organization — and when the senior executives want to blame everybody and everything else for those problems — we have them look in the mirror to identify one of the primary sources. They need not look at anyone else or ask any question except one: "Do I have integrity myself?"

Conclusion

These seven chronic problems are curable. They are also common — the competition likely has as many cancers as you do. Success in business is a relative thing: it is not measured against an ideal such as excellence; it is measured against the competition. And since most organizations have these problems to some degree, people learn to live with chronic problems all their professional lives. They may even have long tenures, unless the pain gets too acute.

I'm confident that enlightened leaders can cure these seven chronic problems, not just treat the symptoms, and create better societies. But to do that, they've got to change hearts, build trust, revise the structure and systems. Most leaders are trying to do that to some degree. They are trying to create a profitable, informed, skilled, productive, cooperative, quality organization. And they are beginning to value people, the top line, as much as they value the profits, the bottom line.

Chapter 30

Corporate Constitutions

A written corporate constitution can be a priceless document for both individuals and organizations. As Thomas Jefferson said about the Constitution of the United States: "Our peculiar security is in the possession of a written Constitution."

Mission statements, whether personal or corporate in scope, empower people to take control of their lives and thereby gain more internal security.

In writing a mission statement, you are drafting a blueprint, raising a standard, cementing a constitution. The project deserves broad involvement. In my experience, every company that has conscientiously involved their people in formulating a mission statement, has produced a fine constitution. The principle is basic to our society: govern (manage) by the consent of the people. People have a sense of what is right, and, if involved, will come up with a noble document.

For example, at the Pillsbury Company — a fast-growth, diversified corporation that grew from 40,000 to 100,000 employees in the last decade — executives woke up one day with "the uneasy feeling that our concern with financial goals in the 1970's had come at the expense of helping our people adapt to the dramatic growth of the company. We decided there had to be some statement, a public declaration of what Pillsbury should stand for. It would have to be simple, short, give people permission to dream dreams, take risks and think creatively and signal a change in our culture from conservative, cumbersome and bureaucratic to people-oriented, innovative and supportive of individual initiative."

Pillsbury took one year and involved their top 200 managers with participation throughout the company to create a one-page constitution, their mission and values statement.

And what difference has it made? Reports Virginia Ward, vice president of Human Resources, "We now feel a sense of ownership throughout the company for our mission and values. We are more effective in our management of people because of the principles inherent in our mission and values. There is a spirit of optimism and excitement about the future."

Such is the power of a corporate constitution. We have in America a glorious constitution. John Adams said that the Constitution of the United States was written for a moral people. Most corporate mission statements also assume there is a basic morality, integrity, and sense of social responsibility in people.

A mission statement focuses your energies and lets you enjoy a sense of orientation, being, purpose. It prevents being distracted and side-tracked. It also focuses your personal energies and resources. You don't spend time and money and effort on things that don't return and aren't related to your reason for being.

Use your mission statement to direct and unify your life. You build more internal security by being more self-directed. If you build your own security around the weaknesses of others, you allow their weaknesses to control you. If you build on weaknesses of your competitors, you actually empower them. On the other hand, if you operate from your own statement of mission and values, your life is not so buffeted by external forces. In fact, your focus will begin to shape the events of your life.

The mission statement becomes a framework for thinking, for governing. Review it periodically and ask, "Are we doing the best we can to live by this? Are we preventing problems? Management by quick fix leads to management by crises. Crises come one after another just like a pounding surf. Troubles come so frequently that life begins to blend into one huge problem. Cynicism and fatigue set in.

For example, we once worked with a business that wanted to create cost-consciousness. So they put on a drive, and everyone became cost-conscious and forgot new business. Then the new drive was to get new business. Everyone went out to get new business and neglected internal relationships. The next frantic drive was human relations. One drive followed another. Cynicism became pervasive until people would no longer support a drive. Their energies were diverted into politicking, polarizing, and protecting turf.

This can also happen in families. Too many families are managed on the basis of quick fix, instant gratification, not on sound principles and rich emotional bank accounts. Then, when stress and pressure mount, people start yelling, over-reacting, or being cynical, critical or silent. Children see it and think this is the way you solve problems — either fight or flight. And the cycle can be passed on for generations.

This is why we recommend that you have a family mission statement as well. By drafting a family constitution, you are getting to the root of the problem. If you want to get anywhere long-term, identify core values and goals and get the systems aligned with these values and goals. Work on the foundation. Make it secure. The core of any family is what is changeless, what is always going to be there. This can be represented in a family mission statement. Ask yourself, "What do we value? What is our family all about? What do we stand for? What is our essential mission, our reason for being?" If you identify your essential purpose and set up shared vision and values, you can be successful with any situation that comes along. The mission excites people. It gets them to deal with problems and to talk them through in a mature and reasonable way, rather than fight or flight. If there is a dream, a mission, a vision, it will permeate that organization and shape its actions.

Principles are timeless, universal laws that empower people. Individuals who think in terms of principles think of many applications and are empowered to solve problems under a myriad of different conditions and circumstances. On the other hand, people who think in terms of practices tend to be limited in effectiveness to specific conditions under which the practice is effective.

Principles have infinite applications, as varied as circumstances. They tend to be self-validating, self-evident, universal truths. When we start to recognize a correct principle, it becomes so familiar to us, it is almost like "common sense." The danger is that we may cast it off early instead of looking deeply into how the specific principle may be valuable in our current circumstance.

This can be easily seen when we talk about the principles involved in developing personal and corporate "constitutions." There are certain underlying principles which are applied whether in the life of an individual or of an organization. Processes grow out of principles and give life to principles.

A mission statement helps people achieve success because it answers key questions like, "What do I want to do? What do I want to be?" Becoming the kind of person you want to be and doing the things that you desire to do actually define success.

The same is true with an organization. Unless organizations have some identity, some compelling mission, they accomplish far less that they might. To accomplish things based on objectives is not enough. To unleash the productivity in an organization, the focus needs to be on, not only what do you want to do, but what do you want to be. Thus, the corporate constitution deals with the questions of why.

For example, our firm has done some work with Walt Disney Imagineering. Initially, of course, Walt was the catalyst for the whole Disney organization. Since his death over 20 years ago, the

Disney Corporation has worked to complete his ambitious dream, the Epcot Center. After completing the center, the production and design team went from 2,200 engineers, artists and technicians to around 500. Morale was low.

To create new growth a group prepared a mission statement for the company, but few bought into it because they weren't involved. They then began a several-month process of writing a mission statement, involving all levels of the organization. Today they are motivated by a new mission. The spirit of the new Disney approach is: "We seek not to imitate the masters; rather, we seek what they sought." Clearly this was needed to move forward.

A corporate mission statement provides meaning for the enterprise. Meaning is the challenging need of the modern worker. It's not enough to work to eat or stay on the job because you're treated well. Nor is it enough to have an opportunity to contribute your talents and to unleash some of your potential. People want to know why. Meaning is the essential ingredient in modern times to organizational success.

The same thing applies to nations. The Declaration of Independence, the Constitution of our country, define what we're about, what we're trying to achieve and why. The underlying principles of constitutionalism, individualism, and volunteerism are still the cornerstones of our society. Many things that we value are manifest in the Declaration of Independence and the Constitution.

How to Write Your Own Constitution

There are some specific steps individuals and companies must go through in developing a constitution: first, expand perspective; second, clarify values; third, test it against yourself; and fourth, test yourself against it.

Expand perspective. We become so involved, both individually and organizationally, with the day-to-day preparations of life that it's usually necessary to stand back to gain or expand perspective and remind ourselves what really matters.

These "perspective experiences" may be planned or unplanned.

Unplanned experiences may include the death of a loved one, a severe illness, a financial setback, or extreme adversity. At such times, we stand back and look at our lives and try to ask ourselves some hard questions. What do we consider to be really important? Why are we doing what we're doing? If we didn't have to do what we do to get money, what would we do? Through this self-evaluation process, we tend to expand our perspective.

Proactive people can expand their perspective through such planned experiences as gathering the views of others involved in the organization or situation. They start contemplating, "What is most important to the organization? What contribution can we make? What is the meaning of what we do? What are we about? What do we want to be? What do we want to do? The many views expand perspective. As individuals search for the best within them and the best within the organization, real synergy takes place. Synergy is the process of valuing the differences and creating the best possible solution.

"Management by wandering around," a common practice at Hewlett Packard, is another good way to expand views on the organization. Often people are reluctant to provide much open information because they do not feel part of the governing body of the organization; they question whether their values or their views are really needed or appreciated; or they feel at risk in sharing those views. One way to overcome this reluctance is to put together some questions and have buzz groups discuss them and submit their findings. Those can be compiled, considered, and responded to. When people see that what they contribute is taken seriously, they tend to want to contribute more.

This process of expanding perspective, of gathering the views of others, and trying to get a handle on what is the best, highest, and noblest within the organization, is a process that should not be rushed. It takes time, several months in a large organization.

Clarify values. After perspective has been expanded and many new views contemplated, some individuals need to be charged with the responsibility to write a draft of an organizational mission statement, taking into account what has been gathered, and seen, and shared so far.

This draft then needs to be sent back to the members of the organization, with the caption, "We don't like it either." It is the exact wording that clarifies and gives tremendous focus to the mission statement. One that is not well defined and refined will not be as valuable and useful in decision making. The best mission statements are the result of people coming together in a spirit of mutual respect, expressing their different views, and working together to create something greater than any one individual could do alone.

Test it against yourself. Take a more final draft of the mission statement or constitution and test it by asking, "Is this in harmony with my values, with the things that motivate me? Does it capture the heart and soul of the company? Does it represent the best within the organization?

Think of the constitution in terms of two overlapping circles. One circle can represent the value system of the organization and the other circle can represent the value system of individuals. The more the circles of the individuals and the organization overlap, the more effective the organization tends to become. The mission statement needs to be tested for fit.

Test yourself against it. After the mission statement has been through this process, most people now need a chance to live with it for a while and to test the organization against it. Since these shared values are the heart and soul of the company, all policies, programs, strategies, structure and systems should be in harmony with them.

Over time, this process of writing and refining a mission statement becomes a key way to improve the organization. You do it periodically to expand perspective, shift emphasis or direction, amend or give new meaning to time-worn phrases.

By having a constitution, you have continuity. This is one of the major benefits of managing and leading by a mission statement developed by a participative process. It provides long-term continuity and helps executives maintain a long-term competitive advantage because they have direction and purpose. And, when individual values are harmonized with those of the organization, people work together for common purposes that are deeply felt. They contribute more as a team than they would individually. Productivity doesn't just get a little better, it gets dramatically better.

An On-going Process

As you change and grow, your perspective and values may undergo metamorphosis. It's important that you keep your mission statement current and congruent with your values. Here are some questions to help you.

- Is my mission statement based on proven principles that I currently believe in?

- Do I feel this represents the best within me?

- Do I feel direction, purpose, challenge and motivation when I review this statement?

- Am I aware of the strategies and skills that will help me accomplish what I have written?

- What do I need to do now to be where I want to be tomorrow?

Keep in mind that you can never build a life greater than its most noble purpose. Your constitution can help you be your best and perform your best each day.

Chapter 31

Organize Around Shared Values and Goals

I was once asked to conduct a training program for all managers and sales people in a large retail organization made up of several stores. The top management, after extensive fact gathering and analysis, had concluded that the sales people needed to upgrade their professionalism, their knowledge of the products, and their methods of influencing people.

Surveys showed that the sales people were often rude, abrupt, and officious — and management thought they needed to learn some good human relations skills.

Immediately, I questioned their conclusions. "What is the root cause of these symptoms?" I asked. "Is it lack of skills, or is the problem structural and systemic?"

I also questioned their data. Their primary source of information was customer survey, interpreted by themselves. Since this data really didn't get at the cause, I continued to press them for more data.

"Who are your top sales people?" I asked.

In almost every instance, the department heads were selling the most. This pleased top management, because they had often said that sales was the primary role of department heads, that they should only spend about a fourth of their time in administrative and supervisory duties and the rest of their time in sales. And so top management was delighted that these department heads were "such good models," being the top sales people in almost every case.

That was a major red flag to me. I wondered why the department heads were also the top sales people, and so I did my own anonymous survey among the sales people. A basic theme emerged and reoccurred so often that it became painfully obvious: the problem was not lack of skill and professionalism but rather the real problem was with the structure and system.

"Creaming" was the word sales people used to describe how the company was structured and how the compensation system worked. Everyone was paid individual commission on top of the base salary. Department heads were making the most sales because they would stand behind the cash register during slow periods and "cream" all the sales that would come in, delegating all the "dirty duties" to the sales people.

Essentially, this was a win-lose structure and compensation system. Sales people were demoralized because of it, and their attitudes were reflected in their treatment of customers.

The problem was in the compensation system, not in the sales people. People problems can take a long time to correct, but structure and system problems can be corrected almost immediately. This problem was corrected overnight, and once corrected, the attitudes of sales people started to improve. Moreover, these same people started developing more effective ways of selling, which required some training. Of course, they were then eager for training and benefited enormously from it. But it took a change in the compensation system (toward the win-win principle) to instill such a mindset.

What was the change? We simply put department heads on a group incentive system, meaning they made money themselves only when their sales people were making money. It was a very simple change, and yet the net effect within a few weeks was that everyone was making more money, including the company.

Sacred Cows & Scapegoats

This scenario is played out daily in one organization after another, whenever top management misperceives the underlying cause of a problem.

All too often, managers look upon structure and system as "sacred cows," and yet they are constantly trying to shape up people.   In fact, one executive recently introduced me to a group of his people gathered for a training seminar by saying, "Now, all of you need this, so pay good attention and get it!" He then walked out of the room.

It is my experience that whenever people are undergoing training, they are saying inside themselves, "The people who really need this aren't here."   But I have concluded that about half the time, the real problem has little to do with people, even the ones who "aren't here" (the scapegoats).   It usually has a lot to do with the structure and the systems of the company (the sacred cows): with whether or not they are supportive of company values and goals.

In their book, *In Search of Excellence*, Tom Peters and Bob Waterman indicate that their research design is based on the McKinsey 7-S consulting model:

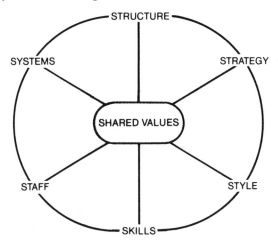

Like the hub of a wheel, shared values constitute the center of this circular model. That's as it should be. Shared values powerfully influence and shape the strategy, structure and systems (hard S's), as well as the staff, skills and management style (soft S's) of an organization.

When I apply the McKinsey model to organizations, I find it most illuminating to ask, "How interrelated and interdependent are these seven S's? Is there a set of common values and goals at the center? If so, do the other six elements complement these? Is there a resulting harmony and synergy in the company as a whole?"

These are critical questions. Consider, for instance, how important to a great orchestra are shared values and goals — and a common desire to work together harmoniously in order to produce beautiful music. If one important element in the symphony is amiss or missing, it dramatically affects the quality of the production. If the conductor's style were adversarial, combative or confrontive, or if the motivations of the orchestra members were to stand out individually rather than blend in harmoniously, the result would be cacophony or noise.

On the other hand, if there is a deeply internalized set of values and goals in all members of the organization, and the other six S's are harmoniously working together, marvelous synergy — beautiful music — will result.

Six Reinforcing Systems

Let's now discuss some of the most fundamental systems of organizations and the principles that must undergird these systems if they are to be effective and harmonious with other systems so as to produce organizational synergy.

The win-win agreement is part and parcel of the performance, planning and review system. This "psychological contract," together with the one-on-one visit that establishes it, is the single most important system, because it sets up the constitutions, the rules, the agreements from which other systems form.

Let's now look at six other systems common to most organizations.

1. Information. The key here is to achieve accuracy and balance and eliminate bias. This is virtually impossible if financial accounting is the primary or only information system in the organization. To have a balanced picture of what is happening, executives must supplement financial or physical resource accounting with human resource accounting or Stake-holder Information Systems — a system that tells you what is happening inside the organization and inside the minds and hearts of all stake-holders. The more accurate, complete, current and relevant the data, the better it is for decision-making. Good data makes for good decisions (assuming wise judgment).

2. Compensation. There are at least four kinds of compensation: money, recognition, opportunity and other perks of position and office, and responsibility. We might condense these four into two: financial and psychic (psychic would include opportunity, responsibility and recognition). An effective compensation system has both financial and psychic rewards built into it. It rewards synergistic cooperation and creates a team spirit. It is based on performance, and on clear, up-front, win-win agreements — not on seniority and credentials. "Pay for performance" means that the people who produce the profits share in the profits.

3. Training and Development. Effective training and development programs are characterized by four features. First, the learner is responsible for the learning, and the instructor and institution are seen as helpful resources. Second, the training is learner-controlled rather than system-controlled, meaning the learner can go at his or her own pace and choose the methods for meeting the mutually agreeable objectives. Third, the learner is required to teach what is learned, as teaching the material to a third party greatly reinforces commitment while improving retention. And, fourth, there is a close correlation between the goals of the training program and the career plans of each individual.

4. Recruiting and Selecting. When companies are organized around shared values and goals, people are recruited and selected systematically. Their values, abilities, aptitudes and interests are married with the requirements of the job. What they enjoy doing, and do well, is closely related to what they do for the company. The interviewing and screening process is based on the win-win principle: hiring must be in the best interests of both parties. This means personnel directors and their staff members explore work records in depth (testing may also be appropriate) to detect patterns. These should match the patterns for success in the particular industry. Discrepancies should be openly discussed. And, before making a decision to hire, promote, demote, or fire, a manager should seek counsel, in confidence, from respected colleagues and supervisors.

5. Job Design. Just as homes are designed to meet the needs and individual tastes of people, so should jobs be designed in order to tap as many of the interests and skills of people as possible. People should have a clear sense of what the job is about, how it relates to the overall mission of the company, and what their personal contribution could be. They also need to know what resource and support systems are available to them. They then should enjoy some degree of autonomy in determining what methods to use to get desired results. Feedback, like the wiring in a home, should be built in from the beginning, as well as provisions for growth and new opportunity.

6. Communication. One-on-one visits — with the purpose of working out the win-win agreement and reporting on progress — are important keys to effective organizational communications. Of course, other elements are also needed. These might include regular staff meetings with agendas and action-oriented minutes; employee suggestion systems that reward ideas that result in savings; open-door and due-process policies and procedures; annual skip-level interviews; anonymous opinion surveys; and *ad hoc* committee brainstorming.

All of these systems — and any others that are in place within the organization — will function more effectively if they are planned and organized around shared values and goals.

Chapter 32

Transformational vs. Transactional Leadership

One of the more popular lines of toys for children in past years has been the Transformers. These colorful units are really two toys in one: they change like chameleons from one thing to another — from robot to jet plane, for example — simply by maneuvering certain parts.

In the corporate world, "transformers" are also quite popular. At least, in the management magazines, one encounters them virtually on every page — and with good reason. "We all have a need to reinvent what we're up to," says John Naisbitt. "It's a matter of survival."

Certainly the world is undergoing revolutionary changes. Any careful observer will note the metamorphosis that is taking place in virtually every industry and profession. In *The Aquarium Conspiracy*, author Marilyn Ferguson describes it as a great shuddering, an irrevocable shift, a new mind — a turnabout "in consciousness in critical numbers of individuals, a network powerful enough to bring about radical change in our culture."

It is a change so fast, so profound, so complete, that it will almost overwhelm the careful observer. Reportedly, more change will take place in the next few years than has taken place in the past few centuries. And yet, some people are oblivious to it. Like fish who discover water last, they fail to perceive the obvious. They do not sense the difference between then and now, today and tomorrow.

In my opinion, these revolutionary changes will alter forever the way many companies operate. People and products that are not in touch with these changes will fast become obsolete.

249

Transforming with the Trends

While some cynics may accept obsolescence as an inevitable consequence of change, proactive executives innovate and increase market share. The trick is first to identify the trends and then to transform with the trends.

For example, *PC Magazine* reported that the microcomputer, even more than the mainframe and minicomputer before it, will "transform computing, those who use computers, and even the nature of our society and life in this century."

The "megacomputing trends" suggest that by the end of this century "there will be a computer on almost every desk — and at least as many computers as TV sets in the home. The personal computer will increase personal productivity by 20 percent; executives will begin using the computer more enthusiastically; and voice input will play an important role — transforming every telephone into a full-fledged computer terminal for both input and output."

The effective executive will note the computing trends and make necessary transformations. Many social observers are describing the "megatrends" and giving us a sense of how dynamic and radical these changes are. To simplify matters, I will consider three categories — economic, technological, and social/cultural — and contrast traditional and emerging patterns within these categories.

Traditional	**Emerging**
Economic	
Industrial-age rules	Information-age rules
Stable economy	Uncertain economy
Stable markets/suppliers	Fluid markets/suppliers
Assembly-line production	Personalized delivery of services
Domestic competition	International competition
Brawnpower	Brainpower
Technological	
Mechanical technology	Electronic technology
Predictable technological innovation (10 years)	Rapid, unpredictable technological innovation (18 months)

Social/Cultural

Acceptance of authoritarian hierarchical roles	Rising expectation of employee involvement
Stable male workers	Women, minorities, baby boomers
Growing birthrates	Declining birthrates
Externally driven/material values	Internally driven/quality-of-life values
Corporate drift from dominant social/economic values	The reaffirmation of dominant social/economic values

The scope and scale of these emerging trends require leaders of organizations to adopt a transformational style.

Implications for Managers and Executives

Implied in these changes is the need for a major shift in management thought and practice. Many companies and their managers are not transforming with the trends. For example, our society values democracy, and yet most companies practice autocracy; our society values capitalism, but many organizations practice feudalism. While our society has shifted to pluralism, many companies seek homogeneity. Perhaps the most fundamental need is to understand man's full nature. Motivational theory has shifted its orientation from stomach (physical and economic) to heart (good human relations, good treatment) to mind (identify, develop, use, recognize talent) to spirit (a sense of transcending purpose or meaning).

An enlarged concept of man's nature triggers another shift in the role of the manager from hero to developer, from commander to consultant, from order-giver to mentor, from decision-maker to value-clarifier and exemplar. The new manager is moving away from confrontive dialogue to empathic dialogue, from retaining power to sharing power, from adversarial relationships (win-lose) to collaborative relationships based on mutual interests (win-win).

We might think of this "paradigm shift" in terms of a continuum with external control on one side and internal control or commitment on the other side — from superficial human relations to full utilization of human resources.

The new leader is learning to "read" each situation and to adapt accordingly. An excellent model of this new leadership style is Ken Blanchard's *Situational Leadership II.* As he describes it, this model suggests that the leader must adapt his style to suit the ability and maturity (competence and commitment) of his people. Such a leader must have good diagnostic skills, a large repertoire of management styles, and the courage and flexibility to use the appropriate one.

Personal Precedes Organizational Change

It's almost axiomatic to say that personal change must precede or at least accompany management and organizational change; otherwise, the duplicity and doublemindedness will breed cynicism and instability. Life's imperative is to grow or die, stretch or stagnate.

Attempting to change an organization or a management style without first changing one's own habit patterns is analogous to attempting to improve one's tennis game before developing the muscles that make better strokes possible. Some things necessarily precede other things. We cannot run before we can walk, or walk before we can crawl. Neither can we change our management styles without changing personal habits.

Psychologist William James suggested that to change personal habits, we first make a deep internal commitment to pay whatever price is necessary to change the habit; second, we grasp the very first opportunity to use the new practice or skill; and third, we allow no exceptions until the new habit is firmly imbedded into our nature.

Of course, change – whether personal or organizational – carries some degree of risk. Because of that risk and the fear of failure, many people resist change. Those who adapt well to changing environments generally have a set of changeless values within them and are congruent in behavior with those values. This integrity boosts their self-esteem and provides a bedrock of security from which they deal effectively with changing circumstances.

Companies on the "cutting edge" often enjoy a competitive advantage. Not surprisingly, these are often young companies, trend-setters.

While well-established companies like U.S. Steel or General Motors won't transform in the same way, all companies must, as John Naisbitt says, "reinvent" or transform themselves. Those driven by momentum and memory may find themselves going right over a cliff.

Transformational vs. Transactional Leadership

Transformational leadership is not the same as transactional leadership. The former basically means that we change the realities of our particular world to more nearly conform to our values and ideals. The latter focuses on an efficient interaction with the changing realities.

Transformational leadership focuses on the "top line" and is value-centered. Transactional leadership focuses on the bottom line and is event-centered. Transformational and transactional leadership may be contrasted in other ways, as the chart shows.

Transformational Leadership
- Builds on man's need for meaning;
- Is preoccupied with purposes and values, morals, and ethics;
- Transcends daily affairs,
- Is oriented toward meeting long-term goals without compromising human values and principles;
- Separates causes and symptoms and works at prevention;
- Values profit as the basis of growth;
- Is proactive, catalytic, and patient;
- Focuses more on missions and strategies for achieving them;
- Makes full use of human resources;
- Identifies and develops new talent;
- Recognizes and rewards significant contributions;
- Designs and redesigns jobs to make them meaningful and challenging;
- Releases human potential;
- Models love;
- Leads out in new directions;
- Aligns internal structures and systems to reinforce overarching values and goals.

Transactional Leadership
- Builds on man's need to get a job done and to make a living;
- Is preoccupied with power and position, politics, and perks;
- Is mired in daily affairs;
- Is short-term- and hard-data-oriented;
- Confuses causes and symptoms and concerns itself more with treatment than prevention;
- Focuses on tactical issues;
- Relies on human relations to lubricate human interactions;
- Follows and fulfills role expectations by striving to work effectively within current systems;
- Supports structures and systems that reinforce the bottom line, maximize efficiency, and guarantee short-term profits.

Obviously, both kinds of leadership are necessary. But transformational leadership must be the parent as it provides the frame of reference, the strategic boundaries within which transactions take place. Without an overarching system of values and goals and without a clear picture of what kind of transformation is needed, executives and their managers will tend to operate on social and political agendas and timetables.

The goal of transformational leadership is to "transform" people and organizations in a very literal sense — to change them in mind and heart; enlarge vision, insight, and understanding; clarify purposes; make behavior congruent with beliefs, principles, or values; and bring about changes which are permanent, self-perpetuating, and momentum-building.

I am personally convinced that one person can be a change catalyst, a "transformer" in any situation, any organization. Such an individual is yeast that can leaven an entire loaf. Transformational leadership requires vision, initiative, patience, respect, persistence, courage and faith.

Chapter 33

A Pattern for Excellence

It's high time for many individuals and companies to make a quantum leap in performance, a healthy change of habits, a major shift in patterns; otherwise, it's business as usual — and that's simply not cutting it anymore.

Victor Hugo once said, "there is nothing so powerful as an idea whose time has come."

When the book *In Search of Excellence* took this country by storm, capturing the imaginations of people throughout our society, it was a clear indication that the time had come for the idea and the ideal of excellence.

The question now is "how?" — how do we change to achieve excellence?

I have found that if you want to improve a little, change your attitude or behavior. But if you want to improve in major ways — I mean dramatic, revolutionary, transforming ways — if you want to make quantum improvements, either as an individual or as an organization, change your frame of reference. Change how you see the world, how you think about people, how you view management and leadership.

I'm suggesting that you change your *paradigm*, your scheme for understanding and explaining certain aspects of reality.

For example, suppose we have a street map of Los Angeles. It gives us a certain paradigm of the city. It is most helpful in finding our way around. But suppose you are in business, and you are more interested in identifying high tech businesses in the city. That street map is just about worthless to you. You need a new paradigm, a different kind of map, a map of the business community.

Thomas Kuhn introduced the idea of "paradigm shifts" in his landmark work, *The Structure of Revolutions*. Basically, he concluded that every significant breakthrough is a breakwith. In other words, the scientific community had a certain paradigm of the way things were, a map of the territory. But a lot of the data couldn't be explained. And a lot of purposes could not be served. So they needed to get another map, another paradigm. And as soon as the paradigm shifted, it opened up a whole new area of insight and knowledge and understanding, resulting in a quantum difference in performance.

Again, if you want to make small improvements, change your attitude or behavior. If you want to make fundamental, deep, revolutionary, transforming, quantum improvements, change your paradigm — shift your frame of reference.

Consider the following three examples from history.

• Throughout the ages, hundreds of thousands have died of disease and infection. In war, for every man killed in battle, dozens more lost their lives to disease and infection. Likewise, in childbirth, thousands of mothers and newborn babies have lost their lives. The problem was that medical doctors were slow to accept the paradigm-shifting notion that fermentation, putrefaction, infection and disease could be caused by bacteria too small to see. It wasn't until Louis Pasteur in France and Philip Semmelveiss in Austria and others changed the paradigm in the minds of physicians that medical science made any significant progress against disease and infection.

• It was a paradigm shift that gave birth to this land of freedom. When Thomas Jefferson wrote in the *Declaration of Independence* that government derives its just powers from the consent of the governed, he and those who signed that document set up a new pattern of government. There would be no divine right to rule on this land. No imposed overlords. The only public officials would be those chosen by the voice of the people. Out of that paradigm has come the freest people and the most prosperous country in the history of the world.

- Using the wrong paradigm has crippled entire nations. In 1588, Spain was the most powerful nation in Europe. Its coffers were full of gold from the New World, and her ships were the mightiest vessels on the seven seas. But the English weren't intimidated, and when the remains of Spain's proud Armada limped back into port, it was obvious that the paradigm had shifted. The nimble ships and resourceful, innovative English captains were the new rulers of the waves.

In our day, we have seen similar shifts in the business world and from some of the same causes. Some of the world's mightiest corporations have put their trust in their cash reserves, capital assets, technologies, strategies, and buildings, only to witness, as did the Spaniards, smaller companies with a different paradigm — one better suited to the current marketplace — humble them in their battle for customers.

Think of the paradigm shifts in your own life. If you are married, remember what it was like to be single. What happened to your paradigm of life when you married? If you have served in the military, remember when your name and role were changed as you progressed from private to officer. You see an entirely new world. You view your responsibilities differently. You look at life through a new paradigm — a new map — resulting in fundamental, dramatic, revolutionary changes. If you are a grandparent, remember when your first grandchild came? You were called by a new name and perceived a new role.

Having a new name and role, a new paradigm, your behavior and your attitudes shift dramatically. In fact, the fastest way to change people's paradigm is to change their name or their role.

Remember what it was like when you first became a manager? Didn't you begin to see everything differently. And that was a revolutionary change. The same problems we complained about before, we saw differently as we assumed the responsibility to resolve them.

Crises, too, can bring about paradigm shifts, as we are forced to determine what our priorities in life really are. For example, consider the case of Anwar Sadat. When he was president of Egypt, he swore in front of millions of people on television, "I will never shake the hand of an Israeli as long as they occupy one inch of Arab soil. Never, Never, Never." And the crowds would chant, "never, never, never." But in his heart, Sadat knew that he was living in a perilous, interdependent world.

Fortunately, he had previously learned how to work with his own mind and heart to bring about a paradigm shift inside himself. He learned it as a young man while he was imprisoned in a solitary cell in the Cairo Central Prison. He learned how to get into a meditative state of mind, to look at the program in his head against the reality of the day, and to bring about within himself a paradigm shift to see the whole situation differently. And this eventually led him to that unprecedented bold peace initiative at Tel Aviv and to the peace process which eventually resulted in the Camp David Accord.

What has all of this got to do with management and leadership? I suggest that it strikes at the very heart of the matter. I submit that if we focus our attention on techniques, on specific practices, on to-do lists, on present pressures, we might make some small improvements. But if we want to move ahead in a major way, we need to shift our paradigm and see the situation in a totally new way.

Four Management Paradigms

I'd like to suggest four basic management paradigms and suggest that while each of them has its merit, three of them are fundamentally flawed.

First, the scientific management paradigm. Using this paradigm, we see people primarily as stomachs (economic beings). If that's my view of my people, my task as a manager is to motivate them through the great jackass method, the carrot and the stick — the carrot in front to entice and intrigue them, lead them to their benefits, and the stick behind. Notice that I am in control. I am the authority. I am the elite one. I know what is best. I will direct you where to go, and I will do it through the carrot and stick. Of course, I must be fair with the economic rewards and the benefit package. But it's all designed to meet the needs of one's stomach.

Second, the human relations paradigm. We acknowledge that people are not only stomachs but also hearts (social beings). We see that people have feelings. Hence, we treat people not only with fairness, but with kindness, with courtesy, with civility, with decency. But it may only mean a shift from being an authoritarian to being a benevolent authoritarian because we still are the elite few who know what's best. The power still lies with us, but we are kind to people as well as fair.

Third, the human resource paradigm. Here we work not only with fairness and kindness but also with efficiency. We see that people have minds in addition to stomachs and hearts. In other words, people are cognitive, thinking beings. With this larger understanding of man's nature, we begin to make better use of their talent, creativity, resourcefulness, ingenuity, imagination. We begin to delegate more, realizing that people will do what's necessary if they're committed to a particular goal. We begin to see people — their hearts and minds — as the main resource. Not capital assets, not physical properties, but people. We begin to explore ways to create an optimal environment, a culture which taps their talents and releases their creative energy. We recognize that people want to make meaningful contributions. They want their talents identified, developed, utilized and recognized.

Fourth, the whole person paradigm. Now we work with fairness, kindness, efficiency and effectiveness. We see that people are not just resources or assets, not just economic, social, and psychological beings, but also spiritual. They want meaning, a sense of doing something that matters. People do not want to work for a cause with little meaning, even though it taps their mental capacities to their fullest. There must be purposes that lift them, ennoble them, and bring them to their highest self.

Using this paradigm, we manage people by a set of proven principles. And what are these principles? They are the natural laws and governing social values that have gradually come through every great society, every responsible civilization over the centuries. They surface in the form of values, ideas, ideals, norms, and teachings that uplift, ennoble, fulfill, empower, and inspire people.

Tom Peters suggests that as the center of power shifts away from the elite authoritarian group — however benevolent they may be — to people, every person, including people on the lowest rung of the corporate ladder, experiences dramatic benefits.

It's nothing less than a 180-degree shift in the way we think about managing and leading. The models and the metaphors of the past have been the manager as a cop, as a referee, as a devil's advocate, as a nay-sayer, as a pronouncer. The words that we found that seem much more appropriate in the excellent companies are the manager, the leader, as a cheer-leader, as a coach, as a facilitator, as a nurturer of champions. The drum beat, and the drum beat that has been so sadly missing, was it all comes from people.

Most surveys in organizations show that people want to be managed by the human resource and the whole person paradigms. They want meaning and purpose in their life. They want their bosses to manage them by principles. But they want the people who report to them to respond to the human relations paradigm. In other words, "I want you (up there) to ask for my opinion, but I want you (down there) to go along with my opinion like a good soldier. Be cooperative and helpful and go along."

The scientific management (stomach) paradigm says, "Pay me well." The human relations (heart) paradigm says, "Treat me well." The human resource (mind) paradigm suggests, "Use me well." The management by principles (whole person) paradigm says: "Let's talk values and goals. I want to make a meaningful contribution."

I suggest that we cultivate the *management by principles* paradigm, which not only embraces the principles of fairness and kindness and makes better use of the talents of people for increased efficiency, but also leads to quantum leaps in personal and organizational effectivenesss.

Chapter 34

Masters of Excellence

From Pinehurst to Pebble Beach, amateur and pro golfers alike seem to share a common attitude: "I'm really a better player than my scores indicate. Once I figure out what's wrong, I'll be back in the money."

Some players have been trying to "figure it out" for years, not realizing that lasting success depends largely on learning and applying a set of correct principles from the outset.

From my experience in executive training and development, I conclude: Build your game on a solid foundation of values and principles and skills, and your future efforts will lead to continued improvement. Build on misconceptions, misinformation, and bad habits, and you will spend a lifetime in fruitless hit-and-miss searching.

The great golfers know how important it is to master the fundamentals. Notes Jack Nicklaus: "After months of tournament pressure, I find that parts of my swing have changed. If I were to continue from year to year without pausing to reevaluate my game, I could multiply my mistakes."

Management, like golf, is a game of building upon the basics, one skill at a time. If your basic skills are weak, your whole game may collapse. Managers, therefore, are advised: "Start every new season by reviewing each part of your swing — grip, stance, head position and the direction your feet are pointing. Get an objective view — a mirror or a second person. Some things you can correct yourself; others will require the help of a pro. Sometimes, by making minor adjustments, you can shave several strokes from the scorecard."

To score well consistently, golfing professionals play the percentages and observe the basic principles of the game.

Sadly, most newcomers to the sport want to skip over the fundamentals, get out on the course quickly, and take their swings. They have little patience for conditioning, training, practicing. Experienced golfers know that there is no shortcut to developing the capability to handle with excellence any situation that might occur on the course.

The Masters Course

I designed an executive course that would feature a natural, progressive development of leadership skills and character traits. The idea was to build slowly and sequentially on an integrated curriculum in an attempt to educate the whole person to "score" well consistently against tough competition.

In designing *The Masters of Executive Excellence*, I carefully reviewed the popular success literature and discovered that many trainers and consultants have severed management from its character roots, giving rise to manipulative influence techniques. I further recognized that management training could be fundamentally improved by integrating personal development with team effectiveness and organizational productivity.

The Masters stresses both timeless principles and timely applications. It contrasts crisis management — the short-term fix — with character, skill and system development — the long-term solution. Unlike many programs, *The Masters* promotes less dependence on the trainers, more interdependence among team players.

Henry David Thoreau wrote: "For every thousand hacking at the leaves of evil, there is one striking at the root." The masters dedicate themselves to striking at the root, getting at the very heart of what ails individuals and institutions. Their goal is to help build winning teams.

Playing the Course

Great golfers play to a specific target; poor golfers play in a general direction. Great golfers play the course; poor golfers play the opposition.

My advice to management: "Don't play your opponent — play the course. The course is your most formidable opponent. Learn to play the course the way it is laid out. Winning golf is not simply standing on the tee, sighting the flag, and then blasting away. Look for ways to avoid trouble in advance. If possible, walk around the course before playing. At least, look ahead or pace ahead to gauge distance and direction. Preplanning and preparation give you an extra edge."

Duffers become deeply involved with a target only when they are close to the green. The rest of the time they are more concerned with the details of their swings than the goals of their shots. Professionals think of their target before and during every stroke. They trust their body and mind to perform as conditioned in practice and visualization.

The strategy of the masters is to plot a course of action that avoids trouble spots and keeps the ball in the fairway in favorable position for the next shot. Professionals play a disciplined game. They know that the true test of their intelligence comes in managing a course wisely — from tee to green, concept to delivery — and in making their share of pressure putts. Their strategy capitalizes on personal and organizational strengths, not on the weaknesses of the competition.

Such a game requires sensitivity, savvy, skill, foresight, follow-through. It also demands honesty. An image may be stylish or fashionable, but it should never be false. In today's competitive tournaments, those who foolishly attempt to substitute expediency for priority, imitation for innovation, cosmetics for character, or pretense for competence will almost always be found and ferreted out.

Hitting from the Rough

The aim of a master trainer is to help you keep in play, place in the money, recover from rough times, and score well consistently in major tournaments.

But in spite of good intention and training, all players occasionally get in trouble. My experience suggests that the best thing to do is seek a direct route to safety. Sacrificing a single stroke isn't the end of the world — or your round. Trouble turns into disaster when a player tries to follow one bad shot with a miraculous recovery that he or she lacks the talent and resource to produce.

Indeed, with just one faulty swing, a player may find himself alone in a crowd, off camera, out of the money, enduring ridicule from the gallery, hacking at a half-buried ball, cursing a bad lie, blasting out of a trap, or even wading into water — all the while fighting the urge to make it up by going for broke, shooting for the pin in spite of the odds.

Golfing masters suggest that when a ball is buried in deep rough, a player should use a more lofted club and make the angle of attack steeper to reduce the amount of resistance the clubhead must encounter before impact. Likewise, the masters of management can make masterful recoveries by reducing resistance and coping expertly with the elements and other hazards.

Winds (social and business trends) can be particularly troublesome. Don't attempt to fight against them. And don't be fooled by surface winds, as these may not reflect what is happening in the line of flight. To be sure, look up. Check the clubhouse flag and keep in touch with the corporate mission.

Putting to Win

From tee to green, most professionals are fairly even; tournaments are won and lost on the greens. From the textbook, we read: "The basic law is to putt with a purpose. Simply slapping the ball with the blade of your putter without having a plan in mind is like playing pin-the-tail-on-the-donkey blindfolded. Good putting requires correct reading of the greens — an art acquired through practice and course play. It means studying the terrain between your ball and the hole and determining how this will affect your putt. To hold the line on short breaking putts, use a firm bold stroke."

Why do the greatest golfers in the world spend so many hours practicing their putting? They realize that putting is the most crucial part of their game because it often affects how well they perform elsewhere on the course. Making a long putt provides a tremendous psychological boost while missing a short putt can be demoralizing.

All management training should have as its purpose to measurably improve your "short game," the finesse strokes that can make such a difference in your bottom-line scoring. These, of course, include the finesse skills of people management.

An Executive Nine

An executive course should be designed to meet real needs and interests, as determined in part by preassessment. These typically fall into four areas of development: personal, interpersonal, managerial and organizational.

To help executives analyze their game and achieve their goals, I have adapted the McKenzie 7S model into a PS model. In golfing terms, it serves as "an executive nine," a short course for keeping on top of your game. As you can see, the PS model also embodies the four areas of development.

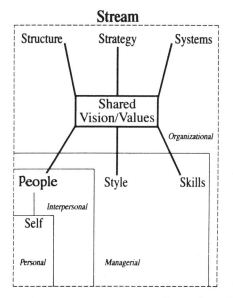

Self: While we have many concerns "out there," we learn that change must start within our "circle of influence," with those things we can control directly. In effect, change and improvement must begin with self.

People: Culture is the manifestation of the personal beliefs of people in three areas: how they see themselves, how they see their coworkers and how they see their organizations.

Style: Participative styles of management create more innovation, initiative and commitment but also more unpredictable behavior. Managers must weigh the benefits of participatory style against the predictability of high control. To talk participation but practice control only creates cynicism.

Skills: Such skills as delegation, communication, and time management are fundamental to high performance. Fortunately, these can be learned and enhanced through training.

Shared values/governing principles: What is the mission and how will we achieve it? Peak performers have a strong sense of mission and values, and in successful organizations, these values are widely shared and supported.

Strategy: The strategy should be congruent with the company mission, with available resources, and with market realities. Moreover, the strategy should be monitored and changed to reflect shifts in the wind, the status of the competition, and the current financial condition.

Structure: How people are positioned in the organization, their roles and goals. Structure should be flexible and follow strategy. Roles and goals should be clear.

Systems: The following six systems should operate in harmony with structure and strategy: information, compensation, training and development, recruiting and hiring, job design and communication. Rarely are these perfectly aligned, however, which leads to various "hooks" and "slices."

Streams: The operational environment needs to be monitored to make sure that strategy, shared values and systems are in harmony with it. If the "stream" changes while the strategy stays the same, a ball or two just might land in the water. And it's hard to win tournaments with penalty strokes.

In Conclusion

Every individual and organization we work with is, to some degree, in transition. Something significant is changing — their products and services, the market, their workforce or their management. Our objective is to empower people with the principles of leadership that will keep them centered on their game, responsive to change, and able to win.

In each Masters session, participants are challenged to apply the key principles in their own game plan. Among other things, they develop the vision, inspiration and courage to change what can and must be changed to make themselves, their management team and entire organization more effective, productive, unified.

Chapter 35

Fishing the Stream

For many years, I've subscribed to the following bit of philosophy:

Give a man a fish and you feed him for a day.
Teach him how to fish and you feed him for a lifetime.

It's an old axiom, but it's as timely as ever. In fact, we currently use the principle in our training. The goal is always to teach executives "how to fish" the stream for themselves.

Streams represent the environments — the ever-changing realities of the marketplace — that you and your organization are working in. You may be fishing many streams. These may include the corporate network, the parent industry, the market, the government, and the community. There are many currents and many streams that affect the success of your organization. To the degree that the strategy, systems, and shared values are in harmony with the streams, your organization is more likely to achieve success.

Rule One, Rule Two

On the surface, a stream appears easy enough to read, and, indeed, the fundamentals are quickly learned. But, as in fishing, the finer points can take a lifetime.

In teaching executives how to fish the stream, I often refer to a simple rule of thumb. I call it *Rule One, Rule Two*. The basic idea is that the shared values or governing principles of the organization ought to be primary considerations — that's *Rule One*. *Rule Two* suggests that everything else — the strategy, structure, systems, skills, and style — are derivatives, that is, they ought to flow with, not against, core values and stream realities.

271

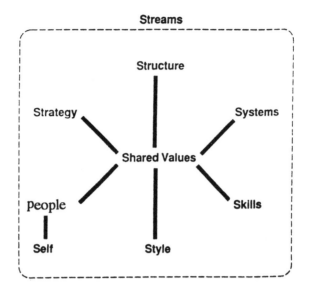

In this PS model, we see that the shared values are central and are considered in the context of the stream. To understand the derivatives, you have to study the source. In fact, executives who are clear on shared values (mission, roles and goals) can better afford to study the stream because they have something that never changes — their value system, their principles. They can afford to study the stream because their security does not come from the hard S's; their security comes from their value system.

But if organizations don't have a central value system based on correct principles, they build on a foundation of sand — their strategy, structure, and systems. It gives them a sense of security. But it's false security. They may have a nice set of flies and trophies on the wall, but all that doesn't matter much if they are out of "sync" with the stream. They will borrow strength from the past, and by doing so will build weakness.

After presenting the PS model and the idea of *Rule One, Rule Two* to executives at a large insurance company, they said, "We've got to build a fundamental security source of shared values in order to have the freedom and strength we need to change whatever we're doing that must be changed."

We have now helped them do that by getting them to formulate their mission statements. And once it gets into their minds and hearts, people won't go back to the old ways. It's also very unsettling and unpopular with some executives. One executive told me that he struggled with it, but he's coming to realize that he's got to manage by principles. It's the only way to "fish the stream" effectively over time.

Fishing & Managing

I've long been impressed with the many parallels between fishing and managing. In reality, senior level executives are really fishing the stream. That is, they're looking at the business in the context of the total environment and devising ways to "reel in" desired results.

As I see it, there are basically two ways to fish, reactively and proactively. The reactive method is a "waiting game," as described here by Gene Hill:

> *I like fly fishing as a nice way to pass time—waiting. It is a respectable thing to do as opposed to being purely idle, stretched out in a hammock or taking a nap on the couch. You at least look serious and industrious—a vest full of instruments, polarized glasses, wading staff and net, perhaps a small canvas creel and the busy little hum of the fly line slicking through the rod guides.*
>
> *"There," you say, "is a serious man," if you should see me poised like a heron in some stream. Far from it. There you see an idler in costume, a man wondering where the time went. Not the past hour or so while exchanging nods with a duck or mulling a two-penny philosophy about a mud-colored snake, but the past five or ten years. He is thinking about his work that has been left undone, his loves unknown, and that just yesterday, he was only a boy."*

In truth, some executives are like this fisherman — idlers in costume. On the other hand, proactive executives better fit the following description:

Consistently successful anglers are not locked into fixed responses to situations, rather they are flexible, constantly reading the water to discover the best place from which to cast into each lie. They, in fact, learn to think like a fish. Often they will approach the water slowly, keeping a low profile, perhaps even casting from a kneeling position."

That's sound advise for any angler: keep a low profile and kneel while casting. Here's more, right from the handbook:

Many contemporary anglers are imitationists with a penchant for minutiae and measurements and with an eye for surface details. But they might be better off if they never weighed, measured or recorded their catches. The experts are usually too busy fishing or observing to count and measure things.

Effective executives constantly read the stream. They look carefully at the business trends and the cultural "megatrends," since these are like the currents. They tune into knowledgeable forecasters — people like Naisbitt and Yankelovich — who monitor the stream and report periodically on current conditions. They get a sense for themselves of what the basic trends are and what will likely happen as a result of those trends.

All of this reading of trends in the environment, like the forecasting of weather, is done for a clear purpose: to better get through the day and prepare for what's to come tomorrow. If you're caught in a rainstorm by surprise, you can look pretty foolish. In a downpour, it's nice to have an umbrella and a water-repellent coat. Likewise, in a downturn, it's nice to have the right apparel and repellents to avoid getting soaked.

Back to the handbook:

Match line, leader and tackle to the type of fishing you do, taking into account such things as the speed of the current, the depth of the water, and the rate of retrieve. If you fish different waters, have more than one line. And give careful thought and attention to the leader, the most important link in the tackle system.

Once you see that the trends are starting to turn, the trick is to adapt — to make your internal operations harmonious with the external environment. The most important trends to look for are opportunities and threats. If the stream starts turning away from your product line, that's a threat. If the stream turns toward a new product line, a new technology, or new market, that's an opportunity. But an opportunity could be a threat if you don't adapt to it.

One of the main problems that I find with organizations is that they don't adapt their structure and systems to the stream. In fact, they're often looking at the stream through their existing structure and systems. Consequently, they don't know where the catch is. They don't see the threats and opportunities because they're looking through the wrong lens.

Even if they can sense a shift, they may be stuck with the wrong equipment, weighed down by high overhead, or burdened by bureaucracy. Whatever the reason, the result is the same — they can't move. Something — be it myopia or debt load or dead-wood "fat" — is keeping them from being flexible and having the freedom to move to adapt to a new stream.

Again, the handbook says:

To be successful over time, an angler must have some understanding of history, biology, geography, stream ecology and, of course, fishing strategy and tactics. Moreover, most could benefit from a crash course in entomology, because imitating the natural food source is the name of the game when fly fishing for trout. Trout are smart, tentative, cautious, hard to fool, and stubborn about not taking flies that look like Easter hats instead of caddis fly nymphs.

For example, it's not likely that General Motors was ignorant of the trends when the low-price, high-quality Japanese cars started gaining market share. Detroit was aware of the trend, but the main problem was that they had all of their systems, particularly their compensation systems for their top executives, geared toward selling big cars. So they continued to manufacture big cars to feed that system.

They didn't adapt to the stream, and their existing structure and systems were ill-suited to the new game — it was like playing golf with a tennis racket.

Now, in retrospect, GM executives are talking about how they've learned some hard lessons from the stream, and how they've gone through many years of team building to regain their competitiveness and recapture a measure of the world market. And they're saying that anybody who's really serious about competing long term is going to have to go through that kind of pain to get the gains. And it's true. Every industry — from steel to health care — must learn to fish the stream.

How? First, they should not look at the hard S's as being sacred cows. Those are all paper concepts, and they can be changed. They are programs. People often don't want to change them because it may mean leaving a comfort zone or entering uncharted waters. But not changing them may be the greatest risk of all.

Nothing Fails Like Success

I'm reminded of another axiom: nothing fails like success. We can abridge all of history into a simple formula: challenge/response. The successful response works to the challenges.

As soon as the stream changes, the challenge, the one successful response, no longer works. It fails. Nothing fails like success. It's intriguing, and it's true. Arnold Toynby documented it throughout history. He noted that as new challenges arise — as the stream changes — the response stays the same because people don't want to leave their comfort zone. They have their perks, their lifestyle, and they don't want to change. They're too tied into it.

Just as an expert fisherman reads the stream, so the professional executive considers the ambient conditions — the light, the temperature, the time of day, the total environment — before selecting tackle and lure. But perhaps nothing in his current tackle box, no bait or lure, is appropriate to the steam. Maybe all an executive has inside his tackle box is old stuff. He sees competitors out there using the search lights and dynamite, and all he's got is the fly rod.

I once observed a fascinating scene on the banks of the Yellowstone River. On one side of the stream was a young man, obviously a tourist, who was diligently casting out a variety of lures and bait from a scenic spot overlooking the river. He wasn't having any luck in the venture, but the very activity of "fishing the stream" seemed to satisfy him — that is, until another man started fishing the stream from the opposite side.

From his decorated cap and vest to his hip-boot waders, I could tell that this man was no stranger to the stream. Moreover, he was catching fish — so many fish, in fact, that he had to let them go because he already had his limit. Now he was fishing for the sport of it.

Meanwhile, the hardluck tourist didn't even get a bite during the time I observed him. And yet he was fishing the same stream, same spot, same day. As time passed, he grew so frustrated that he was about to wade in and try to catch a fish with his bare hands.

The problem is that most newcomers aren't interested in waiting years to learn the art and craft of fly fishing — they want to pass over the fundamentals quickly and get out on the water and start reeling in impressive results. Some schools even cater to such ambition. They promise their students that in no time they'll know all about the different lines and leaders.

Seasoned professionals, however, know that there is simply no shortcut to developing the capability to handle with excellence almost any situation or condition that might occur on the water. Real excellence does not come cheaply. A certain price must be paid in terms of practice, patience, persistence — natural ability notwithstanding.

I conclude with one more bit of advice from an old sage:

Often a strike can only be detected by watching for a slight twitch or pause in the drift of the line. A major fault of most fishermen, novice and expert alike, is striking too hard, suddenly and violently stressing the leader, snapping the line, and breaking off the fish. Set the hook smoothly by simply lifting the rod tip and tightening the line. Keep the point sharp, and in all ways, be gentle.

Chapter 36

Feeding for a Lifetime

I once worked with a large restaurant organization that wanted to make their management style consistent with the philosophy: "Give a man a fish and you feed him for a day; teach him how to fish and you feed him for a lifetime."

This company had hundreds of restaurants, and each had its own manager. While these managers seemed to have full authority and responsibility for running fairly sizable restaurants and employing large numbers of people, they were really only resident assistant district managers.

Almost all of the significant decisions regarding employment and other business practices were made by the district managers who supervised them. Every time they encountered a problem, they ran to the district manager for a "fish." Since the district managers only supervised a few restaurants and were supervised themselves by regional managers, they were trapped in a constant problem-solving or management-by-crisis mode.

This method of operation created a picture of a single career path in most everyone's mind. The procedure was to begin at the bottom, eventually become a restaurant manager and then get promoted up the line. Usually, the higher one went in the organization, the more one traveled. And the more managers traveled, the more marriage and family problems resulted. Once they reached the top of the ladder, they realized it was leaning against the wrong wall. They weren't doing what they enjoyed doing or living where they wanted to live. But such was the price for success.

The restaurants, moreover, tended to be managed on the basis of company rules and procedures rather than consumer needs and wants, because managers lacked the flexibility and incentive to develop and use their own judgment, ingenuity, and initiative to solve or prevent problems. The entire hierarchy was more methods-oriented than results- or consumer-oriented, even though "customer relations" was the theme of most every management meeting. Company politics so dominated the minds of the managers that many decisions were made on political or social criteria.

Remarkably, in spite of all this, the company was doing well relative to their competition, but the people at the top throughout the entire organization knew that there must be a better way.

After diagnosing the problems with them, we reached a general agreement that the operation needed to be decentralized by pushing the authority and responsibility for decision-making as far down the corporate ladder as possible and by strengthening the role of the restaurant manager. It was further recognized that more management training and development was needed to make decentralization feasible and financially profitable.

The change process started slowly and continued over a number of years. The renewed commitment to the importance of the individual manager was communicated not only through the rhetoric in company meetings and literature but also through an increased investment in planning, training, and career counseling programs. In addition, the compensation system was adjusted to reward managers for training the people that reported to them.

It soon became apparent that true decentralization would require managers at all levels to develop new skills. When entire levels of line management and overhead were removed, restaurant managers started supervising about 20 restaurants instead of five or six, making it impossible for them to be involved in day-to-day operating decisions. The resident managers now made those decisions, and they needed training in decision-making and in carrying the full responsibility for managing the restaurant.

The serendipitous effect of this decentralization was to create a dual-career path: the traditional one up the line and a second one that provided resident restaurant managers with more community status and recognition and with more financial incentive for building up the restaurant and developing people inside to take over other restaurants in the corporation. Incidentally, making this second option more attractive to resident managers reduced the number of marriage and family problems in the company.

In the upper echelons of the company, executives were no longer directing, controlling, motivating, evaluating — practices they had been heavily involved in up to this point. Instead, their energies shifted to training and development, counseling, coaching, and responding to requests for guidance. Essentially, they began training their managers "how to fish" and stopped giving them a "fish" a day.

This liberated them to focus more upon planning, organizing, and developing people — responsibilities that had been neglected during the management-by-crisis days.

Perhaps the biggest benefit of the decentralization effort was that it uprooted many of the top people who had served earlier as pathfinders and entrepreneurs and exposed their deeply imbedded but ineffective ways of delegating, communicating, and developing people.

When these pioneers moved on to other endeavors, many wondered what the effect would be. To the surprise of some, the transition not only went smoothly but created a sense of upward mobility, excitement, enthusiasm, and gratitude. Within three days, the organization was essentially reorganized, and soon the quality and the depth of leadership were evident to everyone. People were being called to assume more responsibility, trained in the applications of correct principles, and found equal to the task.

On a personal level, however, this transition was not easy or simple. It involved a great deal of gut-wrenching, uprooting, and growing pains at all levels. But because everyone knew that it would be the best in the long run, both personally and organizationally, and because the people at the top were committed to the strategy, it worked.

In fact, as the vision of what the company could become was transmitted — almost by osmosis — throughout the organization, a strong sense of mission developed within the company. In effect, the company culture changed as new stories and anecdotes were shared continually to confirm the vision.

Such far-reaching results come naturally from the practice of managing and leading an organization by correct principles.

POST SCRIPT

Universal Mission Statement

Executives might want to pattern their personal and professional mission after a 12-word universal statement.

There are three levels of leadership: meta, macro and micro. The universal mission statement is an expression of meta leadership.

Meta. Meta leadership deals mainly with vision and stewardship — with what is being entrusted to you as a leader and as a manager.

Macro. Macro leadership deals with strategic goals and how you organize structure and systems and set up processes to meet those goals.

Micro. Micro leadership deals with relationships, with building the emotional bank accounts so that you have legitimate authority with people — people then *choose* to follow and align themselves with your vision or mission. Effective senior executives give most of their time and energies to issues at the meta and macro levels of leadership. They focus on maintaining and enhancing relationships with the people they work with most.

The universal mission statement is intended to serve leaders of organizations as an expression of their vision and sense of stewardship. It attempts to encompass, in one brief sentence, the core values of the organization; it creates a context that gives meaning, direction and coherence to everything else.

To be functional, mission statements should be short so that people can memorize and internalize them. But they also need to be comprehensive. These appear to be contradictory concepts. How can something be short *and* comprehensive? By being simple, general, generic. We see in the computer world, for example, that the more advanced the technology becomes, the more simple the product becomes. The same thing can happen with a mission statement. And if the mission statement represents your "software," you will begin to see and deal through it.

This doesn't mean that the mission statement will take the place of your organizational goals. But it will direct those goals and provide context and coherence for everything else.

The universal mission statement should deal with all aspects of a person's responsibility, with the long run and short run. It could apply to all organizations, as a common denominator which leaders of organizations could consider as they develop their own mission statements. It reads like this:

> *To improve the economic well-being and*
> *quality of life of all stake-holders.*

Three Parts

I will now comment on the three key phrases of the statement.

1 *Economic well-being.* Why do we address the economic dimension first? Because organizations are primarily established to serve economic purposes. Employment is the way that people derive their livelihoods. It does not take the place of families or churches or fraternal organizations. Jobs are to produce wealth, to produce things that people can use and consume in their daily lives — and hopefully enough money to pay taxes, tuition, and everything else.

We sometimes lose sight of this simple fact. That's what my former professor at Harvard Business School, Abraham Zaleznik, suggested in his article, "Real Work" (*Harvard Business Review*, January-February 1989). Tom Peters and Bob Waterman said the same thing in their book, *In Search of Excellence*: they said that companies exist to make and sell products. And Ted Levitt, author of *Marketing Management*, said that companies exist to get and keep customers. Simple ideas.

2 *Quality of Life.* Individuals and organizations sometimes feel that they cannot deal with quality of life issues unless they are relatively affluent. Historically, that's been the case; probably 90 percent of all people have not dealt with quality of life issues, only with survival issues. Even in the United States today, perhaps only 50 percent of us have and take the time to address quality of life concerns. That's one reason why we have so many legislative and social movements toward more recreation, continuing education, fitness, wellness, leisure, travel and tourism. In large measure, these quality of life industries have developed in America in the last 44 years since World War II.

Business executives should be concerned with the overall quality of life of their stake-holders, but their primary responsibility is to enhance the quality of *work life*; there are other institutions — school, family, church — that deal more with private life.

I see five dimensions to quality of life:

Acceptance and love. People have a need to belong and be accepted, to join with others in common enterprises, to engage in win-win relationships and to give and receive love.

Challenge and growth. People also have a need to experience challenge and opposition, to grow and develop, to be well utilized, to be informed and to be creative. We all know that people possess far more capability, intelligence, resourcefulness and initiative than their present jobs allow or require them to use. Such a waste! Such a low quality of life! Leaders must identify, develop, use and recognize talent; otherwise, people will go elsewhere, physically or mentally, to find their satisfactions, fulfillment and their sense of growth.

Purpose and meaning. People also have a need for purpose and meaning — for making a contribution to that which is meaningful. People can make good money and have all kinds of growth experiences and good relationships but if their work is not intrinsically satisfying or if the outcome does not constructively contribute to society, they won't be motivated in the highest and deepest sense.

The economic dimension is extrinsic. But you don't work just for money. Money is a means to an end. You also work for intrinsic satisfactions — meaning that the nature of the work, the relationships at work, and the sense of contribution to something meaningful are satisfying in and of themselves.

Fairness and opportunity. The basic principles in the field of human motivation emphasize *fairness* regarding economic rewards and *opportunity* regarding intrinsic rewards. Frederick Herzberg, a University of Utah professor who is an expert in the field of motivation, talks about "dissatisfiers" and "satisfiers" or motivators. A dissatisfier would be a sense of inequity regarding economic rewards. When people become dissatisfied, when their higher level needs are not met, they fight the organization in one way or another in order to give their lives its cohesion and its meaning. That's why a person's "economic well-being" and "quality of life" are closely interrelated.

Life balance. Now, if you have fairness, justice and equity regarding economic rewards but you lack challenge and meaning in your organization, what will people do? They'll press for more money, more benefits and more time off — because with money and time they have opportunity to satisfy their interests and find their intrinsic satisfactions off the job. Therefore, the real challenge of leadership is to recognize that these are not only needs of people, they are capacities. And if any of these needs are not fulfilled, the neglected capacity will work *contrary* to their organization.

For instance, if people have a mission statement that focuses only on the economic side and not on the social, psychological and spiritual sides, the mission may actually encourage them to moonlight or to use their talent and energy to try to get more money and a better deal for themselves so they can have more time and find more fulfillment off the job.

3 *All stake-holders.* This universal mission statement deals with all stake-holders. And who is a stake-holder? The best way to answer that is to ask, "Who will suffer if the enterprise fails?"

And who suffers depends on what the situation is. If the owners have plowed their life savings into the enterprise and are at risk right up to their ears, they'll probably be hurt the most if the enterprise fails. Other people can go and get jobs. But the owners may literally be wiped out and may have to start again. They may have to pay off tremendous debts for a long period of time. If, however, the owners are wealthy and have many diversified assets, they may not be hurt if a particular investment or enterprise fails. But the employees might suffer tremendously, especially if they are specialized professionals stuck in a one-industry town with the wrong training and skills. Also, the suppliers may suffer terribly. And the domino effect could be very damaging to many other people in the community.

It takes a lot of judgment, discernment and sense of stewardship about all stake-holders — all who have a stake in the welfare or success of the enterprise — including customers, suppliers, distributors, dealers, the community and the public at large. Because if business leaders become exploitative, they help create a cynical climate, get the media on their backs, and hurt many other companies in the same industry. They may even cause special legislation to avoid dirty dealing on the part of "big business."

The leaders of corporations should have a high sense of responsibility about some social problems and get involved and encourage high involvement by members of the organization. For example, John Pepper, president of Procter & Gamble, once asked me go to the Cincinnati School Board and speak to them about some issues that conern him. Many other organizations want their people involved in volunteer work with social and educational programs because they know that it affects some stake-holders directly and the entire business climate indirectly.

Stake-holders means more than just the shareholders. Most mission statements are geared more to the shareholders — and more specifically, to the short-term quarterly dividend. One reason is that many organizations are owned by small shareholders who count on that income. Losing it could be very dislocating to them. But the whole "goose and golden egg" phenomenon is in operation here: if we focus on the short term and kill the goose, we won't have more golden eggs — and that hurts not only the shareholders but all stake-holders.

Remember the story of the entrepreneur who takes his prime employees to a scenic site that overlooks a beautiful valley. And he tells them, "I appreciate what you've done all these years, and if you continue your devotion and industry, I just want you to know that someday all of this will be mine."

That's just about how some mission statements are worded. One large organization basically had as its mission: "to enhance the asset base of the owners."

I asked the CEO, "If you put that on the wall, would it inspire the devotion of your employees and the commitment of your customers? Would it communicate that you really care about them?"

There is a kind of conscience in organizations, social as well as private, which defines what equity and fairness mean. Any time you have people putting in a greater investment than they are rewarded for, you will have many negative consequences. Or, if there are more rewards than investment, that too is an injustice in the social ecology — and it will eventually have a negative impact on other things.

That's why meta leadership requires a sense of stewardship about the whole package and a careful balancing of many different interests. Meta leadership is not a transactional approach. The human resource movement defines people as assets, as resources; they are that and more — they are intrinsically valuable in and of themselves, not just an assets. If you don't see that people have intrinsic worth, you get into a utilitarian approach. You are "nice to them" as important assets, but you violate their spiritual nature and their sense of intrinsic worth. Ultimately, the human resource approach to leadership is *transactional* — it is not transforming or synergistic.

The principle-centered approach to leadership is *transformational* because it gives people the conviction that they (their respective fates in the company) are not a function of arbitrary personalities but of timeless, correct principles, particularly if principles are embedded into the mission statement and emanate out to management style, practices, procedures, policies, strategy, structure, systems and so forth. People then gain confidence that "this place is run by principles" and that everyone, including the top people are accountable to those principles, as well as to each other.

In fact, I would like to see a new organizational chart: in the center of the chart are correct principles, and on the perimeter would be the different stewardships. The chairman and everyone else are accountable to those principles.

What I'm suggesting is that the universal mission statement, whether it is written or not, is already operating. It's like a natural law: you cannot violate it — or this sense of total economic community — with impunity.

Five Major Benefits

I see five basic virtues of this universal mission statement.

• *Ecological balance.* The universal mission statement helps you to think ecologically about all stake-holders. You know that by constantly attending to the transforming principles, all stake-holders will enjoy synergistic benefits.

• *Short and long-term perspective.* The universal mission statement suggests that if you try to take the short-term approach, you will compromise or kill the goose that lays the golden eggs over the long term.

• *Professional challenge.* These 12 words embody enough challenge for leaders throughout their entire professional careers.

• *Management context.* Within the parameters of the universal mission statement, you can better set policies and procedures, strategy, structure and systems.

• *Personal sense of stewardship.* The universal mission statement generates a sense of stewardship with respect to people and other resources.

Again, I see this as a generic mission statement for leaders, not necessarily for organizations, although leaders might want to build these concepts into their organizational mission statements. They may also want to apply these concepts to their personal and family mission statements. The universal statement doesn't preclude the need for a personal, family or corporate statement in any way. Every organization should have its own mission statement. But it might well be an extension of the universal mission statement:

To improve the economic well-being and
and quality of life of all stake-holders.